Transnational Families, Migration and Gender

New Directions in Anthropology

General Editor: **Jacqueline Waldren**, *Institute of Social Anthropology, University of Oxford*

TRANSNATIONAL FAMILIES, MIGRATION AND GENDER

Moroccan and Filipino Women

in Bologna and Barcelona

Elisabetta Zontini

Berghahn Books
New York • Oxford

First published in 2010 by

Berghahn Books

www.berghahnbooks.com

© 2010 Elisabetta Zontini

Library of Congress Cataloging-in-Publication Data

Zontini, Elisabetta.
 Transnational families, migration, and gender : Moroccan and Filipino women in Bologna and Barcelona / by Elisabetta Zontini.
    p. cm. -- (New directions in anthropology ; v. 30)
 Includes bibliographical references and index.
 ISBN 978-1-84545-618-4 (hardback : alk. paper)
 1. Women immigrants--Europe, Southern--Case studies. 2. Europe, Southern--Emigration
and immigration--Social aspects--Case studies. 3. Filipinos--Italy--Bologna--Social
conditions. 4. Moroccans--Italy--Bologna--Social conditions. 5. Filipinos--Spain--
Barcelona--Social conditions. 6. Moroccans--Spain--Barcelona--Social conditions. 7.
Women immigrants--Italy--Bologna. 8. Women immigrants--Spain--Barcelona. 9. Family--
Italy--Bologna. 10. Family--Spain--Barcelona. I. Title.
 JV7590.Z665 2009
 305.48'89276404672--dc22
                                              2009045271
British Library Cataloguing in Publication Data

A catalogue record for this book is available from the British Library

Printed in the United States on acid-free paper

ISBN: 978-1-84545-618-4 (hardback)

CONTENTS

LIST OF TABLES

List of Maps

ACKNOWLEDGEMENTS

My deepest thanks go to my Ph.D. supervisor Professor Russell King without whose encouragement and support the research on which this book is based would have never taken place. His role in all the phases of this project has been invaluable. I also wish to thank all the members of the Families and Social Capital ESRC Research Group at London South Bank University where part of the writing up of this book has taken place and where my thinking about transnational families has continued to develop. My special thanks go to Tracey Reynolds, Kanwal Mand, Venetia Evergeti, Rosalind Edwards, Harry Goulbourne and John Solomos. The majority of this book was written during a fellowship at the International Gender Studies Centre at Oxford University. I wish to thank everybody at the Centre for their help and support, especially my mentor there Judith Okely. Her interest in my work and our lengthy conversations on my research made me re-engage with my material and gave me the confidence to try to pursue this publication. I also wish to thank her for her comments on an earlier draft.

During the various years that this project took to complete, the friendship of several individuals has been invaluable. At Sussex, my thanks go to Carolyn, Caterina, Imran, Karim, Jaqui, Marie-Jo, Nicola, Nicole and Yorghos. I am also thankful to Jenny Money for her kind support on several occasions. In Bologna, the friendship of Adriana Bernardotti has been invaluable. She provided me with friendship, practical support and shared with me much of her 'local knowledge' of the city. I also wish to acknowledge all the people who made my Bologna fieldwork possible, especially, Vicky of the Association of Filipino Women Liwanag, El Hussain of the CGIL trade union and the volunteers of the Association Famiglie Insieme. In Barcelona, special thanks go to the people who worked in the Housing Service of the NGO Sodepau, Rita of the Association of Filipino Women, SURT, Nora and the Spanish teachers of Ibn Batuta. In Barcelona, I enjoyed the support and friendship of: Abel, Anna, Berta, Dan, Michel, Perla, Roberta, Sergio and Virginia. In Oxford, my thanks go to Jenny, Eulalia and Eliseu.

Acknowledgements

My warmest thanks go to all the women in Bologna and Barcelona who generously found the time to talk to me, letting me into their homes and sharing their life stories with me. Meeting them has been an extremely enriching experience for me and I am deeply indebted to them all.

I am also thankful to my family, my parents Laura and Gianni Zontini and my children Antonio and Roberto who were born during the writing up of this book. Finally, this research has been strongly influenced by Davide Però. It was by living with him during his own fieldwork in Bologna and reading the early drafts of his thesis that I started to develop the ideas about my own project. His commitment to fieldwork, his critical perspectives and his political engagement have always inspired and stimulated me. I thank him for this and for his intellectual, practical and emotional support during the process of this project.

Elizabetta Zontini
July 2009

1
INTRODUCTION: SOUTHERN
EUROPE AND THE NEW
IMMIGRATIONS

Women represent a considerable and growing percentage of the total immigration to Southern Europe, as in many migrations world-wide (Castles and Miller 1998). However, the peculiarity of Southern Europe is the presence of many highly gendered flows: some male-dominated and others female-dominated. This study addresses the causes and consequences of this gender-selective migration for the individual migrant worker and their families and explores the important, but hitherto overlooked, question of women's role and position in transnational families. The analysis is based on a double comparison in two Southern European countries and between two migrant groups (Filipinos who are of Christian heritage and Moroccans who are Muslim) who represent the most and least favoured nationalities in the racialised and gendered niches of the domestic labour market were women of both groups are located, irrespective of their previous qualifications and experiences.

By linking the experiences of immigrant families with the increased reliance on cheap and flexible workers for care and domestic work in Southern Europe, this book documents the lived experiences of neglected actors of globalisation – migrant women – as well as the transformations of Western families more generally. However, while describing in detail the structural and cultural contexts within which these women have to operate, the book questions dominant paradigms about women as simply trailing or as passive victims of patriarchal structures and brings out instead their agency and the creative ways in which they take control of their lives in often difficult circumstances. As Chapter 2 and the next sections of this chapter will show, there is now a respectable body of literature dealing with the macro characteristics of immigrant flows to Southern Europe as well as with the specific features of Southern Europe as an immigration context. This book explores instead the *individual* experiences of migration in such a context; the 'lived accounts' of the migration, transnationalism and settlement of ordinary women.

The questions framing my analysis and which I will seek to address in the course of the book are the following:

- What are the reasons behind female migration to Southern Europe? And following from this, what are the causes and consequences of gender-selective migration to Southern Europe?
- How are women's roles in wider units such as households, families and kinship groups shaping their migration?
- How do migration and trasnationalism in turn affect households and families, and women's roles in them?
- To what kinds of settlement does women's immigration give rise? And what is the role of women in the settlement process?

Answering these questions will, on the one hand, enrich our understanding of the role of women as key actors both in migration and settlement; on the other hand, such answers will help us to understand the type of multicultural societies that are emerging in European countries such as Italy and Spain. The strategy by which I address these issues will be to compare the experiences of women belonging to two groups following different migratory patterns (male-led and female-led), namely Moroccans (a typical male-led group) and Filipinos (a typical female-led group), in two Southern European geographical locations: Bologna (Italy) and Barcelona (Spain). The purpose of this twofold comparison is to show both the similarities and differences uniting and separating women, both between and across groups and in different geographical locations. My epistemological aim is to move away from 'victimising' accounts of immigrants in general and women in particular and show the space for human agency within social, cultural and economic constraints. The strength of my comparative ethnographic approach is that it offers unique detailed data on migration decision making, settlement and on the multiple ways in which different women cope with the consequences of their transnational lives.

I conducted the research through ethnographic fieldwork in the two cities of Bologna and Barcelona, spending approximately six months in each location. During fieldwork I adopted a reflexive, dialogical approach which aimed at revealing the agency of the women I met. The material I present in the following chapters was obtained through a combination of different qualitative methods employed across different levels of society. Such methods include participant observation, life-history accounts and semi-structured interviews conducted both with immigrants and officials belonging to various institutional and non-governmental organisations working in the field of immigration.

This chapter is dedicated, firstly, to a brief exploration of the specificity of contemporary Southern European immigrations, pointing out the relevance of studying migration in this geographical context; secondly, to the description of the main characteristics of this receiving context. An outline of the book will conclude this introductory chapter.

The Specificity of Southern European Immigrations

Southern Europe is an extremely interesting region for the study of immigration in contemporary Europe. First of all, in the emerging regulatory regime of 'Fortress Europe' mass migration has shifted from countries of the North, such as Germany, the UK and France, to countries which until not long ago were countries of emigration, such as Italy and Spain (King 1993, 2001). Here, from the 1980s onwards, immigration has increased steadily year after year. In the period 1990–2000, the 'stock' of immigrants doubled in both Italy and Spain. It increased from about 650,000 to almost 1,300,000 in Italy (Istat 2002) and from 400,000 to almost 900,000 in Spain (INE 2002).[1] This sharp increase is mainly due to the sealing off of borders in Northern Europe and the relatively easier access to the countries of Southern Europe. However, there are further causes directly linked to the particular economic and social transformations of Southern Europe. In Italy and Spain the process of modernisation happened over a relatively short period of time and it has been quite 'intense'. From the economic point of view, success was accompanied by the development of a thriving informal sector (Solé 2001), whereas from the social point of view, profound social transformations were accompanied by a growing crisis of the welfare state. In this setting migrant labour became essential both in the informal sector and in other less attractive spheres of the labour market now left vacant by the local workers. These jobs range across employment in small-scale industries, in the lower positions in the tertiary sector – often requiring undocumented, and thus flexible, labour – and in the care and domestic sector left open by women who have joined the labour force and are not covered by the services of a declining welfare state (King and Andall 1999; King and Zontini 2000; King 2001). Secondly, and partly linked to the reasons presented above, migration to Southern Europe today differs from colonial and postcolonial migration to the UK, France or the Netherlands and from the highly regulated migration of the 'guestworker' era. The migrants to Southern Europe come from a much greater variety of countries, are highly mobile geographically and are often undocumented and employed in the informal sector and, because of these reasons, live in the peripheries and interstices of the receiving societies, under conditions of high marginalisation, exclusion and almost complete absence of social and political rights.

Grillo (2002: 5) has identified five reasons why Italian migration differs from that experienced by countries such as the UK and France. First, as just mentioned, the heterogeneity of the immigrant population is marked (see Table 1.1). No group in Italy exceeds 15 per cent of the total and in Spain Moroccans are the only non-European group to do so (22 per cent).[2] By contrast, in Britain and France just a few groups make up a very large proportion of immigrant and ethnic minorities, although there too there are significant changes and commentators are talking about a new situation of 'superdiversity' (Vertovec 2006). The fragmentation of the immigrant population has obvious consequences from the policy point of view, especially in relation to the design of so-called multicultural policies.

Table 1.1 Legally present foreign population in Italy and Spain, 2000

Italy	Total	Women	Spain	Total	Women
Morocco	194,617	66,624	Morocco	199,782	65,250
Albania	163,868	64,638	UK	73,983	37,231
Philippines	72,275	45,267	Germany	60,575	30,078
Rumania	62,262	31,187	France	42,316	21,491
Tunisia	60,441	17,082	Portugal	41,997	18,302
Ex-Yugoslavia	60,146	25,380	Ecuador	30,878	17,144
China	58,844	26,928	Italy	30,862	10,986
Senegal	39,708	4,438	China	28,693	12,475
Germany	38,183	22,758	Peru	27,888	17,050
Egypt	37,674	10,532	Dominican R.	26,481	18,996
Sri Lanka	36,281	15,755	Colombia	24,702	17,114
Peru	32,706	21,171	Cuba	19,165	11,262
France	29,713	17,798	Holland	16,711	8,277
India	29,341	11,958	Argentina	16,610	8,351
Poland	28,282	19,673	Algeria	13,847	2,523
Macedonia	26,051	8,899	USA	13,743	6,551
Ghana	24,689	9,832	Philippines	13,160	8,110
Total	1,270,553	580,314		895,720	407,423

Sources: Italian and Spanish official statistics, http://demo.istat.it and www.ine.es, retrieved 11/10/2007

Second, the colonial legacy which was at the root of much migration from former colonies to the UK and France has had less relevance in Southern Europe. Here a greater proportion of immigration originates from countries which have no direct colonial link with the country of immigration, although Spain and Portugal are partial exceptions. In Italy the majority of immigrants come from Morocco, Albania, the Philippines, Rumania, Tunisia and the former Yugoslavia. The situation is slightly different in Spain where the link with the former Latin American colonies is more evident. Foreign residents in Spain are divided among a very large Western European group; a North African group (almost exclusively Moroccan); several Latin American groups; and other smaller groups including Chinese, Filipinos, Gambians and Senegalese.

The third difference identified by Grillo refers to the increased number of refugees entering Italy after the end of the Cold War, especially from Eastern Europe and Central Asia. This is less the case for Spain.

Fourth, the demographic composition of the immigration to Italy and Spain differs from that of past migration flows to Northern Europe. The characteristic to which I want to draw particular attention is the asymmetric sex distribution in many immigrant groups, meaning that while some nationalities of migrants are predominantly male, others are almost exclusively female (Table 1.2). This aspect contrasts with older types of immigration to Northern Europe where single-sex migration was predominantly – although not exclusively – a male phenomenon, which usually preceded the arrival of other members of the family. It is also worth noticing that this sex asymmetry, although declining in some groups (e.g.,the Moroccans), seems to be still quite evident at the end of the 1990s, more than twenty years after Italy and Spain become countries of foreign immigration, a point that I believe needs further attention.

Table 1.2 Major immigrant communities by sex, 2000

Italy	No.	per cent	Spain	No.	per cent
Female majority					
Philippines	45,267	62.6	Ecuador	30,878	55.5
Peru	21,171	64.7	Peru	27,888	61.1
Poland	9,832	69.6	Dom. R.	26,481	71.7
Somalia	7,574	62.8	Colombia	24,702	69.3
Dom. R.	8,307	74.7	Cuba	19,165	58.8
Ecuador	6,980	67.5	Philippines	13,160	61.6
Male majority		per cent			per cent
Morocco	127,993	65.8	Morocco	132,473	66.3
Albania	99,230	60.6	Algeria	11,124	81.8
Tunisia	43,395	71.7	Senegal	9,105	82.4
Senegal	35,270	88.8	Romania	6,920	63.0
Egypt	27,142	72.0	Gambia	5,869	66.4
Macedonia	17,152	65.8	Pakistan	6,810	86.8

Sources: My elaboration from Italian and Spanish official statistics, http://demo.istat.it and www.ine.es: retrieved 11/10/2007

The groups that at the beginning of the 2000s were predominantly female were either from Catholic countries like Filipinos, Poles, Latin Americans, Cape Verdeans; from former Italian colonies, the cases of the Somalians and Ethiopians;

or from other Eastern European countries.[3] Female migration to Italy was in fact initiated by the Catholic Church as early as the 1970s when priests started to recruit Filipino and Cape Verdean women to perform domestic work in the rich families of the capital city, Rome (Andall 1998). This type of immigration to Italy – but also to Spain – has continued ever since, also reinforced by the networks and migratory chains established by these early migrants. Immigration of Ethiopian and Somalian women also has a fairly long history and is again connected to Italians returning from the colonies bringing with them 'exotic' domestic helpers. After a decline during the 1980s, immigration from Somalia started to grow again as a consequence of the civil war that devastated the country during the 1990s. The arrival of Eastern European women started after 1989 and by 2005 they had overtaken several of the other *female-dominant* immigrant groups. They came often on a tourist visa and then found employment both as short-term domestic helpers and in the sex trade (Vicarelli 1994). In recent years they have been mainly employed as carers for the elderly. What appears clearly from this brief analysis is that single-sex migration of certain female groups was originated both by historic links (Catholicism, colonialism) and by a constant demand originating in the local labour market and particularly in domestic service and elderly care, but also increasingly in the sex trade (Campani 2000). Other causes will be presented in the course of the book.

The groups that have a male majority tend to come from North or West Africa, from the Balkans and from some Asian countries, and are predominantly Muslims. In recent years a new migration of Eastern European men has emerged in Spain to work in the expanding agricultural industry of the greenhouses of Southern Spain (Hartman 2008). Men often migrate alone to find employment in a variety of low-skilled jobs, ranging from seasonal work in agriculture or in fishing, to work in construction, in factories, peddling, etc. Moroccans, one of the groups studied in this book, are still a male-dominated group. The causes and consequences of these gender-selective migrations are taken up in the following chapters of the book.

Other demographic characteristics of the immigrant population differentiate Italy and Spain from other immigration countries such as France and the UK. In the former there were, until recently, relatively fewer immigrant families and children. In Southern Europe there is still a predominance of young adults among most immigrant groups. This is, however, changing (King and Andall 1999). In 1999 Caritas (1999) started to talk about a tendency towards normalisation in the demographic structure of the foreign population in Italy (see also Caritas 2001; Colombo and Sciortino 2004).

As far as the groups considered in this book are concerned, we can observe (Table 1.1) that Moroccans, in 2000, represented the largest group both in Italy and Spain whereas Filipinos were third in Italy and only seventeenth in Spain. However, their low numbers in Spain can be explained by the fact that they (like some Latin American groups) benefit from privileged access to Spanish citizenship due to the historical link between Spain and their country of origin (Escrivà 2000a). Many of my Filipino interviewees were in fact Spanish nationals; thus they would not appear in statistics counting foreign residents such as the ones reproduced above. Their presence in Spain, especially in large urban areas, is therefore more large-scale than that shown by these statistics.

Both groups have increased steadily over the years. Both Moroccans and Filipinos have more than doubled their presence in Italy over a decade (Table 1.3). As far as their current sex balance is concerned, in 2000 women represented 62.6 per cent of Filipinos whereas men constituted 65.8 per cent of Moroccans in Italy. The sex ratios among Moroccans and Filipinos in Spain were analogous: men represent 66.3 per cent of Moroccans and women 61.6 per cent of Filipinos. What is interesting to consider is the evolution of this sex distribution over time. Moroccans seem to move towards a 'normalisation' of their demographic profile since the percentage of males over females is decreasing steadily. In Italy they represented 88.4 per cent in 1991, 80.5 per cent in 1994, 65.8 per cent in 2000 and 61.9 per cent in 2005. In Spain they went from 85.4 per cent in 1992, 84.7 per cent in 1994 to 66.3 per cent in 2000 and 65.7 per cent in 2005. The same cannot be said for Filipinas since the percentage of females over males does not seem to be decreasing as clearly. In Italy they were 68.7 per cent in 1991, 69.7 per cent in 1994, 62.6 per cent in 2000 and 59.7 per cent in 2005 (Caritas 1994, 1996, 1999; ISTAT 2002, 2006). In Spain they were 66.0 per cent in 1992, 65.3 per cent in 1994, 61.6 per cent in 2000 and 62.1 per cent in 2005 (Escrivà 2000a: 207; INE 2002, 2006).

As far as families are concerned, in 1995 there were more singles (50 per cent) among Filipinos than among Moroccans (47 per cent) residing in Italy. Moroccans married with children in 1995 were one in four whereas Filipinos were one in nine. According to Caritas this has to do with a different integration of the two groups: 'for the former [integration] is maybe more difficult but it tends to be family-oriented; for the latter it is definitely easier but it has mostly a labour character given that children are normally left in the country of origin' (Caritas 1996: 97). This difference emerges also from data on age distribution for the two groups in Spain. The age bracket 25–44 years old was the dominant one for both groups (54.4 per cent for Filipinos and 52.4 per cent for Moroccans) in 2000 but Moroccans showed a much higher presence of children and young people (20.2 per cent are under 16 years old and 17.2 per cent are in the 16–24 age bracket) than Filipinos (11.4 per cent and 11.9 per cent respectively) who in turn had a higher percentage among 45–64 year olds (20.1 per cent as against 9.2 per cent of Moroccans) (INE 2002).

Table 1.3 Moroccans and Filipinos in Italy and Spain in 2000, 1995 and 1990/1991

Italy	2000	1995	1990
Moroccans	194,617	94,237	80,485
Filipinos	72,275	43,421	35,373
Spain			**1991**
Moroccans	199,782	74,866	43,513
Filipinos	13,160	9,681	8,049

Sources: My elaboration from Italian and Spanish official statistics, http://demo.istat.it and www.ine.es: retrieved 11/10/2007

The fifth and last difference characterising contemporary migration to Southern Europe with respect to Northern Europe identified by Grillo (2002: 8) refers to the fact that such migration takes place 'in a world which is more "transnational" than that which previous generations of migrants to Europe or North America encountered', meaning that migrants move more easily and across larger distances than they ever did before, due to the increase in communications and the reduced costs of transportation. Whether contemporary migrations are qualitative different from previous ones in terms of their transnational character or whether most migrants can now be defined as transmigrants is a debated issue (Portes et al. 1999; Vertovec 1999). The answer to these questions is beyond the scope of this book. However, Grillo's observation reminds us of the importance of avoiding 'methodological nationalism' (Wimmer and Glick Schiller 2002) that is limiting the focus of analysis to the receiving society and using the nation-state as the natural framework from which to asses the experiences of migrants. This book, following Glick Schiller (2004) and Levitt (2001) among others, will look at migrants as located in social fields that go beyond the country of settlement and will consider their links, obligations and responsibilities beyond the locales where they are currently living. This seems particularly relevant for the Southern European case where, according to the statistics reported in this chapter, migrants such as Moroccans and Filipinos often move without their families. As the data just reported show and as various authors have noted (Basch et al. 1994; Glick Schiller 2004; Levitt 2001; Smith and Guarnizo 1998; Portes et al. 1999; Vertovec 1999), migration is not necessarily unidirectional, with permanent settlement of entire families in the countries of destination as the logical and final outcome of the process. Fluid relationships between two or more countries are the norm for many immigrant groups (see discussion on transnationalism in Chapter 2), as we will see later on in the book.

The Specificity of the Receiving Countries

Grillo and Pratt (2002) point out that in order to understand the ways in which immigrants are being incorporated into society it is important to consider a number of aspects related to the specific characteristics of the context of arrival. They conduct their analysis in relation to Italian society[4] but the same framework could be applied to Spain[5] (and to any other immigrant-receiving society). The first dimension has to do with the cleavages and processes internal to the receiving society which will inevitably affect those who are newly arrived. The second dimension refers to the ways in which 'difference' has been historically constructed there since ingrained ideas about 'in-group' and 'out-group' tend to serve as a template to interpret and classify newcomers. The third one refers to the institutional response, the way in which governments and local authorities go about 'managing diversity'. This has to do with laws and policies specifically targeting immigrants. Finally, there is the broader political response to immigration, that is to say the ways in which political parties and movements both in government and in opposition deal with the issues of immigration. All these interlocking spheres (together with the economic and demographic ones presented in the previous section) have an important impact on the ways immigrants are incorporated (or excluded) in the receiving societies. In this section I will enlarge briefly on each of these points.

Internal Cleavages and Processes

Pratt (2002) points out that rather than seeing Italy as a static and homogeneous society, we have to think about its plurality and its evolution. He reminds us that there are different ways of 'being Italian', affecting differently the new immigrants (see also Cole 1997). He identifies five issues that, in his view, shape the lives of immigrants. The first one relates to the state and its complex regulatory practices. Italian bureaucratic practices are chaotic, if not arbitrary. Having privileged channels of information and some 'connection' is often the only way to 'get around' otherwise insurmountable barriers (Zinn 2001). Thus to obtain things such as permits, resources or licenses one needs 'the kind of social capital which few recent migrants can possess' (Pratt 2002: 32). Second, in many parts of Italy there are ingrained mechanisms of closure connected with a strong tradition of localism resulting in the fact that those 'coming from the outside' will find it very difficult to find a job, a house and have access to those social networks that in these contexts are crucial to establish a livelihood (Carter 1997; Maher 1996). Third, there is the way in which progressive forces have dealt with the politics of recognition. Pratt argues that in the past the main Italian left-wing party (PCI or the Italian Communist Party) recognised class as the only relevant axis of differentiation. Its political heirs, the DS (Left-Democrats), shifted their attention to questions of ethnicity, abandoning in the process any consideration of socioeconomic inequalities (See Peró 2004).

The fourth issue that affects the life of immigrants in Italy is the role of the Church in shaping responses to international migration. As noted, it was the Church itself which set in motion some of the migration chains to Italy (especially the female-dominated ones). It is also the institution around which revolve many of the most effective organisations that provide assistance and support to immigrants. Yet, Pratt reminds us, there is also the integralist side of the Church which advocates an exclusively Catholic Italy and opposes a plural vision of Italian society. This strand of the Church warns against the dangers of Islam and recently has gone as far as proposing to admit into Italy only those immigrants originating from Catholic countries.

Fifth, there is the North–South divide that still shapes the representation of new minorities. As Carter (1997) and Maher (1996) have shown, Italians tend to make sense of new immigrants in relation to older representations of Southern Italians. Southern Italians were perceived by Northerners as coming from underdeveloped regions. They were described as having 'barbarous' attitudes to women, including their own wives, and as being 'bad-mannered, ignorant, delinquent, violent, and liable to have many children' (Maher 1996: 171). Pratt points out how today immigrants from poor countries are associated with this imagined South whereas immigrants from rich countries get associated with the developed North. The fact that only the former are deemed to have 'cultural problems' points to 'the invisible socio-economic axis which underlies the representation of migration and the politics of cultural difference' (2002: 36).

These issues identified by Pratt in relation to the Italian context are relevant to a lesser or greater extent also in Spain. First, the Spanish state is as bureaucratic and its practices as complex as the Italian. To give just one example, immigrants often receive their work permit when it is already about to expire due to the slowness of the system. This necessitates the worker staying with the same employer until a new permit has been reissued, with obvious consequences for geographical and job mobility. Second, processes of closure towards so-called 'outsiders' are also very evident in Spain where, as in Italy, there is a strong tradition of localism. Third, progressive forces tend to frame the immigrants in ethnic terms, emphasising their difference (Santamaría 2002). In Catalonia left-wing administrations have concentrated most of their activities towards immigrants around the recognition of cultural difference, especially through large-scale 'multicultural festivals' (see Grassilli 2001), neglecting other issues such as granting newcomers access to adequate housing or combating the discrimination they suffer in the labour market. Fourth, the Catholic Church has played the same dominant role as in Italy in putting forward responses to immigration, but in Spain too the solidaristic side of the Church exists side-by-side with a more reactionary one. Fifth, Spain too has its own North/South divide

10

although in Catalonia this is complicated by a strong opposition between central and autonomous governments. Such dualism shapes much of the Catalan political scene, including debates on immigration.

In addition to the five elements just seen, there is a sixth factor that affects the experiences of immigrant women in both Italy and Spain, namely the evolving Southern European gender order. In this region of Europe several key economic and demographic transformations – such as the expansion of the service sector, the casualisation and informalisation of work, birth rate decline and ageing – have proceeded further and faster than in other parts of Europe (King and Zontini 2000: 49). These wider changes, together with transformations in women's role and position in Southern European societies, have induced women to join the labour force in increasing numbers over the last three decades. However, this trend has been matched neither by an adequate development of an accessible and affordable social infrastructure nor by adjustments in the domestic sphere (Barbagli and Saraceno 1997; Vaiou 1996). Southern Europe is characterised by what can be called an 'imperfect transition to gender equality' (King and Zontini 2000).

In order to understand this gender order, it is necessary to consider the Southern European family. Dina Vaiou (1996) believes that, even though one cannot speak of a single model of the family across Southern Europe, there are shared characteristics that help us to understand Southern European women's specific integration in work and everyday life and which differentiate them from their Northern European counterparts. Whereas in Northern Europe it is the state, through the welfare system, that plays the role of safety net, in Southern Europe this function has been historically carried out by the family (Reher 1998). According to Saraceno (1997: 308): 'the family in Italy has always been the implicit resource of the welfare state. Services for both the young and the elderly have developed in a residual manner defined as substitutes of an absent, or malfunctioning family or kinship network'. In Spain, García-Ramón and Cruz (1996) conclude that 'support by the family is essential for understanding women's integration in the labour market ... . For it is not families but specific members within them (mothers, mothers-in-law and eldest daughter) who often make it possible for the female day-labourer to work outside the home' (1996: 260). Sabaté-Martínez (1996) believes that it is the existence of female family networks that allows women to combine paid work with housework since, in spite of cultural changes, 'in practice, only some men are willing to "give a hand to their wives"' (1996: 276). It is clear, as Vaiou points out, that the family 'protective net' goes hand in hand with the persistence of prescriptive behaviour, rights and duties (Vaiou 1996: 68). Within the family it is women who are responsible for domestic and caring work, whether or not they are also involved with paid work outside the home (Facchini 1997; Palomba 1997; Trifiletti 1997).

Both Italian and Spanish families are going through structural changes, which include the disappearance of the traditional extended family even if numerous authors have noted that family members continue to live close to one another, maintaining important economic and emotional links (Facchini 1997; Vaiou 1996). Other important changes include the position of women within Italian and Spanish societies. In the contemporary period, also as a result of the feminist movement, new cultural models have developed with respect to women's attitudes towards family and work. Whereas in the 1960s and 1970s female cultural attitudes placed a higher priority on the needs of the family than on paid work, now women of the younger generations are no longer willing to give up their professional career and their economic autonomy (Trifiletti 1997). However, as Vinay (1996) points out in the case of Italy, they are not placing higher priority on paid work either.

This non-choice between family and work, as Vinay calls it, results mainly in a double day of work (for the family and for the market) and reflects a general unresolved tension between Italian women's expression of productive and reproductive roles.

Andall (2000a) believes that this unresolved tension is a central characteristic of the contemporary Italian gender regime. In spite of the emergence of the Italian feminist movement in the 1960s and 1970s, such tension has still to be fully resolved and, in Andall's view, it is an important contributory factor to the demand for migrant women's labour. In spite of important changes, most care work is still done in the family, mainly by female members. The reasons for this situation are, on the one hand, men's minimally increased involvement in care work and, on the other hand, the failure of the Southern European state to relieve the family (and especially its female members) from the bulk of caring work.

Trifiletti (1998: 178) describes the Italian welfare system as patchy, 'being based on specific groups and originating from patronage ties between particular groups or categories and politicians or political parties' (see also Saraceno 1997). In her view, social care in Italy has never been universally publicly provided. Moreover the national expenditure for social assistance is quite low and declining (it was around 3.5 per cent of the GDP in 1995) (Trifiletti 1998: 177). Two areas of social care seem important to understanding immigrant women's insertion into the labour market: care services for the elderly and care services for children.

Care services for the elderly (of increasing importance in a country whose population is rapidly ageing and with one of the lowest birth rates in the world) are traditionally characterised by neglect on the part of public authorities. Until 1985 the ways in which the elderly had access to public care were through nursing homes and home care. The former – normally run by organisations linked to the Catholic Church – however, were limited mainly to independent old people and their coverage was low. In 1997 only 3.6 per cent of those over 75 were institutionalised. The latter depended on the provisions established by local authorities, there were no clear rules on entitlement and coverage was highly fragmentary. This means that the care of the elderly in Italy is at present on the shoulders of the family. The introduction of a 'payment for care' policy (a subsidy given to people opting to keep a dependent elderly person at home) does not change this situation since families are left alone in organising the care for the elderly person for which they receive the subsidy (Saraceno 1997).

This seems a common pattern across Southern Europe. In Spain, too, the welfare state 'very often chooses to provide people with financial assistance rather than social services', not touching the role of the family as an alternative protective net (García-Ramon and Cruz 1996: 247). In addition to the limitations of the state in providing services, there are also cultural factors that need to be borne in mind, such as the widespread preference for looking after the elderly within the home. Institutionalisation is still seen by many in Southern Europe as the fate of those who have no family which can support them (Reher 1998).

Care services for children in Italy are still marked by their specific evolution. (Trifiletti 1998). A characteristic of the service is the lack of a single policy for childhood. The networks of crèches (0–3 years) and nursery schools (3–6 years) developed as two separate branches of public policy and had no connection to any family policy. Thus, whereas the nursery schools developed as part of the education system and their provision is virtually universal, the same is not the case for crèches which were originally set up to deal with the children of poor working mothers. The crèches are now unevenly distributed across the country. Apart from the lack of coverage, another problem with crèches is their 'rigidity'. In fact, their organisation and opening times are not designed to meet the needs of working families. For instance, long opening hours are not part of the crèche policy. Funding for crèches is also declining, in spite of growing demand. This results in the increase in crèche fees paid by parents and the expansion of private alternatives (Saraceno 1997).

As we will see later on in the book, elderly care and childcare are two sectors of high demand for immigrant women's labour. Immigrant women – by providing the cheap and flexible services that the state does not provide – offer Italian women an alternative to their 'double day' work while being compatible with cultural norms that see the care for the old and the very young as best done at home. Although more is now known about the organisation of foreign domestic work in Southern Europe (Anderson 2000; Andall 2000a), less attention has been so far given to the consequences of these arrangements for the immigrant women who perform these services. Their experiences in this respect will be explored in the ethnographic chapters of this book.

Recognising Difference

Grillo (2002) argues that questions relating to the recognition of difference have to be located in an historical perspective. He notes that Italy has had its own specific 'politics of recognising difference'. The politics of difference or recognition originates in the United States where it was advocated by minorities as a way for oppressed groups to organise autonomously and assert a positive sense of their specificity (see Young 1990; Però 2007). However, Grillo points out that in the Italian context the politics of recognising difference tends to have rather negative connotations. Historically Italy has recognised a difference between the North and the South; between Italy and its former colonies; and between Catholics and non-Catholics – just to give a few examples. Such recognition has been in negative terms, however, revolving around a series of 'xenophobic' counterposing images such as the following, between 'a "Northern", "Western", above all "European", "modern", and "civilized" Italy, Catholic, too, albeit in a complex and sometimes contradictory ways, and a "primitive", "backward", "violent" and "irrational" "South" and "East", that in contemporary terms is readily associated with crime, drugs, and prostitution (Grillo 2002:15).

Spain too has a long history of recognising difference, for instance between autonomous regions, between the peninsula and its former colonies, between North and South, etc. In Spain, too, the way difference has been recognised has been in negative and in inferiorising terms. Anthropologist Dolores Juliano (2000: 386) argues that the main historic 'other' in the Iberian Peninsula has been the Moor. New immigrants are constructed with reference to this historic 'other'. Contemporary Muslim immigrants are thus depicted as 'fanatic and fundamentalist', 'aggressive' and 'discriminatory against women'. To them are opposed the 'democratic', 'civilised', 'progressive' Spaniards (on the construction of immigrants as 'other' see also Chapter 2).

'Managing Difference'

Such ideas of 'difference' shape and resurface in the institutional response to immigration. Many authors have pointed out that both Italy and Spain had difficulties in recognising their changed status from countries of emigration to countries of immigration (Hellman 1997; Maher 1996). Both were slow in legislating and developing policies devoted to the issue of immigration. For several years immigration occurred in a legislative vacuum, with the initiative towards the incorporation of newly arrived immigrants left to the goodwill of local authorities, with scarce resources and little coordination with central government. In spite of the initial shock, however, both Italy and Spain have started to come to terms with the new situation, providing comprehensive legislation and undertaking processes of self-examination.

In the sphere of immigration policy, Italy has passed four sets of legislation (the laws of 1986, 1990, 1998, 2002). Andall (2000a: 54) defines Italy's response to immigration contained in the first three laws as theoretically pluralist (if not in reality). In her view, Italy's legacy as a country of emigration 'leads many to articulate a moral obligation not only to treat migrants well but to respect their cultural difference' (2000a: 54). Grillo too notes that, if in the initial legislative response the stress was on control, by 1998 rights and difference received greater prominence (2002: 16). However, what tended to prevail in practice was a negative recognition of difference. The 2002 Bossi–Fini law shifted again the focus towards control and repressive measures (Colombo and Sciortino 2004; Schuster 2005). However, the implementation of the law was accompanied by a new regularisation programme which became the largest ever in Europe (Schuster 2005). According to Colombo and Sciortino (2004: 67) large sectors of public opinion pressed for the regularisation, worried that the new restrictive law would take away the foreign domestic and care workers who had become vital for an increasing number of Italian families.

In Italy the recognition of difference and the management of this difference (or multiculturalism) seem to be based on essentialist notions of culture. What seems to prevail is 'the idea that cultures are static, bounded entities, and that culture in the anthropological sense determines individual and collective identities and their place in social and political schemas' (Grillo 2002: 23). Thus Grillo points out that the recognition of difference in itself is not necessarily positive, since it can reinforce processes of exclusion rather than challenge them: a trend that Però (1997, 2002a) has documented well in the cases of left-wing multicultural policy making in the areas of housing and political participation. In Bologna the recognition of immigrants' 'difference' resulted in allocating them to second-rate housing schemes (metal bungalows) and in confining their possibility to voice their political demands to parallel (and powerless) political institutions.

As far as Spanish immigration legislation is concerned, it followed a fairly similar evolution to the Italian one, moving from early attempts to control entry towards more comprehensive legislation trying, on the one hand, to control and plan inflows and, on the other hand, to favour the 'integration' of legal residents. Spain had its first 'foreigners law' in 1985 (Ley Orgánica 7/85), which entered into force just a few months before Spain joined the European Community in 1986. According to Escrivà (2000a: 201) this law was strongly influenced by three factors, namely: forthcoming membership of the European Union, strong links with Latin America and geographical proximity to the African coast. New guidelines for border controls where introduced with the 1986 law to guard the southern shores of the European Union. As in Italy, since 1986 immigrants were required to obtain a residence and work permit in order to become legal citizens (Escrivà 2000a). As regards the links with Latin America, these were recognised in the special treatment reserved to Latin Americans, Equatorial Guineans but also to Filipinos. They are entitled to: preferential residence and work permits;

easier renewal of permits and the issuing of longer and more flexible permits; no visa requirements to enter the country (with the exception of Cubans, Dominican Republicans and Peruvians); and a faster application procedure for the granting of Spanish nationality (Escrivà 2000a: 202). However, the geographical proximity with Morocco (also a former colony), and the fear of massive immigration from there, resulted in the denial of the same preferential treatment to Moroccan subjects (Escrivà 2000a).

In a similar vein to Italy, Spain in 1991 promulgated an amnesty law to attempt to solve the problem of the so-called 'illegal' immigrants. Differently from Italy, Spain introduced a quota system already in 1993. The annual quota for non-EU nationals was initially set at 20,000 entrants but was increased in subsequent years. The quotas for 1993 and 1994 were used mainly to regularise those immigrants already present in the territory, rather than for regulating new entries. The quota system was suspended in 1996 when a new regularisation was launched and it was reinstated again in 1997 (Escrivà 2000). A new extraordinary legalisation process followed in 2005 (Hartman 2008).

In spite of the numerous similarities noted above there is, however, a difference worth noting between Italy and Spain (and especially Catalonia) on the issue of the management of diversity. This is the Catalan opposition to and criticism of the idea of multiculturalism. Such opposition does not originate exclusively in right-wing circles as is the case in Italy, but rather it seems to occupy a shared position across the political spectrum. The Ajuntament (Council) of Barcelona (which at the time of fieldwork was socialist), for instance, declares itself against multicultural policies which result in the creation of separate services for the immigrants, and stands instead for making the normal services available to everybody (interviews with Council officials 2001, and Grassilli 2001).

The same stance was adopted by the Generalitat (2001: 118) (which was nationalist), which, anticipating neo-assimilationist discourses now prevalent also in the UK (Goodhart 2004; Phillips 2006) in its four-year plan on immigration, struck a posture explicitly against what it called 'Anglo-Saxon multiculturalism' and suggested aiming for 'a balance between social cohesion and diversity'. They propose instead a 'Catalan way to integration' (Generalitat 2001: 118):

> We have to promote our own style of *convivència* based on democratic values, on our own language and culture which has developed through the centuries and which has been enriched by foreign inputs as will continue to happen in the future. ... All this will mean for immigrants a process of adaptation without rejecting their origin and their identity.

What emerges from the above quote, however, is that what seems to worry the Catalan authorities is not the potential exclusion and marginalisation of immigrants but rather the protection of the 'Catalan cultural identity' which they consider threatened by immigrants' 'cultures'.

Politicising Difference

Political forces have responded to the issue of immigration in different ways. We have already seen above how the main Italian left-wing party (DS) framed the issue of immigration. The party which has made the issue of immigration its main political tool and which has had the greatest impact on popular discourse has been the Northern League of Umberto Bossi (King and Andall 1999: 154). This party has adopted a clear anti-Southerner and anti-immigration stance with a political programme advocating strong autonomy from central government, strict immigration controls and the reduction of the number of immigrants in Italy. Its explicitly anti-Southerner and anti-immigrant stance has had two important consequences, according to Pratt (2002). First, it has articulated and rendered as commonly accepted the fact that Northerners are different from Southerners and that the relationship of the latter with the central state is unacceptable. Second, it has legitimised xenophobia.

This is a path that Catalan political forces have wanted to avoid. They in fact agreed not to use the issue of immigration as an electoral tool. All political forces represented in the Parliament of Catalonia signed the *Document de la Comisió d'Estudi sobre la Política d'Immigració a Catalunya* ('The Document of the Study Commission on the Politics of Immigration in Catalonia') which sets guidelines on the handling of immigration. All parties agreed to adhere to such guidelines (Generalitat 2001; Parlament de Catalunya 2001). In practice, however, important political Catalan figures have made anti-immigrant declarations and at the time of fieldwork there was a growing 'concern' with the issue of immigration and a general climate inclined to support new restrictive measures.

Given the social and political characteristics and conditions of the Southern European context just described, we can anticipate that the Moroccan and Filipino women at the heart of this book will be involved in transnational activities, as economic uncertainty and social and political subordination are considered important factors shaping migrants' propensity to develop and sustain transnational links (Glick Schiller et al. 1992). However, the implications of transnational living and identities for migrants' incorporation were not debated or considered in the prevailing discourses on migration at the time of fieldwork. This book will consider the transnational practices of two different migrant groups as well as spell out some of the consequences of transnationalism for migrant women and their families as well as for the settlement process.

Research Settings: Bologna and Barcelona

Bologna

Bologna is the capital city of Emilia-Romagna, a region located in the north-central part of Italy. Economically, it belongs to the richest area in Southern Europe and is characterised by a widespread wealth and one of the lowest unemployment rates of Southern Europe. Its economy is founded mainly on the industrial sector (based on a well-developed structure of small and medium-sized industries) and the tertiary sector. Its province and region also have a very strong agricultural sector. Emilia-Romagna is often indicated as an exemplary case of the 'Third Italy' model of flexible accumulation (Brusco 1982; King 1987: 197–202). Its production is decentralised in small- and medium-sized units – several of which are cooperatives – closely interconnected to one another.

Politically, Emiglia-Romagna belongs to the so-called Red Belt and Bologna has a long tradition of left-wing administration. The PCI-PDS, in fact, governed the city continuously from the end of the second world war up to the recent historic defeat of 1999 and then again from 2004. Its policies were always innovative and the social services of the city gained a reputation for being outstanding by the average Italian standard, especially in relation to the working classes, women, old people and gay and lesbians (Ginsborg 1990; Kerzer 1980; Jaggi et al. 1977; Però 1997).

Although less than other Northern Italian cities such as Turin and Milan, Bologna has experienced important immigrations in the past. In fact, between the 1950s and 1970s it received significant inflows of internal immigrants arriving from the impoverished regions of Southern Italy (Però 1999). The foreign population residing in the municipality of Bologna in December 2000 numbered 16,190, or 4.3 per cent of a total population of 379,964 (Comune di Bologna 2000). In the dynamic Bolognese economy immigrants find jobs easily, especially in low-skilled occupations avoided by the local population. The main sectors of activity for men are construction, manufacturing industry and agriculture. Women are employed mainly in the care and domestic sector (Però 1997).

In 2000, the two largest immigrant groups were those studied in this book, Moroccans and Filipinos (see Table 1.4). They maintained the same leading positions they had in the past, since immigration first began in the 1970s. As far as the sex composition of the two groups is concerned, we can see that Moroccans were still a predominantly male group (women represented 38.1 per cent of the group) and Filipinos a mainly female one (58.8 per cent). Both groups, however, seem to be moving towards more balanced sex ratios, although slowly. In 1997 Moroccan women represented only 30.2 per cent of their group, and Filipinas 60.3 per cent of theirs. In 2004 Moroccan women were 41.5 per cent and Filipinas 56.7 per cent.

Table 1.4 Foreign nationals residing in Bologna, 1997 and 2000

Country of origin	31/12/2000 Total	31/12/2000 Women	31/12/1997 Total	31/12/1997 Women
Morocco	2,100	802	(1) 1,473	446
Philippines	1,689	1,159	(2) 1,303	786
China	1,356	660	(3) 890	430
Albania	898	360	(6) 418	132
Bangladesh	765	203	(9) 298	70
Jugoslavia (Serbia -Montenegro)	692	337	(4) 657	319
Tunisia	634	147	(5) 512	70
Sri Lanka	630	279	(7) 374	161
Pakistan	539	92	(8) 356	30
Greece	420	139	-	-

Sources: Comune di Bologna (2001); Osservatorio Comunale delle Immigrazioni (1998, no. 1).

As far as the management of the 'new immigrations' in the city is concerned, the Council of Bologna anticipated the national legislation and from the early 1990s showed a concern for the recognition of cultural diversity and a commitment to the social integration of immigrants (see Municipal Charter, Comune di Bologna 1997, cited in Però 2001). In order to achieve these goals the Council of Bologna designed a number of policy initiatives targeting the immigrants. In 1994 it created the ISI (Institution for Immigration Services) as a unitary service for immigration. However, Però (2001, 2007) noted from his ethnographic research that the formal claims made by the Council through the ISI in favour of multiculturalism and the integration of immigrants were largely inconsistent with its exclusionary policy practices, a point confirmed by Grassilli's research (2002) and by my own. The cases of the Forum (Però 2000a) and of that of the housing policy for immigrants are two examples of questionable Bolognese policies towards immigrants. In the sphere of housing, when in 1990 the Martelli law was passed allocating funds to local authorities for the setting up of shelters for immigrants, the Council quickly intervened by 'recycling' a few disused public buildings and subsequently by creating brand new centres. Around 1990 in Bologna there were about 1,000 'first shelter' beds distributed in eight CPAs *(Centri di Prime Accoglienta)* (Però 1997). However, what were meant as temporary accommodations (they were initially designed for sixty days) become long-term arrangements, with some immigrants having already spent more than a decade in them.

Moreover, it has to be pointed out that the Council's housing policy scarcely addressed the needs of immigrant women. Of the twelve centres, ten were for male workers, one was for families and one was for women and their children. The one specifically for women has only twenty-five places. It is clear that the target population of the Centres of First Shelter were and, due to the inertia of the policy still are, single men (Zontini 2002).

Barcelona

Barcelona is the capital city of Catalonia, an area of Spain which since 1979 has had the juridical status of autonomous region. Together with the Basque country, Catalonia is one of the main industrial regions of Spain and in recent years has been an economically and culturally very dynamic region. Barcelona's main economic sectors are industry (mainly small and medium-sized) and the expanding sectors of tourism and services. Like Bologna, it has a tradition of left-wing administration, having always had socialist Mayors from the first free local elections held in 1978 after the death of Franco up to the present. Unlike Bologna, during fieldwork it did not belong to a left-administered area of the country (it does now) but was rather an enclave surrounded by a nationalist-administered region, located within a conservative state. In spite of its political isolation, Barcelona's local administration has excelled in innovative policies and ambitious programmes in recent years.

Although Spain was until very recently a country of emigration, Barcelona, like Bologna, has a tradition of being an immigration region, having witnessed important internal immigration flows both in the nineteenth and twentieth century (Pascual de Sans et al. 2000; Solé 2001). During the era of postwar economic expansion that went from the 1950s to the early 1970s, it received its most important immigration from the poorer regions of Spain. Recent foreign immigration to Barcelona is still much less than the estimated internal migration received by the city before the 1970s. In January 2001 the foreign population of the city numbered 74,019, 4.9 per cent of a total population of 1,508,805 (Ajuntament de Barcelona 2001). Differently from Bologna, immigrants have hardly penetrated the industrial sector; instead, they are employed in tourism and services, as well as in construction (Pascual de Sans et al. 2000). In 2001 the largest immigrant group in the city was the Ecuadorian one which had grown at a spectacular rate since 1996 when it was only the twenty-fourth biggest group (see Table 1.5). As for the two nationalities analysed in this book, Moroccans were the second largest group, consolidating the position they had in 1996, whereas Filipinos, although they increased their numbers, moved down from fourth to seventh place. There are no data by sex for 2001, but looking at the partial 1997 data we can see that Moroccans remained a predominantly male group (women are 44.5 per cent of the group) and Filipinos a mainly female one (58.4 per cent). Contrary to what has happened in Bologna these two groups do not seem to be moving towards more balanced sex ratios. In 2006 Moroccan women went down to 41.7 per cent of their group and Filipinas stayed at 58 per cent. What is interesting to note is that even though they belong to a masculinised group, Moroccan women represent one of the largest female groups in the city. Contrary to common stereotypes, Moroccan women in 1996 were the group with the biggest number of employed women, followed by Peruvian and French women (Domingo and Brancós 2000).

Table 1.5 Foreign nationals residing in Barcelona, 1996 and 2001

Country of origin	01/01/2001	31/12/96	Women 1997
Ecuador	8,204	378	-
Morocco	7,165	3,838	1,550 (44.5 per cent)
Peru	6,879	3,937	1,865 (61.3 per cent)
Colombia	4,708	937	-
Dominican Republic	4,136	2,507	1,177 (76.9 per cent)
Pakistan	3,405	1,072	-
Philippines	3,176	2,878	1,116 (58.4 per cent)
Italy	3,142	2,811	-
France	2,943	3,299	-
Argentina	2,504	1,870	-

Sources: Elaborated from the following: Ajuntament de Barcelona (2001), Domingo and Brancós (2000), Observatori Permanent de la Immigració (1998).

The way in which Barcelona responded to immigration seems, at first sight, quite different from Bologna. In fact, in policy documents and interviews with Council officials, it emerges that the Council of Barcelona opposes the creation of specific services targeting immigrants and rather wishes to promote their full integration in the regular services of the city by adjusting the latter to their presence. This policy is reflected in the Council document *Un Plan Municipal para la Multiculturalidad* (Barcelona City Council 1999, quoted in Grassilli 2002) which stressed that cultural diversity should be accompanied by equality of opportunity.

This refusal in principle to deal with immigrants as a special category seems to be dictated partly by the fear of excluding immigrants and partly by more political concerns connected with the desire of preserving a Catalan cultural identity which is perceived as threatened by the arrival of foreigners. However, in spite of the claims, Barcelona does have special services and institutions targeting immigrants which, in spite of the different immigration policy, resemble quite closely those of Bologna.

Bologna dealt with immigrants' access to housing in a very problematic way, as was previously discussed. Barcelona City Council opted instead for not intervening at all, in spite of the Plan Municipal's recognition that housing is an area 'where more should be done'. Thus, no public initiatives in this sphere took place during the period of my fieldwork. Rather, the Council embarked on important projects of inner-city regeneration that, given the increase in property prices that they favoured (as we will see in Chapter 5), made immigrant's access to housing even more difficult.

In Barcelona social integration and equal opportunity were stressed and a differentiated treatment of immigrants refused. In practice, however, the institutional support for immigrants' access to 'normal' services in condition of equal opportunities was minimal. Thus, I can conclude that in spite of apparent differences, the ways in which the two cities have responded to the 'new immigration' seem to be rather similar. Both cities hardly projected the 'model policy' on immigration that one could expect from two cities that have long enjoyed the reputation of being among the most progressive and innovative of their countries.

Outline of the Book

This book is organised as follows. Chapter 2 situates the study within debates on gender and migration, transnationalism and settlement as well as family studies. The chapter brings together literature from various disciplines and combines themes that, at least in the European context, are normally considered separately. Based on such literature the chapter seeks to develop a theoretical framework for the book that, while drawing on geographically diverse material, takes into account the specificity of the Southern European context.

Chapter 3 initiates the ethnographic examination of Moroccan and Filipino women's experiences as they emerged from the fieldwork I conducted in Bologna. The themes treated are as follows. First, I examine the reasons why migrant women came to Bologna and the mechanisms they use (both legal and illegal) to get there. Second, I look at immigrant women's position in the local labour market. Finally, I examine women's central role in so-called 'transnational families'.

Chapter 4 presents the findings of my Barcelona fieldwork. It follows the structure of the previous chapter, starting with immigrant women's migration histories. The case of Barcelona confirms the importance of the interplay between economic motives and other factors, such as women's roles and positions within families and kin groups, in order to understand the reasons behind these women's migration. Second, the chapter explores the role of women as key economic actors both for their own families and for Spanish middle-class families who benefit from their services. The final section deals with how women's roles in 'transnational families' influence women's behaviour and choices.

Chapter 5 interprets in a comparative context the ethnographic material from Chapters 3 and 4. The chapter brings together the experiences of each group of women in the two cities and highlights the similarities and differences among them in relation to the three key themes discussed in the ethnographic chapters (the reasons behind women's migration, their insertion in local labour markets, and the characteristics of new immigrant families and women's roles in them). The aim of the chapter is to summarise in an explicitly comparative context the main findings emerging from the field research.

Finally, Chapter 6 links my findings with wider theoretical debates on gender, migration and transnationalism going back to the research questions presented in this introduction as well as in Chapter 2.

Notes

1. These figures are indicative for two reasons: first, there are recognised problems with existing records of immigrants; and second, such figures do not include so-called 'illegal' immigrants who are, by definition, difficult to quantify (King 2001; King and Andall 1999). The figures for 2002 are the relevant ones for the period when fieldwork was conducted. The foreign residents in 2005 were 2,402,157 in Italy (Istat 2006) and 3,730,610 in Spain (INE 2006).
2. In 2005 the top five immigrant groups in Italy were Albanians (316,659) followed by Moroccans (294,945), Romanians (248,849), Chinese (111,712) and Ukrainians (93,441), with Filipinos (82,625) now in sixth place (Istat 2006). In Spain they were Moroccans (557,219), Ecuadorians (479,978), Romanians (312,099), Colombians (288,190) and Argentineans (260,386), with Filipinos in thirty-first place (25,522) (INE 2006).
3. In 2005 the groups with a female majority in Italy were in descending order: Ukrainians, Filipinas, Polish, Ecuadorians and Peruvians (Istat 2006). In Spain they were: Ecuadorians, Colombians, Bolivians, Peruvians, Dominicans (INE 2006). In Italy the groups with a male majority were: Moroccans, Albanians, Chinese, Tunisians and Senegalese (Istat 2006). In Spain they were Moroccans, Rumanians, Argentineans, Bulgarians and Chinese (INE 2006).
4. See also Carter (1997), Cole (1997), Maher (1996).
5. See Santamaría (2002), Juliano (1998).

2
TRANSNATIONAL MIGRATION, GENDER AND SETTLEMENT: TOWARDS AN UNDERSTANDING OF THE SOUTHERN EUROPEAN CASE

Recent literature on transnationalism has attempted to break down the divide between sending and receiving societies, offering a unified perspective on the migration experience which encompasses the multidirectional relationships that individuals maintain across countries. However, a large body of literature, especially in Europe, continues to focus on either the migration process or on aspects related to settlement. This chapter aims at reviewing and bringing together these two areas of research in order to develop a framework that looks at settlement in Southern Europe from both a gendered and transnational perspective. The chapter starts with a review of early attempts to 'gender' migration theories and shows how such approaches still influence current Southern European literature. I then move on to consider more recent developments in the field, concentrating on those approaches that go beyond the structure and agency impasse, and develop meso-level theories that combine micro- and macro-level perspectives. I review the different meso-level units that are considered crucial for understanding the migration process; namely the household, the family, social networks and migratory institutions. I also consider how these new approaches have been taken on board in Southern European studies and with what results. The first half of the chapter concludes with the presentation of a possible model for interpreting female migration, based on a combination of the different elements previously discussed. The second half deals with settlement seen as a gendered and transnational process, paying special attention to two issues that I see as closely linked: women's position in the labour market and women's role in the family (which often extends across borders). The chapter concludes by summarising a framework for a gender analysis of migration and settlement in Southern Europe that combines the insights gained from authors interested in the migration process with those from scholars working from the perspective of receiving societies.

Early Attempts to 'Gender' Migration Theories: Migrant Women as Economic Actors

Writing in the early 1980s authors such as Annie Phizacklea (1983) and Mirjana Morokvasic (1983, 1984) were among the first to point out the male bias in migration research. Morokvasic (1984) highlighted how women were neglected in most migration research and how, when they were included, they were described in a stereotypical fashion. Using a tradition/modernity framework to explain migrants' experiences, this male-centred literature invariably associated migrant women with the pole of tradition, describing them as dependent on male migrants, uneducated, unable to speak the language of the new society, and anchored to their 'culture'. If mentioned at all, women were thus only considered in their roles as wives and mothers, that is, in their roles within 'the family'. Feminist researchers wanted to challenge such images, showing the diversity of women's experiences and how, in many cases, women were initiators of migrations in their own right and active protagonists in the labour market (Buijs 1993; Morokvasic 1983, 1984; Phizacklea 1983). Morokvasic's call to see female migrants as economic migrants, and not as mere dependants, has been taken on board in Southern Europe, especially by (female) scholars who, during the 1990s, started to direct their attention to the growing presence in the region of migratory flows composed predominantly by women.

Two elements can be identified with respect to this Southern European literature. On the one hand, authors' desire to redress previous 'mistakes' resulted in an almost exclusive focus on immigrant women's economic function. This translated into a particular attention paid to the role of women in two niche sectors of Southern European economies: domestic service and sex work. Other aspects linked to the migration experience thus became largely marginalised, notably those related to 'the family' and women's role and position in it. On the other hand, researchers focusing on Southern Europe applied Morokvasic's framework of analysis to some groups of women, but not to others, which continued to be described in a stereotypical fashion as passive followers and victims of their tradition. I am referring here to North African women whose economic function continued to be neglected well into the 1990s. Studies produced particularly in Italy during the early 1990s, developed a typology of migrant women which divided them in two supposedly opposed categories: autonomous and dependant migrants. To the former group belonged women of feminised groups such as Filipinas, Latin Americans and Cape Verdeans, who were described as solo migrants moving for work reasons; to the latter belonged mainly Moroccan women who were described as migrating to follow their husbands.

In the few studies carried out in Italy on female migration before the 1990s, women's migration was framed within push factors, such as poverty and destitution in their countries of origin. It is only in the mid 1990s that pull factors within Southern Europe are recognised and explored (Andall 2000a; Anthias and Lazaridis 2000; Catarino and Oso 2000; King and Zontini 2000; Herranz 1996; Parella 2000; Vicarelli 1994). The desire to explore the structural conditions favouring migration to Southern Europe and to show that women were key economic actors at the centre of the region's transformations, resulted in a number of studies focusing on migrant women's insertion in the local labour market, especially in domestic service.

Chell (1997) explicitly sets out to vindicate Morokvasic's claim of the importance of female economic migration, looking at Filipino and Somali women's insertion in the domestic labour sector in Rome. She frames their migration within push (poverty in the Philippines and war in Somalia) and pull factors (increased demand in feminised jobs) and demonstrates how both groups of women are key economic actors, not only supporting themselves but also taking care economically of entire families left behind. In the same year Escrivà (1997) used a very similar theoretical framework to analyse Peruvian women migrating to Barcelona. She too centres on their productive role, documenting their insertion in the Catalan domestic service market.

It is particularly in Spain that, through a number of doctoral theses (Escrivà 1999; Gregorio 1996; Herranz 1996; Ramirez 1997; Ribas 1996) and related articles, immigrant women's central role in specific sectors of the local labour market has been explored. Herranz (1998), for instance, analyses the feminisation of migration to Madrid in relation to the growing demand in the domestic service sector in the city. Catarino and Oso (2000) focus on domestic service, comparing immigrant women's insertion in the sector in Spain and Portugal; and so does Parella (2000) who centres on the local structural conditions to demonstrate that immigrant women are suffering a triple discrimination in the Spanish labour market based on social class, gender and ethnicity.

The ethnicisation of domestic service is a theme taken up also by Gabriella Lazaridis (2000) in the first collection published in English on the topic of gender and migration in Southern Europe. She too frames the migration of Filipino and Albanian women to Greece within push and pull factors. After having analysed the structural factors present in Greece she concludes that immigrant women 'are trapped in a condition of inferiority, immobility and ultra-exploitation' (2000: 72). Similar frameworks are adopted also by Chell

(2000) and Ribas (2000a) writing in the same volume, with reference to Italy and Spain respectively.

The emergence of the dichotomy of autonomous versus dependent female migrants in the Southern European literature has its origins at the beginning of the 1990s. We can find it, for instance, in the works of Favaro and Bordogna (1992) and De Filippo (1994) when they sketch different models of female migration to Italy. Elena De Filippo (1994: 65) identifies four such models: '*women head of households* (that is to say Eritrean, Cape Verdean, Filipino domestic helpers), *travel mates* (Ghanaians, Nigerians, Côte d' Ivorians who came to Italy with a member of their family); *wives* (Moroccans and Tunisians who arrived for family reunification) and *tourists* (Polish women)'.

We can already see the emergence of the dichotomy between supposedly 'independent' women who migrate to work, such as Filipinas, and 'passive' women, like Moroccans, who merely follow their husbands (see Giannini 1994). With regard to the latter group De Filippo (1994: 68) says: 'Very different is the condition of Muslim women who come to Naples within the framework of a migration project defined by the men of their families. They are the wives … .'

We have to wait until 1998 to see a critique of the model that conceptualised Moroccan women migrating to Italy as passive followers of their husbands, steeped in tradition, and economically inactive. Schmidt di Friedberg and Saint-Blancat (1998) analyse the changes brought about by migration for Moroccan women residing in Veneto both in relation to work and the family. This study distances itself from modernisation theories and shows how Moroccan women are neither anchored to tradition nor uncritically embracing the culture and values of the receiving society (see also Busato 2001).

Gregorio (1998) adopts a similar approach to that of Schmidt di Friedberg and Saint-Blancat, arguing against modernisation theories in the context of female migration to Spain. She shows that the Dominican women she interviewed in Madrid are both changing and adapting to the new society and retaining cultural values of their society of origin. Other Spanish studies also challenge the passive role of Moroccan women, viewing them as autonomous social and economic actors: Herranz (1998) looks at Moroccan women's participation in the domestic service sector in Madrid, and Ramírez (1998) focuses on Moroccan migrants' associationism.

Yet, as late as 2000, we still find interpretations that reproduce the simple dualistic model where the autonomous female migrants who move to work are contrasted with those who follow their husbands. The latter group, as usual, is associated with North African women. De Filippo and Pugliese (2000) stress the importance of looking at immigrant women as economic actors but this does not seem to apply to Moroccan women whose migration continues to be interpreted in relation to that of the male members of their families: 'North

African women arrived in Italy for family reunification within a migration project almost always defined by the men of their families' (De Filippo and Pugliese 2000: 66).

This brief overview of the Southern European literature of the 1990s on gender and migration has shown that the theoretical approaches developed in the 1980s in the Northern European context were taken on board and adapted to the local context. However, this was less the case in relation to Moroccan women who, well into the 1990s, continued to be described in a stereotypical fashion and viewed merely as dependants whose experiences could be inferred from those of the male members of their families. In contrast, the main problem with the approach that aimed to show that migrant women were important economic actors was that it tended to over-emphasise economic factors influencing migration, paying scant attention to 'non-economic' elements that, as I will show, are particularly relevant for understanding female migration. In their attempt to go beyond the equation 'women = wives and mothers', these latter authors went to the other extreme, focusing almost exclusively on women as autonomous economic subjects and on their involvement in the labour market. Another criticism that can be applied to this literature is that, by looking at immigrant women from the perspective of the receiving societies, it tended to focus on structural factors determining their position, paying almost no attention to the agency of these women and the ways they interpreted and acted upon their circumstances.

In my work I acknowledge the importance of the economic dimension, seeing it at the root of much female migration. However, I also see the need to go beyond it so as to include also sociocultural factors. This book, contrary to much of the existing Southern European literature, seeks to utilise the *same interpretative framework* for analysing Moroccan and Filipino women's migration. Rather than assuming and viewing Filipinas as 'active workers' and Moroccans as 'passive followers', I will consider the economic *and* non-economic factors influencing the migration of *both* groups. And I will enrich this comparison by making it in two cities in two different Southern European countries. The experiences of these women will be compared against each other (rather than against a supposedly 'modern' European woman) to show the similarities and differences that emerge among women confronted with the same structural constraints in the context of arrival. In doing so, I hope to dispel those stereotypes and misconceptions that are unfortunately still recurrent about female migrants.

Beyond Structure and Agency:
Households, Families, Networks and 'Migratory Institutions'

While Southern European scholars were preoccupied to show the economic nature of female migration (denied in mainstream accounts of European postwar migration), scholars working in other geographical areas were trying to move beyond previous conceptualisations by paying renewed attention to social factors influencing migration and giving centrality to households and families as analytical units. These authors were becoming increasingly dissatisfied with current theories of migration which, focusing mainly on economic factors, were not capable of explaining important features of current migratory flows, such as their self-sustaining nature or their gender-selectivity (see Anthias 2000; Brettell 2000; Chant 1992; Chant and McIlwaine 1995; Kofman et al. 2000; Phizacklea 1998; Tacoli 1999; Wright 1995).

The main criticisms that feminist scholars have applied to the neoliberal approach are, first, that it assumes that men and women move for the same reasons (they are supposedly moving to the destination that offers the highest net economic returns); and second, that, in so doing, it fails to take into account non-economic constraints around choice and also the presence of structural forces affecting decision making. Structuralist accounts are criticised for the opposite reason, namely their over-socialised view of migration (seen as a consequence of the need of capital for cheap labour) that leaves no room for human agency. Their exclusive focus on production and their consequent marginalisation of the issue of reproduction are also seen as problematic by feminist scholars.

What the new approaches have in common is their attempt to resolve the structure/agency opposition in order to provide accounts of migration that, while recognising the structural context within which migration occurs, leave space for the appreciation of human agency. Increasingly authors are referring to these ways of conceptualising migration as structuration approaches (Chant 1992; Kofman et al. 2000; Phizacklea 1998; Wright 1995). The name derives from a concept employed by Giddens (1984) 'to express the mutual dependency, rather than opposition, of human agency and social structure' (Wright 1995: 771). Such a model presupposes that structures are both constraining and enabling.

These approaches have been taken on board and further developed by feminist scholars who see them as particularly fruitful for the study of immigrant women. They believe that what is needed is a new approach that synthesises the positive elements of previous models, that is to say, a model that sees migrants as social actors and not as passive victims, but which also considers the social, political and economic power structures, at the national and international level, which limit and influence their actions. Several authors are thus becoming interested in a meso-level of analysis where micro- and macro-level factors influencing migration can be integrated. If all seem to agree on the need to reconcile structure and agency, the way to go about it does not seem to be clear, however. The issue on which authors seem to diverge is what exactly has to be included in what Thomas Faist (1997) has called the 'crucial meso-level'. Authors seem to focus their attention on four different units of analysis, which I will briefly review in the remainder of this section: the household, the family, social networks and so-called 'migration institutions'.

Households

In order to explain the reasons for migrating some authors have shifted their attention from the individual as decision maker to the household. In this approach the household is seen as the main unit mediating between the individual and the larger structural setting in which he/she is living. The household strategies approach developed mainly in the US to account for the ways in which decisions about migration were taken. In its early conceptualisations the household was seen as a cooperative unit where members pooled resources and took joint decisions, such as migration, for the well-being of the unit as a whole (Boyd 1989).

Feminist scholars criticise this view of the household as a cooperative unit and have elaborated more sophisticated and gendered versions of the household strategies model. Chant and Radcliffe (1992), for instance, define the household as: 'a social institution which organises resources (land, labour, tools, capital and so on) and recruits and allocates labour in a combination of reproductive and productive tasks. Gender divisions of labour are crucial to this pattern of livelihood and provide a basic template for household decisions about who will migrate and who will stay' (Chant and Radcliffe 1992: 22–23).

The importance of their approach lies in the fact that it pays attention to the nature of gender roles and relations in different cultural and economic contexts; it considers production as well as reproduction; and it points out the existence of power relations within households. For these reasons, it can be used as an important starting-point for the understanding of female migration in a variety of contexts. In a later publication Chant and McIlwaine (1995) further develop the household strategies approach to migration and use it to explain gender-selective migration (both rural–urban and international) in the Philippines. The validity of their approach lies, in their view, in the fact that it shows the crucial role of economic, labour and power disparities between men and women in shaping gender-selective migration and the relevance of the question of kinship obligations, especially among migrant daughters. Other elements influencing female migration, little considered generally, are issues of moral propriety and sexuality. Chant and McIlwaine believe that in order to refine the model it is important to identify what are the core factors that affect women's migration and to this end systematic application of the model in a range of places is needed.

Tacoli (1999) responds to this challenge in the context of Filipino migration to Italy. She believes that the household strategies approach is a good starting-point for explaining Filipino women's international migration. Within the factors that constrain individual choices and are articulated within the household, she sees normative gender roles as particularly important for explaining who moves and who does not. However, she identifies some limitations in the model. First, she found that the household is not the only institution where decisions about migration are taken, since non-kin networks also proved important in the Filipino case. Second, since it was originally developed to account for internal migrations, the household strategies approach does not deal adequately with the role of state policies in both sending and destination countries in shaping international migration.

Hondagneu-Sotelo (1994) posed an earlier criticism of the validity of the household strategies approach which she found only marginally relevant in accounting for the migration of Mexican families to the US. Although authors such as Chant (1992) recognise that households are not fully cooperative units and are divided along gender and generational lines, they still maintain that there is some level of cooperation and that members tend to share the same goals and objectives. Hondagneu-Sotelo (1994: 94–95) refutes this point:

> After looking at dynamic relations inside the household to see how various types of migration are formed, it is virtually impossible to retain the image of a unified household planning and enacting a particular migration strategy in calculated reaction to capitalist market forces. Opening the household 'black box' exposes a highly charged political arena where husbands and wives and parents and children may simultaneously express and pursue divergent interests and competing agendas. How these agendas become enacted draws attention to the place of patriarchal authority in shaping migration.

In Hondagneu-Sotelo's view not all decisions (such as that of migrating) are taken for the household's good. In her study, single migrants were never sent north as a result of calculations by other members of their household, nor did they do so out of moral obligation. What was common was that individuals responded to opportunities that opened up for them, such the invitation of a friend or a job offer. Subsequently they justified their move with explanations that included the well-being of their household, even if that was not their concern when they left. The second criticism that she makes of the household strategies approach is its emphasis on the household as the site where all decisions are taken, neglecting both intra-household relations and connections to wider social networks.

Feminist anthropologists (Bjéren 1997; Indra 1999; Moore 1988; Yanagisako 1979) have long criticised the use of the household as a prime analytical unit. Their main criticisms have been on households as cooperative pooling units and on their cross-cultural validity. According to Gunilla Bjéren (1997), the first point has been more widely taken on board in migration research, whereas the fact that households can take many forms and have different functions in different locations does not seem to have had the same impact.

The question that seems to remain open in the literature thus far discussed is to what extent decisions about migration are taken at the household level. Authors who have worked on Asian migration, such as Chant, MacIlwaine and Tacoli, seem to consider the household very important in this respect, whereas authors who have worked with other groups in other world regions, such as Hondagneu-Sotelo, seem to disagree. Have these different interpretations to do with the groups studied? In other words, is household-level decision making more relevant for some groups and less for others? What can the study of the Southern European experience add to this debate? With reference to this book, do households play the same role for Filipino and Moroccan female migration? And what are the other contributive factors? I shall attempt to answer these questions, both immediately below and elsewhere in the book.

Families

'The family' is a notion as much contested as the household. Sociologists of the family are now moving away from simplistic understandings of family as an objectively knowable entity, focusing instead on the complexity and variety of 'family practices' (Bernardes 1997; Gillies 2003; Morgan 1996). Anthropologists consider it of little cross-cultural validity since 'who is thought to be "family" and what that implies varies – between groups, individuals and contexts' (Bjeren 1997: 236). However, in spite of the weak accuracy of the term, some authors have pointed out that many migrants do frame their migration in a 'family relations' rhetoric and thus they believe that 'the family' remains an important meso-level unit for analysing how decisions about migration are taken and negotiated. It is particularly in studies on Asian migration that a renewed focus of attention on the family seems to have developed. Root and De Jong (1991), from the perspective of their analysis of Filipino internal and international migration, stress the importance of emphasising a family level of analysis. Yet the family migration model they develop does not make any reference to gender and power inequalities within families as having a role in predicting who will migrate and who will not.

Hania Zlotnik (1995), in a special issue of the *Asian and Pacific Migration Journal* dedicated to 'Migration and the Family', provides the female perspective on the issue. She identifies four reasons why a family perspective is important for the analysis of female migration. They are:

1) women are major participants in 'family migration' as defined by Governments and, albeit benefiting from family reunification provisions, they are also constrained by them; 2) migrant women are important economic actors and their participation in economic activity is closely related to the needs of their families, so that the choices that migrant women make regarding work cannot be understood without taking into account the situation of their families and their roles within them; 3) women are increasingly becoming migrant workers in order to improve the economic status of their families or at least to ensure that their basic survival needs are met; and 4) women rely on their families to provide various types of support that both make migration possible and condition its outcome. (Zlotnik 1995: 269)

Zlotnik believes that the role of families in the migration process is understudied, for two reasons: the strong influence of economic theory on research, resulting in an emphasis on productive activities and a consequent marginalisation of reproductive ones; and a view that migration involves transactions between nation-states and individuals, rather than between states and family groups, resulting in the fact that statistics collected by states do not allow researchers to make links among different family members and therefore to carry out quantitative analyses on family issues and strategies in migration.

Zlotnik (1995) reviews the international literature on women in family migration and on solo work-related migration. Rather than reproducing the passive vs. autonomous dichotomy identified in some Southern European literature, she shows how, on the one hand, women in family migration are not always in the position of dependants and how, on the other hand, a family perspective appears crucial in understanding women migrating alone for work. Zlotnik also starts to open up discussion on some of the implications of migration for family dynamics, such as the effects of migration on household composition, on the children left behind or on marital stability. Lim (1993), too, points out, but does not really explore, the potential interactive or feedback effect of migration on sex roles, on the structure and function of the family, and on the roles and relative position of individual women in it. Some of these issues have started to be explored in the emergent literature on transnational families (see section on immigrant women and the transnational family below) and will be looked at in detail in the ethnographic chapters of this book.

Both Lim (1993) and Zlotnik (1995) have stressed the importance of the family for understanding female migration. This is because it is in the family that women's subordination to male authority is more obvious and acquires special importance. Hondagneu-Sotelo (1994) shares this view and argues that patriarchal gender relations in families and communities determine how structural pressures and opportunities lead to particular patterns of migration and settlement. Lim sees the family as a socialising unit where 'culture' is mediated and transformed into action and where age and sex roles are assigned and expressed. It is within the family that 'migration motivations and values are shaped, human capital is accrued, information is received and interpreted, and decisions are put into operation' (Lim 1993: 230).

Within the European context, Kofman (1999, 2004) is one of the few interested in exploring issues relating to the family and migration, although recently there has been some new interest in the topic (see Ackers 1998; Ackers and Stalford 2004; Bailey and Boyle 2004). In her view, although it is one of the very few ways of having legal access to Western European countries, family migration has long been neglected theoretically, empirically and methodologically. She believes that the fact that women have been dominant in this form of migration is a possible explanation of the limited attention given to it by both academics and policy makers.

What roles families have in shaping migration and how in turn migration shapes family dynamics are questions that remain little explored. Whether families constrain or enable female migration and how families develop and are maintained across geographical borders are all issues that need further investigation. Thus, as far as this book is concerned, questions that need answering include the following: what is the role of families in Moroccan and Filipino migration to Southern Europe? How do families evolve and adapt as a result of migration? Are there differences between the two groups?

Social Networks

Although she criticises 'the family' as an analytical unit, Gunilla Bjéren (1997: 237) acknowledges the importance of kinship relations in shaping migratory processes: 'South to North migration does take place in networks based on kinship or pseudo-kinship, which I would call *effective* kinship links between people localised within social fields encompassing two or several countries. The image I want to use is of effective kinship networks crossing at "residential nodes".' Bjéren draws attention to other important meso-level units of analysis, namely social networks. As I pointed out earlier, other authors too, such as Tacoli and Hondagneu-Sotelo, have come to realise that decisions about migration are not taken exclusively within households and families, and that immigrants' participation in wider networks seems crucial.

The study of social networks is not new; they were in fact at the base of much research on chain migration conducted during the 1960s and 1970s. Yet, in recent decades, they are receiving new attention due to the limited efficacy of the main theories of migration to explain contemporary migrations and the potentiality of social network analysis for bridging macro- and micro-level perspectives on the migration experience.

According to Boyd (1989), who has written an influential review on the topic, family, friendship and community networks underlie much of the recent migration to industrial nations. The importance of networks lies in the fact that they bridge people and locations through time and space; they provide assistance and information about potential destination(s); they lower the costs and risks of migration. Not only are they important in the migration process but they may also facilitate and favour settlement since, through their networks, new migrants can get access to important resources, such as housing and work in an unknown setting (see Loizos 2000).

The functioning of networks helps scholars to explain the self-sustaining nature of migration in a way that economic theories alone cannot do. Migration flows have been shown to continue even when the economic element that caused them ceases to exist. That was the case, for instance, in Western Europe after the end of the labour recruiting policies of the 1960s and 1970s. In spite of the setting up of policies that discouraged further entries, immigration continued to grow. The types of ties that migrants maintain with non-migrants are very important for predicting further migration since, with the number of social ties expanding between a sending and receiving area, migration becomes within the reach of ever more families in the sending area, thus contributing to the self-sustaining nature of migration (Böcker 1995). It is therefore important to look at how these networks are maintained. Boyd (1989) has identified the following ways: by the flow of people who migrate and settle in a destination and the return migration of those who move back to their country of origin; by visits that relatives and friends make back and forth; by marriage contracted by settled migrants with people of the country of origin; and finally by remittances. Chant and Radcliffe (1992) add another element: by the flow of goods and presents that takes place in both directions (see Levitt 2001).

Attention to social networks also emerged from the need to go beyond previous conceptualisations of migration as occurring unidirectionally from a country of origin to one of destination. Researchers became aware that migrants maintain fluid relationships with several locations, often actively participating simultaneously in two or more societies. Such considerations are the basis of reflections on transnationalism (see for instance Basch et al. 1994; Smith and Guarnizo 1998; Levitt 2001; Portes, Guarnizo and Landolt 1999; Vertovec 1999), a topic I return to later in this chapter.

Writing at the end of the 1980s, Monica Boyd pointed out the 'little systematic attention ... paid to gender in the development and persistence of networks across time and space' (Boyd 1989: 657). Boyd believed that the working of networks is strongly gendered and thus the sex of the person providing pressure, aid or information about migration may influence the outcome of the decision making. This is because 'migration decision-making processes are shaped by sex-specific family and friendship sources of approval, disapproval, assistance and information' (Boyd 1989: 657).

Few studies have taken up Boyd's call and provided gendered accounts of the functioning of networks in migration. Chant and Radcliffe (1992) have acknowledged the relevance of gender in what they call source–destination linkages, noting that migrant women appear to be more committed than men to maintaining ties with home areas: 'sometimes this may relate to the fact that children are being reared in home areas, but it may also have to do with the widespread observation that women attach more importance to the family than men and/or are expected to do so within the general framework of kinship obligations' (Chant and Radcliffe 1992: 17). Hondagneu-Sotelo's work (1994) on Mexican migration to the US has shown how networks are not equally accessible to women and men since 'immigrant social networks are highly contested social resources, and are not always shared, even in the same family'(1994: 189). Because of the exclusive nature of some of the male networks, Mexican women are thus starting to develop their own networks. Thanks to the growing and consolidated nature of these women-to-women networks, some Mexican women are now able to circumvent or contest domestic patriarchal authority and achieve their objective to migrate north. Hondagneu-Sotelo (1994: 55) concludes that 'gender, together with age, intervenes in immigrant networks in ways that both facilitate and constrain migration opportunities for Mexican women and men'. Recently, Pessar and Mahler (2001) have offered a gendered perspective on transnational migration more generally, focusing on what they called 'gendered geographies of power'. By this they mean 'a framework for analysing people's social agency – corporal or cognitive – given their own initiative as well as their positioning within multiple hierarchies of power operative within and across many terrains' (2001: 8).

Southern Europe is characterised by gendered migrations, with some groups being predominantly male and others predominantly female. To what extent can we differentiate between male and female networks? Can we detect the existence of female chain migration? To what extent do social networks play a part in Moroccan and Filipino women's migration to Southern Europe? Are there differences in the ties used and maintained by these two national groups?

Migratory Institutions

In spite of the recognised importance of social networks in favouring migration, Kofman et al. (2000) believe that they 'do not by themselves provide an adequate bridge between structure and agency because they fail to take into account the increasingly formalised nature of migration' (Kofman et al. 2000: 29). In these authors' view, migration is increasingly facilitated and shaped by a myriad of organisations and agencies that operate in the 'business of migration' and therefore cannot be seen as influenced only by the informal sharing of information and contacts between relatives and friends characteristic of social networks. Lim and Oishi (1996: 90) state that:

> the growth of an 'immigration industry' in Asia has greatly facilitated female migration, both legal and illegal. Were it not for recruitment agents, overseas employment promoters, manpower suppliers and a host of other legal and illegal intermediaries, Asian labour migration since the mid-1970s would not have reached such a massive scale.

Some Asian governments are directly involved in promoting labour exports as a way of earning foreign cash that can be used to service their foreign debts. They have designed special policies and have opened up agencies to facilitate the link between their workers and distant employers. They have also favoured the private sector's involvement in the business of migrant recruitment. In the Philippines alone there are approximately seven hundred registered recruiting agencies (Lim and Oishi 1996), plus a growing number of illegal agencies and intermediaries operating both in the countries of origin and destination. The growth of such illegal channels may partly be due to the difficulties involved in legal migration, such as its high costs or its time-consuming procedures. Because of that, both migrants and their employers often prefer to resort to illegal channels. Lim and Oishi believe that it is women more than men who use such channels due to their lack of alternatives and limited access to information.

Although Lim and Oishi (1996) see the institutionalisation of migration as a key cause of the current Asian female migrant flow, they still recognise the importance of social networks in accounting for the self-sustaining nature of Asian migration. They believe that migration networks are gendered and that nowadays women move as part of chain migration more than men. However, few studies seem to have dealt with this issue in depth, especially as regards gender differences in the use of informal (and possibly illegal) migration channels (Kofman et al. 2000: 31).

Authors talking about the institutionalisation of migration seem to draw their insights mainly from material on Asian migration. Is it possible to frame other migration flows, such as the Moroccan one, in these terms? How are women affected by this type of migration? Women are said to use these migratory institutions more than men but there seems to be almost no material available documenting their experiences in getting access to such channels and in entering Europe through them. This book will seek to shed some light on this aspect of the migration experience.

Southern European Studies

As far as Southern Europe is concerned, only a few studies have adopted the approaches thus far described. Such studies have shown the importance of going beyond reductionist interpretations of female migration and have provided interesting examples of how personal, socioeconomic and sociopolitical elements interconnect in the experiences of different groups of migrants arriving in the region. The most interesting study in this respect is that of Cecilia Tacoli (1999) who, as I mentioned earlier, has applied the household strategies approach to Filipino migration to Rome. She shows the inadequacy of supply and demand factors to explain female migration to Italy; such factors determine the context within which migration occurs but are not capable of providing answers to questions such as why some women move while others do not.

Tacoli maintains that, in order to understand gender-selective migration from the Philippines, it is not enough to look at labour demand within Italy; it is also necessary to look at power inequalities within households in the country of origin and sociocultural expectations of gender there (see also Ribas 1999). Filipino migrants maintain very strong relationships with their households in home areas. Such households can be described as '"multi-local" units where membership relies on notions of commitments and obligations' (Tacoli 1999: 660). Such commitments and obligations are shaped by gender and Tacoli shows how women maintain much stronger links with their households than their male counterparts. One example is the sending of remittances: young single migrant women remit on average more than double that of their male counterparts. Such moral obligations towards relatives are so strong that older single migrants still send substantial remittances home, directed towards nephews and nieces. Not having their own children – who are generally seen as an insurance for old age – they contribute financially to other members of the younger generation, and thus fulfil their family obligations and at the same time invest in potential support from them in the future.

Although she believes that the household is an important unit of analysis for understanding migrants' decision making, Tacoli has noted the importance of looking beyond it so as to include the role of kin and non-kin networks. Such networks are vital for inserting the new migrant in the foreign labour market, providing him or her with information, money, accommodation and employment opportunities. The presence of such female networks may also contribute to migration's social acceptability. Kin networks are also crucial in the country of origin since they may provide important services such as childcare to emigrant mothers or help in looking after newly-built migrant properties. They also provide moral support and information about home areas to the emigrants and in so doing they contribute to keeping alive the link with home communities.

In Tacoli's study gender ideologies appear crucial in shaping individuals' constraints and opportunities. But if on the one hand they limit the actions of migrant women, on the other hand the latter are also able to use them to pursue personal goals. Filipino women appear to use strategically their normative roles to pursue 'self-interested' goals. By sending large remittances they fulfil their roles as 'dutiful daughters' and 'sacrificing mothers' while at the same time they enjoy the freedom and independence offered by migration.

Decimo (1996) has shown how personal and structural factors are deeply interwoven in migration chains; her study is of Somali women in Naples. Like the Filipinas described by Tacoli, they too are enmeshed in strong reciprocal relations and have a key economic function for their families, dispersed by the war which has devastated their country. Such an important economic role shapes their choices and strategies in the immigration context. By studying the solidarity networks maintained by these women, Decimo is able to show how Somali women manage not only to support themselves in a precarious social and economic context in Naples, but also to send substantial remittances to their families. Decimo shows how Somali women emphasise and use strategically their belonging to a number of spheres – households, kinship groups, clans, ethnic groups, religion – in order to solve unexpected problems and conduct their lives in the immigration setting. It is women who are at the centre and help maintain the networks built on such identifications. Hellermann (2006), however, reminds us that social networks can also have a negative side as they can exercise control over women's behaviour and possibilities of agency, as she noted in her case study of Eastern European women in Portugal.

Decimo has noted how, due to limited possibilities offered by the Italian context, Somali women's only avenue for improving their situation is that of migrating to other Western countries with more developed welfare states, or at least to have their dependant relatives relocated there. This is a theme explored by Andall (1999) who shows how Cape Verdean women effectively 'shop' for destination countries. Her work confirms the inadequacies of simplistic push and pull factors in explaining migration. Several of her interviewees changed destination countries during their migration experience. What emerged as important factors behind further migrations for Cape Verdean women were, for instance, the importance of being near family and friends, or the chance to reunite the family, or the possibility to combine productive and reproductive work. These are all non-economic considerations. Italy is a source of regular employment for these migrants, but a rigid labour market and generally weak social services make it a less than ideal final destination. As was the case for Somali women, Cape Verdean women manage to acquire information about potential destinations and ways around restrictive entry regulations through their key positions in social networks that link various groups of the Cape Verdean diaspora.

In an interesting article on Cape Verdean grassroots businesswomen, Marqués et al. (2000) show how women can use personal networks not only for survival reasons but also to conduct business. Their work focuses on a migrant group that is deeply rooted in the local community in Cape Verde but which carries out business in a number of countries in Africa, Europe and America that have Cape Verdean immigration. The authors show how these trading women successfully combine and enhance their businesses with family ties bounded by 'moral obligations'(2000: 3). While moving back and forth through the Cape Verdean diaspora these women not only buy and sell goods but also carry around letters, packages and remittances as well as first-hand information about family members scattered around the globe. In so doing they strengthen Cape Verdean networks and contribute to their maintenance.

Their work challenges the dichotomy of a sending and receiving society as well as highlighting the gendered nature of networks. Cape Verdean men and women, in fact, seem to be using different types of networks. Men are in more formalised networks involving politics, sports activities and cultural manifestations, whereas women are at the centre of informal networks based on commercial activities and restricted to the ethnic community. Above all, Marqués et al. demonstrate how women are far from passive and in fact are crucial actors for the maintenance of transnational networks.

All the studies presented so far deal with female-led migrant groups showing the important economic role that these women have for their families and the inventive strategies that they adopt to fulfil this role in the context of migration. Salih (2001, 2003) focuses instead on the (female) transnational practices of a male-dominated migrant group, namely Moroccan women residing in Italy. She too demonstrates how the possibility for these women to have access to transnational movement is shaped by normative and cultural regulations. In some cases women are 'forced' to stay put since solo female migration is negatively looked upon; while in others their migration is 'expected', such as when their husbands are already residing in Italy. At first sight, these findings seem to support the picture of the Moroccan migrant (and non-migrant) woman as 'passive' and 'dependant'. However, Salih also explores other roles and dimensions. She notes how transnational movements are shaped by the fulfilment of specific roles in the domestic sphere. She also documents the transnational practices carried out by these women and the ways in which, through regular visits, exchange of goods and food, they create a 'home' that includes both Italy and Morocco. However, Salih refuses a celebratory description of trasnationalism since she believes that 'transnational spheres are not only contingent upon migrants' vulnerability which derives from the transformation of the global economy, but are inscribed in specific cultural and normative constraints' (Salih 2001: 669; 2003).

Towards a New Framework for a Gendered Analysis of Migration

The previous pages have reviewed a number of gendered approaches to migration, stressing the importance of different meso-level units. Although all very useful and insightful, these approaches still do not provide a clear answer to exactly what should be included in the meso-level when analysing female (or indeed male) migrations. The authors who offered the most important tools for developing my own framework for interpreting female migration to Southern Europe are Kofman et al. (2000). They propose a convincing way for linking structural aspects and individual agency and solving some of the problems thus far discussed, such as the neglect of state policies in influencing individual and family decisions about migration and the scarce consideration of the increasingly formalised nature of much contemporary migration.

Kofman et al. believe that it is important to consider simultaneously the following aspects: the migrants' individual stories, motivations and resources; their networks (including social and informal as well as institutionalised ones); but also the wider relations between countries of immigration and emigration with special reference to economic as well as legislative aspects.

The significance of this approach lies, on the one hand, in their attempt to stimulate meso-level types of analysis that, as they acknowledge, have yet to be fully incorporated into European research; and on the other hand in the fact that they add the study of 'migratory institutions' to meso-level approaches, thereby contributing to a refinement of contemporary migration theories.

My research acknowledges the importance of the three levels of analysis discussed above for interpreting female (and indeed everybody's) migration, yet the former two will be privileged in this book. The reason for my choice is that I believe that much more work is available on the broader structural conditions shaping Southern European immigration (see for instance Baganha 1998; Iosifides and King 1996; King and Black 1997; Mingione 1995; Pugliese 1993; Reyneri 1998) than there is on the lived experiences of migrants and on the ways different individuals negotiate the constraints and opportunities offered to them.

Beyond Migration and Settlement:
Transnational Perspectives from the Receiving Society

Whereas the previous section dealt with the actual migration process, this section centres on migration as seen from the perspective of the receiving society. In spite of the recognised interconnection between countries of origin and of arrival, a characteristic of existing European studies on gender and migration is that they tend to focus either on the migration experience itself or on the immigrants' presence within a given territory (be it a city, a region, or a state), with individual studies focusing on aspects such as racism and theories of integration and exclusion. However, new theories on transnationalism and diasporas challenge such divisions and highlight the need to view migration beyond the exclusive focus of the receiving society. Such transnational approaches are more advanced in other geographical contexts, such as North America (Basch et al. 1994; Smith and Guarnizo 1998; Levitt 2001; Portes, Guarnizo and Landolt 1999), and are only now starting to emerge with reference to Europe generally (Goulbourne 2002; Mand 2002; Reynolds 2004; Sorensen 2005; Zontini 2004b) and Southern Europe in particular (Salih 2003; Riccio 2001; Zontini 2004a).

Brah (1996) believes that settlement is not in contradiction with transnational movements since people can be both migrants and settlers, a process that Glick Schiller (2004) has called 'simultaneity' (see also Levitt 2001; Levitt and Waters 2002). This is why Kofman et al. (2000: 42) argue that 'the migratory process should not be seen in isolation from the formation of ethnic communities in the migration setting and from the social structures in which these take place'. Unfortunately, however, these two aspects are rarely treated simultaneously in the European literature, which tends to be still dominated, especially in the UK, by the 'ethnic relations' paradigm, as a number of authors have recently pointed out (Anthias 2000; Kofman 2000; Kofman et al. 2000). This paradigm centres its attention on immigrant 'communities' settled in the receiving country and on their relation with the majority society. Such an approach cannot fully comprehend the nature of contemporary migration flows characterised by a diversity of migration experiences (see Vertovec 2006).

Among studies with a British focus, feminist scholars such as Floya Anthias, Nira Yuval Davis and Pnina Werbner have centred their attention on questions of citizenship and processes of inclusion and exclusion of ethnic minority women. One of their areas of interest has been the implications of multiculturalim for ethnic minority women. Their conclusions are that the current ideas on 'culture' and 'community' that seem to underpin multiculturalist projects disadvantage women in a number of ways. First, multiculturalism tends to homogenise all members of the specific minority without taking into consideration differences of class, gender, age, etc. Corporate representation of groups means that internal dissent has to be minimised in order to achieve the advancement of the group as a whole. Second, and linked to the previous point, multiculturalism privileges specific individuals within groups who are constructed as representing the interests of the whole group. This would not be a problem in itself if, as Tariq Modood (1997) has argued, the representatives were democratically selected. However, Yuval Davis (1991) laments the fact that often such an approach has advantaged fundamentalist leaders who are seen as the most dramatically 'different' and therefore the most authentic 'other'. In her view, community leaders end up controlling women in the name of culture and tradition. In fact, multicultural insistence on the protection of 'the cultural needs of the community' can be highly detrimental to women. This is because 'ethnic culture' is normally organised around rules that are highly gendered, including rigid prescriptions relating to sexuality, marriage, and the family (Anthias and Yuval Davis 1992; Lutz et al. 1995; Yuval Davis 1991, 1997; Yuval Davis and Werbner 1999).

These considerations, important in the British context, bear little relevance to the Southern European one. In Italy and Spain, multicultural ideology has not 'permeated theory, policy and action' (Beckett and Macey 2001: 309). Such ethnic-relations theorising is British-centred and based on Britain's colonial legacy. Multicultural 'group' policies are not widespread in Southern Europe. So-called 'ethnic groups' are so many and numerically fragmented that the type of coalition building that British feminist scholars advocate across different groups (see Lister 1997 on 'transculturalism') is inevitable and already a reality. 'Community' leaders are weak, their influence diluted in small and scattered groups. Moreover, in many female-dominated 'communities' such as the Filipinos and Latin Americans, the leaders are often women (Campani 2000). In these cases, whether multiculturalism still disadvantages women should be investigated rather than assumed. This is, however, beyond the scope of this book.

Another problem with British theorising in relation to the Southern European context is that it centres exclusively on ethnic minority women, paying scant attention to the processes of exclusion experienced by immigrant women. Although ethnic minority women and immigrant women may share a number of experiences – such as their presence in gendered and racialised labour markets – there are important differences between the two, not least the fact that the former enjoy full formal social and political rights and the latter do not. The fact that many immigrants in Southern Europe (including women) are undocumented enhances the relevance of this difference. Whereas feminist debates in Britain centre on new notions of citizenship that can offer women *more* than formal rights, in the Southern European context the issue for immigrant women is their access to basic rights such as the right to enter, reside and work there.

In the debate on citizenship an approach that seems more relevant for the situation of immigrant women in Southern Europe is the one developed by Stasiulis and Bakan (1997). Their idea is that citizenship should not be seen in a static way but rather as a negotiated relationship:

> Subject to change, it is acted upon collectively, or among individuals existing within social, political and economic relations of conflict which are shaped by gendered, racial, class and internationally based state hierarchies. Citizenship is therefore negotiated on the international as well as national levels. (1997: 113)

The authors analyse how Filipino and Caribbean women negotiate their citizenship rights in Canada. They show, on the one hand, how Western states – like Canada – try to exclude these women from citizenship rights, but also how, on the other hand, such women are far from passive. In fact, they negotiate entry in spite of stricter border controls, they try to improve their living and working conditions in spite of regulations that tie them to live-in domestic work and they struggle to obtain landed-immigrant status in spite of their recruitment as contract workers.

The importance of having access to formal and substantive rights for immigrant women and the need to pay attention to their agency are highlighted also by Lutz (1997). She believes that in the debate about multiculturalism too much attention has been given to cultural rights. In her view, the key issue for many migrant women is access to formal and substantive rights. It is migrant women's precarious position within receiving societies that poses obstacles to their incorporation. At the same time, denying the existence of differences between majority and minority women is also problematic, for it assumes the values and norms of the majority as the norm to which migrant women have to comply. This carries the risk of imposing on immigrant women a notion of 'equality' that takes Western women as the norm against which to measure the successes of immigrant women. According to Lutz (1997), the different positions of migrant women – e.g., in terms of class and in terms of the enjoyment of formal and substantive rights – have to be taken into account. She rejects 'orientalist' assumptions about Muslim immigrant women seen as victims of their 'culture' and of the leaders of their community. She believes that such assumptions obscure migrant women's agency and do not help to achieve a better understanding of the real nature of their oppression. In her view, a contextualised analysis of the situation of immigrant women is needed, one that does not focus exclusively on the cultural resources of the immigrants but includes also the situation and the possibilities offered by the receiving society. In fact, she believes that certain 'ethnic' values, such as female chastity, become significant as boundary markers of a group only in the (re-)

organisation of the ethnic community in the host country. The importance attributed to these boundary signifiers should not be regarded as a cause, but rather as a consequence of marginalisation and exclusionary attitudes. In Lutz's view the focus has to be put on the relation between majority and minority women and on the relation of the 'community' to the wider society.

Both Lutz (1997) and Morokvasic (1991) argue that in order to understand migrant women's agency, instead of focusing on their unconditioned adoption of specific (Western) values and behaviours, a more fruitful approach for a feminist analysis is one that looks at their resistance and at change that is produced by it (see also Freedman and Tarr 2000). Lutz (1997) talks about a feminist analysis based on the idea of a 'differentiated' universalism, meaning an approach that neither denies difference nor reifies it.

Among immigrant groups residing in Europe, Muslim women are those whose agency is most often obscured in both academic and popular accounts. In a European climate characterised by 'cultural fundamentalism' (Stolke 1995), gender relations and sexuality become central in defining boundaries between who is considered 'modern' and 'European' and who is assumed to be 'traditional' and incapable of being included in the nation: 'Religion has become the key signifier of incompatible differences. Islamic groups, regulated by patriarchal structures, are singled out as being too distinctive in their daily lives and social norms to be able to cohabit with groups whose practices are derived from Christian traditions' (Kofman et al. 2000: 37).

To counteract widespread oversimplified accounts about immigrant women in Europe, several authors have stressed the importance that should be placed on agency in studying processes of settlement. However, in spite of this recognition, few studies in the European context have documented empirically the active role of women in such processes. This is not the case in other geographical contexts where the important role of women in facilitating settlement has been fairly well documented (Pessar and Mahler 2001). Hondagneu-Sotelo (1994), for instance, has looked at Mexican settlement in California from a woman-centred perspective. Settlement, in her view, is a process that takes place when women and children join the men already residing abroad and which is characterised by 'the unification in one country of family residence and employment, and the maintenance and reproduction of labour' (1994: 18). Hondagneu-Sotelo asks what is the role of women in settlement? And what role do gendered practices have in such a process? Her conclusions are that settlement is a contested process, with men and women having different and often contradicting views on the issue. The former often wish to return whereas the latter work towards consolidating settlement, and do so in three ways: first, by consolidating stable employment for themselves; second, by gaining access to and utilising private and public forms of assistance; and finally by constructing community-wide social ties.

Ganguly-Scrase and Julian (1998) share Hondagneu-Sotelo's view of settlement as a gendered process. Women have been central actors in the settlement process of Hmong people in Hobart (Australia). As is the case for Mexican women, they too 'have played active roles in all spheres of social life namely health, education, work, and kinship' (1998: 637). It is women who negotiate with social services and who build and maintain social ties which go beyond the Hmong community. Yet, the authors lament, it is men who remain the spokespersons of the Hmong.

Buijs (1993), too, shows how settlement is gendered. Her example of Chilean women in the US echoes the experiences of Hmong women in Australia and of Mexican women in the US. They too learned new skills and had new experiences in the immigration context such as learning a new language, learning to drive or having a job for the first time. These achievements increased their self-esteem as well as their position within their families, thereby contributing to changing gender roles and expectations. On the other hand, men found it more difficult to adapt to their new circumstances and their lives continued to be more oriented towards the country they left behind. If the cases of the migrant women reported above appear as successes, Buijs reminds us that migration can also diminish the status of women. Palestinian refugees in Berlin, for instance, enjoyed far less freedom of movement than they had in their country of origin (Abdulrahim 1993) and so did Bangladeshi women residing in London (Summerfield 1993).

Buijs concludes that whether migration results in the improvement of the status of women depends not only on the constraints found in the host society in influencing their adaptation but also on their cultural background and their relationship with their male kin. She adds that if we want to look at immigrant women's status it is important to do so from their point of view; in so doing we will be able to understand that the cultural forms that an outsider might judge as 'oppressive' may not necessarily be so in the eyes of the women concerned.

Women's settlement is therefore influenced by their relationship with the society of arrival and by the changes in gender roles and relations shaped by the migration experience. Two areas seem crucial in this respect: women's insertion in the labour market and the reconstruction of family relations in the society of arrival. Unfortunately, studies on female immigration in Europe tend to divide between those with a family focus and those with a labour-market one. I believe that such a marked separation is problematic for an accurate understanding and representation of the migration experience, not least because it unwittingly acknowledges a separation between a private sphere (of the home and the family) independent from the public one (of the market), a dichotomy that feminist theorists have long criticised. For interim analytical reasons only, in the remainder of this chapter I will treat the issue of women in the labour market and in their families separately. It is, however, one of the principal goals of this book to make explicit the links existing between women's roles and position within their families and their position in the labour market.

Immigrant Women in the Labour Market

In spite of stereotyped assumptions of the contrary, immigrant and ethnic minority women have constituted a high proportion of the European labour force since the late 1960s. They were, and still are, 'confined in low skill and low pay, to home working or shift work' (Anthias and Yuval-Davis 1992). Yet, if thirty years ago immigrant women in Europe were distributed in a number of feminised and low-status jobs, today the range of jobs available to them is if anything even more narrow (Kofman et al. 2000). Phizacklea (1998) argues that restrictive immigration policies and prevailing notions of immigrant women's place in European post-industrial labour markets restrict their possibilities mainly to two areas: sex work and domestic service.

Wichterich (2000) notes how current global restructuring, with the internationalisation of the labour force that it implies, has reintroduced an occupation that in many Western countries was disappearing, namely the housemaid. The demand for domestic workers is expanding in all Western countries, as studies undertaken in a variety of countries such as Hong Kong, Singapore, several countries in Northern and Southern Europe, the US and Canada confirm. Domestic work is now part of a global chain of care (Ehrenreich and Hochschild 2003; Hochschild 2000; Lutz 2002). The difference between maids now and their counterparts of the past is that, whereas before they were predominantly young, single and poorly educated, today they are often married, with professional experiences in their countries of origin and high educational qualifications. The problems associated with domestic employment, however, such as long hours, low pay and sexual harassment, unfortunately remain the same (Anderson 2000, 2001; Parreñas 2001a).

Another characteristic differentiating present-day domestic workers from their predecessors is that the latter were internal migrants whereas the former are foreigners, non-citizens in the country where they are working. This point has been seen as crucial by authors researching domestic work. Anderson (2000) argues that workers' immigrant status is a key variable in determining their living and working conditions (see also Andall 1998; Phizacklea 1998). The fact that the worker is a non-citizen reinforces the power inequalities between her and her employer and exposes her to potential abuse. She is forced into long hours of work and low pay and, if she complains, she can be threatened with deportation. Even if she has entered the country legally with a job contract, her permit is normally tied to a specific employer; if she loses her job she also loses her right to stay.

The growing demand for domestic workers poses difficult analytical and moral questions for feminist scholars and points to the complex relationships between gender, class, ethnicity and nationality (Anderson 2001). Domestic work challenges the premise of gender over other axes of differentiation and

48

clearly leads to the situation whereby some women may be participating in other women's oppression. Anderson (2000) stresses how, thanks to immigrant women who work as welfare providers, middle-class women of the receiving society can exercise their full citizenship rights and have access to the public sphere (see also Andall 2000a).

As far as the insertion of immigrant women in Southern European labour markets is concerned, there are several recent studies that have centred particularly on domestic work (Andall 1998, 2000a, 2000b; Campani 2000; Carmona 2000; Catarino and Oso 2000; Chell 1997, 2000; Escrivà 1997, 2000b; Lazaridis 2000; Parella 2000; Vicarelli 1994). What emerges from these studies is how domestic work seems to be almost the exclusive type of (legal) work available to immigrant women both in Italy and in Spain, and how the demand for this type of work has continued to increase from the 1960s up to the present. The reasons given for this growing demand are related to the rapid changes undergone by Southern European countries in the last thirty years (see Chapter 1).

As I have said earlier, women from many immigrant groups seem confined to domestic work or to other types of very feminised jobs such as care work for the elderly (in fact, another important social change in Southern Europe is the ageing of its population which today is characterised by a high life expectancy and one of the lowest birth rates in the world). However, this does not mean that all immigrant women are involved in this sector of the labour market in the same way. On the contrary, there are important differences that, in my view, are quite revealing about the nature of the receiving societies. The existing literature documents the presence of a kind of hierarchy of different ethnic groups that is dictated by stereotypes and racist assumptions present in Italian and Spanish societies and which are taken up by local employers. This hierarchy in turn is reflected in levels of pay and working conditions. Racism against women intersects with sexism to produce particular forms of exclusion which are differently set against different ethnic and class groups, as Lazaridis (2000) has demonstrated in her research on Filipinos and Albanians in Greece.

At the top of what we can call a 'hierarchy of the marginalised' we find Filipinas; they are generally described as docile, serious, with a strong work ethic and as easily adaptable (Anderson 2000; Chell 1997; Parreñas 2001a). Other groups like Cape Verdeans and Latin Americans seem to rank somewhere in the middle, whereas Somali and other Muslim women, like the Moroccans, seem to be at the bottom of the list. The racist categorisation of preferred and less preferred ethnic groups is further complicated by the legal status of these women. Eastern European women are particularly desired by certain employers. This is not only because they are white and seen as easily adaptable and hardworking, but also because they are cheap and prepared to work very long hours due to the fact that they rarely have a work permit (usually they come in on a tourist visa) and therefore are very dependant on their employers (Vicarelli 1994).

Another important differentiation is that between the women engaged in 'live-in' and those who perform 'live-out' domestic work. Few women seem to be in secure enough positions to be able to work as hourly paid live-out maids. This is obviously a more expensive arrangement for the immigrant because it entails having to pay for her own accommodation and lodging, but it is also seen as a preferable option by many women because of the harsh conditions of live-in domestic work (for an analysis of this see Andall 1998, 2000a; Anderson 2000; Chell 1997; De Filippo 1994). For all the Cape Verdean women interviewed by Andall (1998), live-in domestic work was considered to be difficult and demanding. The hardest part of their job was for these women to be on call for virtually twenty-four hours per day. They had to be – as De Filippo (1994) puts it – workers 'night and day', always available for serving the needs of 'their' family and never allowed to have any privacy.

The fact that the majority of immigrant women perform the same kind of job does not imply that they are an homogeneous group, nor even within each immigrant group. The heterogeneity among immigrant women in Spain has been highlighted by Ribas (2000a and b) in her work and this aspect has to be stressed in order to counter the generalised and stereotyped descriptions of different ethnic groups that prevail in Italy and Spain. Her interviewees differed as regards their socioeconomic position within the country of origin, some of them coming from rural areas, others living in cities, some being highly educated whereas others had only few years of schooling, and so on. They also differed in their motivations for their migration and in respect of the projects that they have for the future. Statements like 'Filipinas come to work and save money' and 'Moroccans come to follow their husbands' – common still in academic literature – are far too simplistic and do not explain reality in full. Many Moroccan women, according to Ribas, migrated alone to further their education, to travel or simply to have new experiences, defying the stereotype that sees them always as victims and incapable of any independent action (De Bernard 1995; Ribas 2000a; Schmidt di Friedberg and Saint-Blancat 1998).

What seems striking about the Southern European case is how little room there seems to be for these women to engage in anything else than care and domestic work (with the exception of sex work). An important aspect that emerges from the literature is the difficulty for these immigrant women of combining this type of productive work with reproduction and the changes in family structures that migration seems to imply. Such changes and new arrangements need further attention, in my opinion. The following section deals with these issues, which will be then explored empirically in Chapters 4 and 5.

Immigrant Women and the Transnational Family

The difficulties in having a family life encountered by immigrant women are not specific to the Southern European context. Glenn (1994) argues that in the US too immigrant women's value as cheap labour has been given prominence over their value as mothers.

> Historically African-American, Latina, and Asian-American women were excluded from the dominant cult of domesticity. Because they were incorporated into the United States largely to take advantage of their labour, there was little interest in preserving family life … ; people of color were treated as individual units of labor, rather than as members of family units. (Glenn 1994: 5)

Questions of difference and diversity, now considered important for interpreting the experiences of women, are also crucial for the analysis of immigrant families. As we can infer from the above quotation, experiences such as mothering are not universal but are shaped by issues of ethnicity and class (Reynolds 2005). This is why generalising about the family from the experiences of white middle-class women appears problematic. Poor racialised women have different concerns from white middle-class women. For instance, whereas the latter in the US 'struggled for the right to limit pregnancy through birth control and abortion', the former 'have contended with their rights to have babies at all' (Glenn 1994: 17). These considerations seem quite relevant for interpreting the Spanish and Italian cases and to counteract 'modernisation' types of analyses that cast immigrant women's concerns about the family as 'traditional' and opposed to what are conceptualised as 'modern' Western values (for a similar critique concerning the depiction of transnational families in Britain see Smart and Shipman 2004).

Issues of difference and diversity do not apply only between majority and minority groups, however. As Foner (1997) demonstrates in her study on immigrant families in the US, family patterns differ from one group to another, 'despite [the] common structural conditions they face and despite common social processes and dynamics of family life' (1997: 962). She therefore sees the family as: 'a place where there is a dynamic interplay between structure, culture, and agency, where creative culture-building takes place in the context of external social and economic forces as well as immigrants' premigration cultural frameworks' (Foner 1997: 961).

Among the reasons why family and kinship patterns change in the process of migration, Foner identifies external factors such as economic conditions and opportunities and the influence of dominant cultural beliefs and values on issues such as marriage, family and kinship relations. The legal system also has an important external impact since immigration laws can impose the receiving society's assumptions of who is thought to be family and therefore allowed in under family reunification regulations (see Kofman 2004). Socio-demographic features of the group are also important. Marriage and family patterns are in fact influenced by sex and age ratios. If the sex ratio of a group is unbalanced – as is the case for Filipinos and Moroccans in Spain and Italy – the consequences will be either marriages outside the group, 'singlehood', the import of spouses from the home country or transnational partnership.

Among the new family patterns emerging, there are some that are a direct result of transnationalism. Foner gives the example of Dominicans in New York who live in what are called 'multilocal binational families', that is to say, families in which parents and some of the children live in the US whereas other children live in a household with other relatives in the Dominican Republic. In these multilocal families members distributed in different households across national boundaries participate in family events and decisions from a distance (see also Reynolds 2006; Zontini 2006; and Reynolds and Zontini 2006).

As this example shows, transnationalism complicates the definition of households and families. If normally the household can be defined as 'a group of people who share the same residence and participate collectively, if not always co-operatively, in the basic tasks of reproduction and consumption' (Chant and McIlwaine 1995: 4), in transnational households one parent, both parents or adult children may be producing income abroad while other family members carry out the functions of reproduction, socialization, and the rest of consumption in the country of origin (Parreñas 2001a). Thus, transnationalism forces us to reconsider our understanding of households and families based on the idea of co-residency and physical unity and to take into account the possibility of spatial separation.

Within the literature on transnationalism, Faist (2000) identifies the emergence of transnational kinship groups as one of three types of transnational social spaces arising from international migration. Glick Schiller et al. (1992), called for the examination of 'the implications of current day transnationalism for kinship relations, family organisation, and the form and content of networks' (1992: xii). They noted how family networks are stretched, reconfigured and activated across national boundaries to cope with economic uncertainty and subordination (Glick Schiller et al. 1992: 54).

These calls for considering kinship relations and family organisation were slow to be taken up by migration scholars who continued to be predominantly interested in the economic dimensions of transnationalism. In recent years, however, a rich literature has begun to develop focusing explicitly on the functioning and daily practices of transnational families. Several feminist scholars, for instance, have shown that women are involved in both productive and reproductive work, which help to maintain their families transnationally.

Alicea (1997), for instance, draws on Di Leonardo's work to show the crucial importance of women's kin and care work for sustaining their transnational families. Di Leonardo defined *kin work* as:

the conception, maintenance, and ritual celebration of cross household kin ties, including visits, letters, telephone calls, presents, and cards to kin; the organisation of holiday gatherings; the creation and maintenance of quasi kin relations; decisions to neglect or intensify particular ties; the mental work of reflection about all these activities; and the creation and communication of altering images of family and kin vis-à-vis the images of others, both folk and mass media. (Di Leonardo 1992: 248)

Kin work seems to assume a crucial relevance in the context of geographically dispersed families. The very existence of transnational families does, in fact, rest on kin ties being kept alive and maintained, in spite of great distances and prolonged separations. Bryceson and Vourela (2002) have recently highlighted this, and advanced two concepts to study transnational family making, namely 'frontiering' and 'relativizing'. The first refers to 'the ways and means transnational family members use to create familial space and network ties in a terrain where affinal connections are relatively sparse' (Bryceson and Vourela 2002: 11). The second refers to the ways 'individuals establish, maintain or curtail relational ties with specific family members' (2002: 14). Goulbourne and Chamberlain (2001: 42), in their study of transnational Caribbean families, have found that 'geographical distance is no barrier to being a "close" family and informants stressed the importance of [transnational links], the "tightness" of the emotional bonds, and the level of "trust" expected and experienced between family members'.

Although, at times, there are men who do the 'kin work' (see Goulbourne 2002), in the aggregate women seem to do more of it (Di Leonardo 1984). Also, kin work is a gendered activity, with men and women normally focusing on different aspects of it. For instance, in her study of transnational Sikh marriages, Mand (2002) noted how women were relegated to the organisation of the domestic and local side of wedding celebrations whereas men took up the more prestigious public and transnational side. Often women tend to have a greater share of kin work than men. Salih (2001, 2003), for instance, describes the preparation work that migrant women do before their annual visit during the August holidays in Morocco. Such preparation (which involves things like buying presents for relatives left behind and the planning of gatherings and celebrations) normally starts one or two months before the date of leaving, with some women dedicating to it almost the entire year.

Caring work involves those tasks related with looking after the young, the sick and the elderly. When done by family members, it is usually an unpaid activity, which in most societies is generally relegated to women. Performing caring work in a transnational family thus means women having 'to monitor and meet the physical and emotional needs of individuals in more than one household [in more than one country] and balance their time and energy between these' (Alicea 1997: 318). Authors have noted that geographical distance does not mean the cessation of caring, and a new scholarship on 'transnational care-giving' is emerging documenting how caring practices are achieved in spite of geographical distance (Baldassar and Baldock 2000; Goulbourne and Chamberlain 2001; Reynolds and Zontini 2006; Zontini 2006). These authors focus on the experiences of established migrant groups such as Italians in the UK and Australia (Baldassar and Baldock 2000; Zontini 2006), Caribbean in Britain (Goulbourne and Chamberlain 2001; Reynolds 2005) or EU citizens across the European Union (Ackers and Stalford 2004), showing how transnational families are maintained and reproduced in spite of geographical separation (Baldassar 2001; Bryceson and Vourela 2002; Burholt 2004; Mason 2004; Wilding 2006; Zontini 2006) and what kind of resources circulate within them (Reynolds and Zontini 2006; Zontini 2006). Their work has focused on caring work that occurs both intergenerationally (e.g., between adult children and ageing parents or grandparents and grandchildren) as well as intragenerationally (e.g., among siblings). This work is thus primarily concerned with reciprocal and caring relationships that occur across (rather than within) households. This is because the groups considered are now established minorities in their countries of settlement, where they tend to have the most immediate kin (young children, partners). For this group of migrants, transnationalism seems to be a way of maintaining family obligations and responsibilities, as well as a form to renovate their ethnic identity and maintain a sense of cultural connection and belonging to their places of origin (Mason, 2004; Reynolds and Zontini 2006). Transnational life for them is thus something more than a consequence of their marginalisation, legal barriers or other impediments.

The work on transnational motherhood (Erel 2002; Hondagneu-Sotelo and Avila 1997; LARG 2005; Parrenas 2001a), transnational childhood (Parrenas 2005; Suárez-Orozco and Suárez-Orozco 2001) and, recently, transnational fatherhood (Pribilsky 2004) brings instead the attention to the separations that occur within the household when migrants (now increasingly mothers) leave their children behind to work abroad. Recent work is also starting to pay attention to transnational partnering, looking at the implications that transnationalism is having on couples which now have to learn to live apart together (Pribilsky 2004; see also Gambaurd 2000; Sorensen 2005).

This literature is showing that the task of parenting becomes particularly difficult for 'transnational mothers' (Hondagneu-Sotelo and Avila 1997), that is to say, those mothers who, due to their work commitments in immigration countries, have to leave their children behind to be cared for by relatives in their countries of origin. These mothers have to learn to cope with the pain of family separations and the feelings of helplessness and loneliness that they engender (Parreñas 2001a). Erel (2002) reports how Turkish mothers in this situation suffer as result of the peer pressure of 'good mothering'. In many societies dominant ideologies of the family stress the importance of the mother–child dyad. Those mothers who live separated from their children often feel guilty of being 'bad mothers' and suffer as a consequence (LARG 2005; Parreñas 2001a). Not all women, however, internalise this image of the 'bad' migrant mother and several actively struggle to reconceptualise the idea of mothering (Erel 2001; Hondagneu-Sotelo and Avila 1997; Parreñas 2001a, Reynolds 2005).

Recent studies have shown that families separations are particularly difficult for children (LARG 2005; Parreñas 2005; Suárez-Orozco and Suárez-Orozco 2001). Suárez-Orozco and Suárez-Orozco (2001) conclude that separation due to migration is a painful process that leaves children longing for missing parents and, when family reunification occurs, for the missing care-givers who had taken up the parental role during parents' absence. According to Parreñas, children of transnational migrants seem to suffer more in mother-away (rather than father-away) families. This is because, in her view, children 'struggle to accept the reconstitution of mothers as more of an economic provider and less of a caretaker of the home' (Parreñas 2005: 164).

Transnationalism also affects partnering, although it seems, in a gendered way. As is the case in mother-away families, couples seem to be more under strain when is the wife migrating. While Pribilsky (2004), analysing Ecuadorian men's out-migration to the US, talks of improvement in couples' relationships following male migration, Gambaurd (2000) talks of the slowness, difficulty and often painful nature of the negotiations surrounding changing gender roles and family structures brought about by female migration from Sri Lanka. Pribilsky (2004) describes how couples learn to live side-by-side redefining roles, relationships and family life in order to meet their goals of success in migration. Sorensen (2005) and my own work also point to the fact that transnationalism may reduce strain in couples and can be used as an exit strategy by women in unsatisfactory and abusive relationships.

The literature on global care-chains highlights some of the problems inherent in the development of transnational families (Ehrenreich and Hochschild 2003; Hochschild 2000). These authors draw attention to the global transfer of care work that is occurring from poor countries to rich ones when women leave their families to work as nannies, cleaners and elderly carers in the affluent homes of the West. They talk of a global transfer of emotional resources which leaves poor countries in a situation of 'care drain'. The victims of these global arrangements are going to be the children left behind who will have to bear the 'inevitable trauma' (Hochschild 2003) of these separations. Although very important, this analysis may run the risk of stigmatising transnational families generally and migrant women in particular (Parreñas 2005; Sorensen 2005). Parreñas talks of the impossibility of a return to the nuclear family and a dependence many families have on the work of migrant women abroad. Women do send emotional support as well as money back to their children, who are also cared for by the extended family. In order to minimise suffering for those involved, these arrangements have to be supported (through policies) rather than stigmatised (LARG 2005; Parreñas 2005; Sorensen 2005).

As far as the Southern European case is concerned, some authors have pointed out that immigrant women's work in support of local families has a profound impact on their private lives and on the possibility of enjoying a family life of their own. The Cape Verdean women interviewed by Andall (1998) were often single-parent working mothers with young children, a condition uncommon in Italy and for which few public structures are in place (see also Maher 1996). This means for immigrant women either postponing procreation, sending their children to residential homes or sending them back to be raised by relatives in the country of origin. Similar difficulties were noted by Victoria Chell (1997) with reference to the situation of Filipino and Somalian women in Rome. She too noted how migration was having an impact (often negative) on the family relationships of the migrants.

Andall (2000a) demonstrates that in Italy immigrant women's maternal identities have been marginalised precisely to enable them to fulfil a labour function. Through their work for Italian families they allow Italian women to fulfil different roles while at the same time enjoying a family life. For migrant women instead, their maternal identity has to be subordinated to the requirements of their job. Having a baby may result in the loss of the job. This can have dramatic consequences for these women since alternative forms of employment to live-in work are so few. Andall (1999) has noted how the desire to be close to family and friends or to achieve a better balance between productive and reproductive work was for Cape Verdean women a motor for further migration both internally within Italy and abroad, in their case usually to the Netherlands. There, a more developed welfare system, but above all the presence of relatives and of a more flexible labour market, made it possible for many of these women to reunite their families and fulfil their migratory projects. Andall concludes that 'when family formation is restricted ties to the new society will be weak thus facilitating the tendency to consider alternative migratory options' (1999: 249).

The case studies dealing with immigration in the Southern European context all mention the stretching of immigrant women's responsibilities brought about by transnationalism. Many authors have noted how familial relationships and responsibilities of female migrants span more than one country, sometimes more than two. This is the case for the Cape Verdean women interviewed by Andall (1999) who have family responsibilities and connections in Italy, Cape Verde, Portugal and the Netherlands. Migration can be seen both as having given new possibilities and more control to women, in many cases the major earner of the family, but also as something that has not altered their fundamental role as those who have to 'sacrifice' themselves (through international migration) for the good of the family and their children. Moreover, having to be both wage-earners and responsible for maintaining a transnational family may be seen as a further burden for immigrant women.

Anthias (2000) has written about the tension between women as migrants and women as settlers. Despite today's tendencies towards transnationalism and multiple loyalties to several countries, for many migrant women the objective of reuniting or forming their family in one location seems to be a desired outcome of their migratory project. In spite of the problems and difficulties highlighted above, the 'familisation' of migration to Southern Europe seems to be a new but now clearly evident phenomenon. Yet this phenomenon has received very little attention in the literature.

Some of the few studies available on immigrant families in Italy and Spain (especially in Italy) seem to portray them as 'problematic' and as a potential burden for already stretched social services. Tognetti Bordogna (1994) focuses on what she considers 'new problematic families', namely reunited immigrant families and mixed marriages. As far as the former are concerned she writes that: 'The reunited family is considered in the legislation but not by social policies even though it is a noticeable reality also numerically *and it is certainly problematic*' (1994: 134; my emphasis).

What seems to worry this author is that the presence of immigrant family members, such as elders and children, will increase demand on social services. New policies of integration, she laments, will have to be designed for them and adequate housing will have to be provided. She seems to be very preoccupied about the potential 'burden' that immigrants may represent for Italian society, yet she chooses to neglect immigrants' role as providers of cheap services currently replacing those of a poorly developed welfare system. Similar views seem to be held by Favaro (1994) who focuses on immigrant women and mothering. Her analysis follows a tradition/modernity framework where Italy represents the pole of modernity and immigrant women that of tradition. Irrespective of their origin, she believes that for immigrant women 'mothering is both more important and "more banal" than it is for autochthonous women' (Favaro 1994: 148). She differentiates Italian women who can and do fulfil several roles and a generic 'immigrant woman' whose only goal seems to be 'the reproduction of the members of her community' (1994: 148).

An exception to these stereotyped visions of immigrant families in Southern Europe is Decimo's (2001) work on the role of the family in facilitating Moroccan settlement in Italy. She notes the importance of family strategies for understanding the migration of Moroccans (both males and females). For them the family unit appears of crucial importance and considerable efforts are dedicated to fulfil it. The family is seen as a source of stability that deploys an important affective function in an unwelcoming receiving environment. Second, it is an economic unit, where various household members (including women and adult children) contribute resources that will then be redistributed and consumed within the household. Such resources are not just strictly economic but they derive also from access to crucial public resources (such as housing) that some families can gain access to. Third, as a social unit, the family plays a key role in the process of social stratification. Families give the possibility to their members of differentiating themselves from other Moroccans: drawing lines between 'us' and 'them'. Decimo argues that by activating processes of inclusion and strengthening kinship relations and at the same time processes of exclusion and differentiation, Moroccans fight against the potential social levelling caused by migration.

Conclusions

This chapter has summarised and brought together a range of different debates on gender and migration, transnationalism and settlement so as to formulate an appropriate and relevant framework for interpreting the experiences of immigrant women in Southern Europe. The first goal of this chapter has been to link and present in a unified way theories that normally are considered separately. In fact, with the exception of the recently published volume by Kofman et al. (2000), in the European context theories of migration and transnationalism are generally looked at in isolation from those dealing with integration, social inclusion/exclusion and settlement. I believe, instead, that why people migrate bears relevance on how and if they settle in a particular society. Hence they should all be seen as part of the same process. Another dichotomy that this chapter has tried to dispel has been that between 'work' and the 'family'. Such a division applies both to the categorisation of migrants – those who migrate to work vs. those who migrate to follow their family – and to the activities that are seen as needing to be investigated in the context of arrival – studies with a labour market focus vs. those with a family one. In this book I maintain that virtually all migrant women are engaged in some form of productive and reproductive work and that these two spheres are highly interdependent and therefore to be considered together.

The second goal of this chapter has been to highlight the necessity of developing a Southern European-based theory about (female) migration, i.e., one which is capable of reflecting more closely the situation characterising that geo-cultural area and which is more autonomous from the British-based one which at present tends to dominate European theorisation about migration.

Such a theoretical framework involves considering the following. First, the migration process, paying attention to different meso-level units ranging from households and families to social networks and institutions. All these units will be considered as gendered, with unequal power relations within them. Second, the settlement process. This will not be viewed in isolation but will be framed in relation to the transnational obligations and relations maintained by the migrants. Migrant women (of all groups) are considered as key economic actors and thus their involvement in the local labour markets will be described. However, the book seeks to show above all the interrelation of employment with women's crucial roles in their families and kinship groups. Throughout my research the active nature of women and the strategies they deploy to negotiate their different roles and often difficult positions will be highlighted. The next two chapters will present the results of my ethnographic research. Chapter 3 is based on material gathered in Bologna and Chapter 4 in Barcelona.

3
IMMIGRATION, WORK
AND FAMILY IN BOLOGNA

❦

The Family Divided and the Long Pilgrimage around Italy

We move from one country to the next without knowing how our future will be. What is the meaning of our life now that our family is divided in three different directions?

My older brothers stayed behind in Morocco, the three of us left for Italy. My mother and I, though, stay here in this unknown town waiting full of anxiety for news about my father who, in the meantime, has moved to another place in search of work.

We are always afraid that something might happen to him. Our minds are tired of thinking because we don't do anything else but think and think…

My mother and I feel like a tree that little by little is losing its leaves: it will take a lot of time to get them back.

I have to pack and collect my belongings. I leave this house that I will never see again, I have to change it another time.

I ask myself if we will ever have our own place and if we will ever manage to meet again finally reunited.

Every time I move house I lose that little bit that I had managed to build.

As soon as I arrive in the new environment I look around and I feel a vast emptiness that can be filled only if we will ever be all together again.

In those years, those long trips never ended. I moved from one town to the next, first it was Foggia, then L'Aquila, Venice, Trieste and then L'Aquila again and finally here we are in Bologna.[1]

Introduction

Haziza's diary account of her migration experience, quoted above, brings out very clearly the richness of the subjective experience and the sufferings involved in this process of continuous uprooting. This chapter initiates the ethnographic examination of Moroccan and Filipino women's stories as they emerged from my fieldwork in Bologna. Following the theoretical framework developed in Chapter 2, this chapter considers their migration and settlement processes simultaneously. Throughout the analysis special attention is given to women's roles and positions in their (transnational) families and kinship groups. However, to the extent that social and family issues are also bound up often with women's experiences of paid work, the labour market dimension will also form part of my analysis.

As Chapter 2 explained, the actions of the main actors of my research (Moroccan and Filipino women) are contextualised within wider units such as households, families, and kinship or quasi-kinship networks. This is not to deny migrant women's agency but rather to locate the fields of possibilities within which their agency can be enacted. Following feminist sociologists who view the individual as relational, interconnected and embedded in their personal relationships (Clement 1996; Finch 1989; Fisher and Tronto 1990; Griffiths 1995; Mackenzie and Stoljar 2000; Sevenhuijsen 2000; Thorne and Yalom 1992), in the following pages I will show how women's familial circumstances and strategies (both at the places of origin and arrival) are key elements in setting in motion and influencing the process of migration, the types of labour market incorporation, and settlement (or return).

This chapter is organised as follows. The first section deals with Moroccan and Filipino women's immigration histories in order to provide examples on who are the women arriving in Bologna, how they got there and for what reasons. The second section considers women in the context of arrival. Here I pay particular attention to their economic role and position in the local labour market and to housing, as these are crucial in influencing the settlement process. Different ways of getting access to (paid) work and attitudes to work are also analysed. The last part of the chapter addresses specifically the issue of the family: it summarises the role of families in constraining or enabling (or even forcing) female migration but also the changes to family formation and family lives brought about by migration and settlement in Bologna. Throughout the chapter, I build in brief case-histories in order to enrich and personalise the analysis. All migrants' names are fictitious.

Immigration History: Arriving in Bologna

This section addresses two much discussed issues in current literature on migration – the reasons for the feminisation of migration (Anthias and Lazaridis 2000; Castles and Miller 1998; Kofman 1999; Phizacklea 1998; Zlotnik 1995) and the role of networks (Anthias and Lazaridis 2000; Boyd 1989; Castles and Miller 1998; Faist 1997) in favouring migration. It does so by looking at the immigration histories of Filipino and Moroccan women who arrive in Bologna. The following two sets of questions are at the core of my analysis. Firstly, why do women migrate? What is the social and familial context of those who migrate? Are there differences in the motives of Filipino and Moroccan female migrants for going abroad? Secondly, which networks do these women get access to? What is their role in them?

Filipino Women

The Philippines have been a country of emigration for over forty years (Parreñas 2001a). Castles (2000: 7) describes the country as 'the labour-exporter par excellence of the current period' – that is to say, a country unable to absorb its growing labour force and which is consciously choosing emigration as a policy aimed at alleviating the problems associated with economic stagnation and growing unemployment. In the Philippines it has been the government itself which has encouraged and supported foreign migration, not least in order to generate valuable foreign exchange. Emigration from the Philippines, for both men and women, is not condemned or stigmatised but rather accepted and even encouraged, to the extent that international labour migrants have been dubbed the 'new heroes' of the country (Stasiulis and Bakan 1997; Tacoli 1999).

Emigration has therefore become 'a fact of life' for many Filipino families, an experience that touches at least one member of a large proportion of Filipino households (Abella 1993). Both men and women are migrating but their migration is still gender-asymmetric, with men and women going to different countries, taking advantage of the differentiated opportunities offered by a global labour market. According to Castles (2000) Filipinos are in a favourable position to compete in this global labour market due to their high levels of education and occupational training, familiarity with the English language and a high rate of female labour participation.

Figure 3.1 Map of the Philippines
Source: www.worldatlas.com

The majority of Filipino women arriving in Bologna come from large families but their geographical origin and socioeconomic background seem to be quite diverse. Some of them come from very poor rural families which have a low standard of living, others come from urban areas and have a middle-class background. Often the absence of the father, dead or absent with another woman, results in the impoverishment of the family and in the necessity of finding new strategies in order to maintain the family's previous standard of living. Emigration represents potentially one of the most successful strategies in this respect.[2] Judith, for instance, came from a very poor family. She remembers

Table 3.1 Basic biographic data on Filipino women interviewed in Bologna

Filipino women	Age	Place of origin	Internal migration before emig-ration?	Number of siblings	House-hold head	Marital status upon migration	Number of children upon migration
Ester	21	Banacal	Yes	4	M	single	0
Maria	28	Cebu	Yes	5	M	single	0
Mina	30	Cebu	Yes	5	M	married	1
Susan	30	Cebu	Yes	14	M	single	0
Edna	31	Alcala	No	3	M	married	0
Lota	31	Sagada	Yes	3	M	single	0
Melissa	33	Visayas	Yes	6	F	single	0
Rebecca	33	Batangas	Yes	5	M	single	0
Tita	34	S. Maria	No	4	M	single	0
Cristina	36	S. Juan	Yes	3	M	single	0
Vicky	36	Laguna	Yes	6	M	single	0
Judith	37	Manila	No	10	M	single	0
Gloria	39	Barcellona (Philippines)	Yes	7	M	single	0
Jenny	40	S. Maria	Yes	6	M	single	0
Rita	42	Sagada	Yes	7	M	single	0
Sarah	44	Elocosor	Yes	11	M	single	0
Gina	46	Village	Yes	6	M	single	0
Purita	52	Laguna	Yes	9	M	married	4
Flora	53	Alcala	Yes	3	M	married	3
Lori	53	Bulusan	Yes	12	M	married	4

how little money they had when she was little and how she was suffering when she was comparing her and her brothers' situation with that of other children at her school who were better off. Although she remembers the sacrifices they had to make, she admits that mere subsistence was not a problem for them since they could just eat what was produced by the land (which was their own). In the case of Rita, the family situation deteriorated when her father left the house to live with another woman. Her mother had been a housewife until then but then she had to start supporting her seven children on her own. Lota, instead, comes from a middle-class family. Her mother was a teacher and she herself started a teaching career, but she felt that her wage was not enough to support herself, let alone to start a new family there.

As Tacoli (1999) also found in her study on Filipino migration to Rome, the women arriving in Bologna, for the most part, do not seem to come from extremely poor families in the Philippines. Only those whose family can afford the high transportation costs are able to become international migrants. As my research confirms, migration seems to be a strategy deployed to maintain or acquire a middle-class standard of living (compromised by the deterioration of wages and rising prices) or to support the family's upward mobility (as we will see later).

The geographical and occupational origin of most of the respondents' families are rural; 80 per cent stated that at least one of their parents was a farmer. Many of them, though, had moved from the villages to the provincial capitals or to Manila itself in order to study and work. As Castles (2000) has stated, the rural–urban migration that occurred in recent decades originating, among other things, from the use of unsustainable forms of agriculture, was the Filipinos' first step towards international migration. Only three of my twenty respondents came to Italy without having previously migrated from their village to a city. All of the three women who came directly from their village were asked to leave by relatives who were already in Italy and preferred to sponsor their migration rather than having to support them back home.

Some of my interviewees decided to migrate independently whereas for others the decision was taken by other relatives. The women who migrated earlier, when fewer co-nationals were already residing abroad, were pushed by economic necessity and knew very little of what they could expect. They were, in a way, the pioneers; those who opened the paths for the thousands of women who subsequently followed them. Rita's sister was one of these early female emigrants: she had gone to Manila to look for work when the family situation deteriorated as a consequence of their father's departure, and while she was scanning the newspapers she saw an advertisement which read 'domestic workers for Italy wanted'. As Rita recalled, her sister did not hesitate to send her application and after she received an answer from a woman in Turin, she bravely left home for a city in which she knew nobody. By so doing she became the main breadwinner of her household.

Others did not migrate by their own initiative but were simply told to migrate by their parents who needed the income to improve the family's welfare. Parents increasingly became inclined to allow or encourage their children to go abroad after they heard the tales of economic success of those who had previously migrated. The presence of female migrants in destination areas helped to facilitate the movement of other women 'by providing social acceptability and chaperoning' (Tacoli 1999: 664). More often, though, those who put the real pressure on the potential migrant are not the relatives in the country of origin but those who have already migrated and are sending valuable remittances. It is they who at some point decide that it is better to sponsor somebody else's migration within the family rather than incurring the burden of sending regular and substantial remittances on their own. As Tacoli (1999) reminds us, usually the decision to go is neither blatantly coerced nor totally based on personal consideration. Often the two are not mutually exclusive; in fact, in Filipino society the so-called 'debt of gratitude' towards one's own family is strongly felt. The children feel an irrevocable sense of duty towards their parents, so that the migration of young adult children can be motivated by their feeling that they should 'look after the family' (Tacoli 1999: 671).

Once the decision to migrate has been taken, the potential migrant has two options: legal or illegal emigration. Out of my twenty respondents only four arrived legally, contrasting with Lazaridis's (2000) sample of Filipino migrants in Greece who were mostly legal. Those who arrived legally did so thanks to the mechanism of the 'direct call' whereby the employer requests a domestic worker directly from a foreign country. During the first year the monthly wage is fixed – at time of fieldwork at L 1,000,000 – but the employer pays the plane ticket of the worker who in exchange has to honour the contract and work for that employer for at least a full year. Melissa answered an advertisement in the magazine of the Italian embassy in Manila, Gina was selected from a job centre's list in the Philippines, whereas Lota was called directly by her cousin Melissa, who in the meantime had married an Italian and acquired Italian citizenship.

As Gina explained to me, being selected from the job centre's lists is very difficult. In her case it was possible only thanks to nepotism and personal contacts (as seems to be the case with most bureaucratic things in the Philippines). Her aunt knew somebody in the selection committee and therefore her application was favoured. This is probably why most of the women lacking these 'contacts' have to turn to illegal immigration. Up to 1986 (before the first immigration law was passed in Italy) Filipinas could come to Italy as tourists and then get a job when they were already in the country. Subsequently this was no longer possible but this did not result in a decrease in the arrivals from the Philippines – quite the opposite. Immigration agencies started to spring up in the Philippines and the ways in which immigrants were conveyed to the country became more ingenious.

For those who arrived in Italy as clandestine immigrants, the journey has remained a memorable experience: all of my interviewees who arrived in Italy illegally chose to talk at length about their adventure (see also Parreñas 2001a). Here is Edna's account:

> Oh my God, we were many – we were twenty people. As tourists we had the visa only until Switzerland, so once we arrived in Switzerland little by little the agency made us – well, they made us go from the hotel where we were staying by car from Switzerland to Milan – then Milan – well, surely we didn't pass the border... we passed a hill where there was a lot of police – but the taxi driver was really good because each trip one had to go with only four people so that when there is a police station one can hide underneath – they are well organised. ... And then – when we reached the bottom of the hill – slowly we went up – there were already two men who were waiting for us, and then the taxi left as if it came from nowhere ... two of us went with these men whereas Tommy and I, my husband, they left us there for I don't know – a quarter of an hour, we were alone and we started to be a bit worried because if the police comes – because it's not really isolated – there are some trees but you never know if someone is coming ... then the two men came back to collect us – they took us to a villa, it was really a nice villa but they put us in the garage – they closed us in a garage that big and then they took our money ... finally they took us all to Milan station.

As we can infer from this account, the journey of these women into Italy is based on a semi-official organisation which directly links Filipino agencies and Italian 'entrepreneurs'. The 'package' includes the plane ticket to a country just outside the European Union (in the stories I have collected they are Hungary, Switzerland, and the former Yugoslavia), a tourist visa for that particular country, the transfer by car, train, or even on foot until the frontier of destination, and finally the help of guides or taxi-drivers who are specialised in passing the Italian border in the most remote and less-guarded locations. The payment takes place only once the journey has been completed, but the price is quite high.[3] Many women were able to afford it only through the help offered by members of their families, often by those who were already abroad. It is therefore necessary for these women to find a job very quickly in order to be able to start to return the capital they borrowed. They are also under pressure to start remitting money back home.

Seven of my interviewees had moved within Italy before arriving in Bologna. The reasons mentioned for moving were several: in two cases higher wages; in two cases the possibility of getting a job with a regular contract and benefiting from one of the regularisation laws granting the permit to stay to immigrants in possession of a job; in two cases to be closer to relatives; and in one case to follow a boyfriend. The women who came directly to Bologna do not seem interested in moving somewhere else within Italy. As the women in the focus group I conducted at the Association of Filipino Women explained, in Bologna:

there is immigration from the Philippines but also from other Italian cities ... because the wages are higher here in Bologna ... They come from other cities – they ask for lower wages, then they leave that job and go somewhere else – they only do it to start. ... Those that are already here they want a high wage, the employers wants to pay a   low   wage,   so   if   there   is   somebody,   for instance, from Rome, they are really after that person. These Filipinos arrive here and start with a *signora* with a low wage and then they leave.

To the question 'why did you come to Italy?' my respondents replied as follows: four said that they came to work; eight because some relative was already there; six mentioned a combination of these two reasons; one young woman said she came because her parents were already in Bologna and because she wanted to study in Italy; another said that she came in 1996 from Paris where she was working illegally as a domestic because she heard that there was going to be an amnesty for immigrants in Italy and so she hoped to regularise her position.

These are the replies given to the standard interview schedule question, but talking in depth to these women it became apparent that the reasons for coming to Italy were in reality more varied and nuanced. Lota, for instance, explained to me that she wanted to improve her life; since 'that was the story of those who had come before', she decided that she too wanted that experience and to have her own little adventure. Maria stated that she came because some relatives were already in Italy. She then admitted that when she left for Italy (aged twenty-three) her parents did not know about her plan. She did everything secretly with the help of a cousin and her sister. She wanted to get away from her parents' control and she feels that by going abroad she has achieved the greater freedom she was looking for. As Tacoli (1999) has noted, some women use their filial duty towards the well-being of their family in order to fulfil more personal objectives such as satisfying their curiosity about 'seeing the world', escaping parental control, or pursuing a socially accepted path to escape an unhappy marriage (divorce is forbidden in the Philippines).

Once these women have succeeded in realising their migratory project to leave their home country, they have to start coping in the new environment. For many, an immediate problem was the climatic change they experienced when moving from a tropical country to the cold of the Northern Italian winter. However, the real traumatic experience for a lot of Filipinas has been the beginning of their new life as full-time live-in domestics. Before migration these women were often college or university students or they had already started a career, usually in the public sector as teachers or health workers. Once in Bologna and once they succeeded in their actual migratory project to get to Italy, they suddenly found themselves living isolated, far away from home and having to learn quickly both a new language and the work and behaviour requirements – often very demanding – of their new employers.

Here below I provide two examples of biographies of Filipino women addressing the issues presented in the previous pages.

Maria

Maria is twenty-eight and a qualified nurse. She arrived as a *clandestina* in 1991. She has four brothers; two are in the Philippines, one lives in Florence and another is in Canada. It was her father who told her to leave because she had to support her youngest brother who was in Canada studying to become a doctor. She did what she felt was her duty as a daughter and sister and embarked on the dangerous journey that took her to Italy. Here is her account of her adventurous experience.

> I left in 1990 – 1991, in November, by plane. When we arrive there is a car that is waiting for us, we are ten people, they take us to a house that resembles a hotel, then in the evening comes a car – two cars to collect us. Then we went to another house, I think it was in Paris, then they took us to the mountains, I don't know where that mountain was – it was full of snow, then we went to Nice, there were two men who came to collect us … they divided us into groups, five for each group, and then we started to walk in the direction of Italy … we had just started to walk when the police arrived and arrested these two guys – after this episode I didn't see these guys any more. I didn't know what to do … after a while the policemen came back and took me to the police station, in France, they asked me the passport but I don't have the passport because they took it – those two men in Paris. After a while the police let me go so we went – I don't know where we went – oh yes, … we slept outside that night, I don't know where. It is cold and our clothes are light, it is very cold there. Then in the morning we split and we started walking I don't know where and at some point I saw the police again and again they took me to the police station and a policemen asked me: 'Where do you have to go?' I replied: 'Well, I have to go to Italy', and so he showed me the route towards Italy and so we started walking again. We passed through a forest and we heard some dogs … I was very scared. Finally, we passed through a tunnel, one of those where the trains pass, luckily the line was broken down so the train didn't pass – then – I don't remember – well, in the end we arrived in Ventimiglia.

Once in Ventimiglia Maria had to start coping on her own in a foreign country without knowing any Italian. To her surprise, she soon realised that few people could speak English. She eventually managed to find a young man who helped her to buy a ticket for Milan. Once in Milan, exhausted and frightened by her recent experiences, she met a Filipino whom she turned to for help. He phoned Maria's brother (who was waiting for her in Florence) and helped her to get a train to reach him.

She spent the first few days in Italy recovering, but after only a week she got her first job and started sending money regularly to her brother in Canada. With a slight sense of resentment she told me that her brother did not become a doctor in the end but only a medical technician. The positive thing is that now he is working so she has stopped sending him money and can now spend more on herself. The brother who is in Italy works, like her, as a live-in home help. He is married and has a daughter of four. His wife works with him for the same family and their daughter lives in the Philippines with her maternal grandparents. One of the two brothers who are in the Philippines is a teacher and according to Maria he earns hardly enough to survive. The other is currently unemployed. He has paid an agency twice to get a visa to emigrate but on both occasions the agent has disappeared stealing his money. Her family comes from a provincial town two hours away from Manila. Her father drives a jeepney (a kind of taxi) and her mother is a housewife.

Her first period in Italy was terrible and she remembers how she used to cry continuously. Her new job in Florence was in an isolated area out of town and this exacerbated her loneliness and homesickness.

Maria arrived in Bologna thanks to a contact that a Filipino friend gave her. Maria was fed up with the job she was doing in Florence. She could not cope working for a family of four members because the workload was too heavy. She wanted an elderly person because she knew that this type of domestic service is less tiring. Her friend told Maria that in Bologna it was easy to find work with elderly people.

Gina

Gina is forty-six, is married and has a son called Paolo who is now fourteen. She has five brothers and sisters. Her mother remarried after her first husband died. She had two children from the first marriage and five from the second (one has since died). Gina is the eldest from the second marriage. All her brothers and sisters are still in the Philippines. Her parents are both farmers and live in a remote part of the country. She was raised by her unmarried aunt who was living in Manila and working as a cashier in a hospital where Gina was also working before she came to Italy. It was this aunt – whom she called her 'second mother' – who helped Gina to find the job at the hospital thanks to a contact she had with somebody on the appointing commission. In spite of the fact that Gina got the job, after a while she decided to leave after having talked to her other aunt who had come to work in Italy.

I was fed up with my boss in the Philippines, in the hospital, they strangle us, they pay us little, I used to say: 'Tomorrow I'll leave this hospital'. I was fed up also because I wasn't living with my aunt at her place, I was staying in a dormitory, the dormitory and the hospital were in the same compound. So – well, I wasn't even able to go out, my life there was a bit suffocating. Then my aunt who is not married, you know an *old maid* (in English) and she is also half crazy, I said to myself 'What do I do with my life? It's better that I run away.

Gina decided at that point that she needed a change in her life and decided to go abroad 'in search of a bit of adventure' (her words). She started the paperwork for both Italy and Canada. Her aunt helped again, this time recommending Gina to a friend in the job centre.

In that period the head of the job centre was a friend of my aunt, that is why he inserted my name quickly, without queueing, because otherwise it is difficult. Also in my country if you don't know somebody inside it's very difficult. So my aunt told me to go and see this person, she recommended me, so I took him my CV … After a week I got an answer from Salerno. It was my fault that I didn't put down Brescia where my aunt was, I only put down Italy. So my picture and my CV ended up in Salerno, in the job centre in Salerno. So this family went there, there were all the CVs in a line with the pictures and they chose me! They said: 'Let's get this one who is rather pretty'.

She did not tell anybody that she was leaving, neither in the dormitory nor in her family. The only person who knew was her aunt. The decision to go was therefore her own.

Only my aunt knew but not my parents, I had the night shift, after the night shift I run to the countryside, I said goodbye to my parents: 'Why?" they asked. Yes, they knew that I had a plan to leave the country but they did not know that it was that day. I said it happened quickly.

It was 1982 when Gina arrived in Salerno (Southern Italy), far away from Brescia (Northern Italy) were her other aunt was working. Gina did not know Italian and she did not know anybody in that area. Her first year was really hard and she felt very unhappy then. Soon she met a Filipina who was living in the same street and who introduced her to the Filipino community. She also started to attend the meetings of the evangelical community. She is a Catholic but she went just to meet people and to get reassured (her words). She then met her future husband on a trip to Florence and it was partly to follow him (she also wanted to leave Salerno) that she moved to Bologna in 1985.

Moroccan Women

Morocco, like the Philippines, is a labour-exporting country. The destinations of Moroccan migrants are less global than those of their Filipino counterparts, although Moroccans are quite widespread in European destinations, with large numbers in France, Belgium, the Netherlands, Italy and Spain, and sizeable numbers in several other European countries as well. In earlier decades they were predominantly orientated towards the countries of North-West Europe; today they are increasingly arriving in Southern European countries, notably Italy and Spain. Colonialism, the close relationship with France and subsequently the labour-importing policies of this latter country were the key factors which set in motion this migratory process. More recently, the profound transformations undergone by Moroccan society and rapid industrialisation and urbanisation (yet coupled by the persistence of a traditional and agrarian society) are playing a significant role. Rapid demographic growth and rising unemployment make the surplus of the labour force a problem that finds in emigration a partial solution.

Like the Philippines, one can also note in the case of Morocco that those migrating are not the poorest sectors of the population (Dal Lago 1994). Although the main reason to migrate given by most Moroccans is economic, it is usually not a problem of subsistence. It is those who belong to the urban lower- and middle- classes – those who have been exposed to the influence of the 'West' (Jaquemet 1999) – who decide to migrate in order to improve their own or their family's situation or simply in search of adventure and new experiences. Differently from the Philippines, female participation within the labour force is still low in Morocco, although increasing in the urban areas. Moroccan emigrants therefore, at least in the initial stage, are predominantly male. Only in a subsequent phase, the literature tells us, do Moroccan women start to go abroad due to the process of family reunification. This is broadly true but during my study it emerged that there are a considerable number of female migrants migrating on their own, and for a number of different reasons. Moreover, these reasons appeared to be rather different from those of their male counterparts and to be shaped by their gender role within Moroccan society. Their migration abroad (in this case to Italy and Spain), whether to follow their husbands or independently, is therefore worth further analysis.

Figure 3.2 Map of Morocco
Source: www.worldatlas.com

Like their Filipino counterparts, the Moroccan women I met and interviewed in Bologna tend to come from large families (Table 3.2) but this is less the case for younger women and those who migrated to Italy with their family of origin. Women who come from a female-headed household, usually that of a divorcee, also tend to have fewer brothers and sisters. The geographical origins of my Moroccan respondents seem to be less variegated than those of the Filipino migrants. Two cities of origin are over-represented in my group: Casablanca and Khouribga. Khouribga in particular seems to be over-represented both in my sample and in the database regarding Moroccan women who seek employment at Famiglie Insieme (one of the charities where I conducted participant

Table 3.2 Basic biographic data on Moroccan women interviewed in Bologna

Moroccan women	Age	Place of origin	Internal migration before emigration?	Number of siblings	Household head	Marital status upon migration	Number of children upon migration
Malika	18	Casablanca	No	3	M	single	0
Habiba	20	Rabat	No	4	F	single	0
Haziza	20	Khouribga	No	4	M	single	0
Aisha	20	Casablanca	No	3	M	single	0
Buchra	23	Khouribga	No	6	M	divorced	1
Zhora	25	Safi	Yes	4	M	single	0
Nadia	26	Casablanca	No	1	F	single	0
Ilham	28	Kenitra	No	5	M	married	1
Naima	29	Casablanca	No	4	M	married	0
Samira	29	Casablanca	No	5	F	single	0
Fatima	29	Casablanca	No	7	F	married	0
Halima	32	Casablanca	Yes	3	F	divorced	1
Rachida	32	Khouribga	No	6	M	single	0
Nezha	34	Kenitra	No	7	M	married	1
Nabila	35	Oned-Zem	Yes	9	M	single	0
Kalima	39	Casablanca	No	6	M	single	0
Saida	39	Khouribga	No	5	F	divorced	2
Khadija	40	Khouribga	No	6	M	married	0

observation). The role of networks based on family or friendship relationships linking source and destination areas can be an explanation for this.

The socioeconomic origin of my interviewees is very heterogeneous. Some women come from very deprived backgrounds and these are usually female-headed households. For these women, migration was one of the last resorts to try to improve their vulnerable situation. These women were already working full-time in Morocco, under extremely exploitative conditions and earning very little money. Habiba, for instance, comes from a poor neighbourhood in Rabat where she lived with her divorced mother and her elderly grandmother. At the age of five she was already sewing carpets in a factory (like her mother) in order to contribute to the meagre income of her household. Kalima too comes from a poor neighbourhood of a big city, in her case Casablanca, and had worked extremely hard in order to help her family. Before coming to Italy she was a seamstress in a sweatshop where she was working seventeen hours every day.

Other women come instead from middle-class backgrounds: their families had properties in Morocco, their fathers had good jobs (and because of that their mothers could afford to be housewives), they studied and travelled. Sadia, for instance, did not migrate for economic reasons:

> In our country it's not that we don't have enough to eat, that we don't have a house – I have got a house that is now closed, he [her partner] has got a villa, it is a matter of customs, problems with the government, freedom, society is like that, all that – so when we come here we suffer.

Most of the other women I met, however, fall somewhere in between the deprived origins of Habiba and Kalima and the comfortable one of Sadia.

The process of rural–urban migration that most Filipinos have gone through before international migration is less clear with Moroccan women. Five of my interviewees were born in Casablanca and left for Italy from there. One, Habiba, came from Rabat. Two were born in Casablanca, then moved to smaller provincial cities upon marriage and then returned to Casablanca before they left for Italy. Two came straight from Kenitra and only two moved from small towns to Casablanca: one, Nabila to study; and Zohra because of her father's work.

The issue of dependent versus independent migration is also somewhat more complicated in the Moroccan case than in the Filipino one. It seems to have a lot to do with the marital status of the women involved and with their socioeconomic position. Unattached women migrating on their own are still rather rare. Two types of exceptions are, firstly, very educated women who come from progressive families (the case for Nabila who is single and came to Italy on her own with a legal contract after she could not find any suitable job in Morocco and decided to make a change in her life), and a second group of poor working-class women who – somewhat like their Filipino counterparts – migrate in order to support their family of origin. Both Kalima and Samira were single women

76

who came illegally in order to work and in so doing contribute to their household of origin's income. These women, in a way, are 'forced' to undertake independent migration by their economic circumstances.

The other ideal-types of Moroccan female migration are represented by the women who migrate for family reunion (usually the only ones taken into account in the literature on Maghreb migration), and by divorcee women who, due to their weak and despised position within Moroccan society, have few options left open to them in Morocco and therefore try to have a second chance in their life through international migration. I will describe two specific biographical examples of these kinds of migration profile later on.

The legal status of my respondents varies: eleven arrived legally in Italy and seven arrived illegally. Among those who arrived legally there are the ten women who came in under the legislation that protects family reunion. Four of these married Moroccan men while the latter were visiting Morocco during their annual holiday in August, and one reunited with her husband who was already living in Italy. Another subgroup consists of five young Moroccan women (today in their early twenties) who came to Italy to reunite with their parents in the early 1990s. Of these, three came together with their mothers to reunite with the father whereas two came to reunite with their divorcee mothers who were already working in Italy. The last legal route relates to arrival with a legal work contract. Only Nabila arrived in this way – with a contract to work as a live-in maid for a family near Bari. Like the case of Gina (the Filipina whose story I reported in the previous section), this was possible only through some contacts Nabila had with a person who was working at the Italian Consulate in Casablanca. Without such a 'link', she probably could not have arrived legally in Italy.

Unlike the Filipinas who endured the adventurous journeys I mentioned in the previous section, the Moroccan women who went illegally to Italy did so more smoothly. When I asked the question: 'How did you arrive in Italy?' many of my Moroccan respondents simply replied: 'By plane', quite puzzled about what I meant by that question. In fact, these women came in with tourist visas which they obtained in order to visit relatives already living in Italy and then overstayed, becoming therefore illegal immigrants. Three women who came in before the 1990 Martelli Law did so by train, coming in as tourists through the border town of Ventimiglia. Only in one case the fact of having paid a sum of money – about L 6,000,000 – in order to obtain a Shengen visa was mentioned. Since their journeys were apparently less complicated than those of their Filipino counterparts, very few women chose to talk about the experience of the trips that took them from Morocco to Italy.

Nine of my respondents (particularly those who arrived in the early 1990s, i.e., at the beginning of the main Moroccan emigration to Italy) migrated internally within Italy before settling down more permanently in Bologna where the local labour market has a surplus demand both in factory jobs (performed by Moroccan men) and domestic jobs (performed by the women).

As far as the reasons for migrating are concerned, they varied greatly for the women I met. As already mentioned, they are linked to other factors, particularly the woman's socioeconomic position and her marital status (single, married, divorced, widowed). Single women normally migrate with their family of origin; they migrate on their own if they come from poor families and need to support their family of origin; rarely do they migrate independently to study or seek work and better opportunities for themselves. Married women – unlike their Filipino counterparts – do not migrate without their husbands; they migrate either with them or subsequently to reunite with them. Nezha, for instance, arrived in Italy as a consequence of her marriage to a Moroccan man who was already working in Bologna. Divorcees and widows enjoy more freedom to migrate independently but this 'freedom' is the result of the lack of any alternatives for these women due to their vulnerable position within Moroccan society. When a woman is divorced, normally the children are left in her care but often without any economic contribution from her former husband. She has therefore to start earning for herself and migration seems to be a new way that these women (or the most courageous among them) have found to overcome their difficult circumstances. Here is how Saida explained to me the reasons why many Moroccan women decide to migrate:

> Many girls have problems with their fathers because they are very strict, you know, they run away and come here to Italy. Many women have problems with their husbands, and so on, each with her own problems. These are the kinds of problems that all foreigners have – or maybe only Moroccans, I don't know. Anyway, I talked to many women and these are the reasons. When a woman divorces she leaves the country.

Once Moroccan women have arrived in Bologna and start to settle in, they face a number of difficulties. This was particularly the case for those women who arrived at the initial stages of the Moroccan immigration and did not have any friends or relatives to turn to. As Saida recalls, the problems at the beginning were several:

> One had to sleep outdoors, one had to face many unpleasant things, one had to – well nice things don't come immediately – also the language was a problem.

A recurrent and more serious problem mentioned by several of my interviewees has been that of racism. Many of them described episodes of intolerance. Here is one example from Ilham:

> In Bologna people see you always as a foreigner. For instance, you get on a bus where there are a lot of people and you want to get through – well, there are a

lot of people who start protecting their handbags, who start turning to the other side. 'What are they doing?' I wonder. 'I don't steal! What do they think, that I'm a thief?!'

The stories of Saida and Fatima presented below serve to exemplify some of the issues discussed above. Saida found in emigration her only possibility to escape from her abusive husband and support her two children on her own. Fatima had to terminate her university studies and delay marriage in order to help her family in Morocco. Once finally married with a Moroccan man who was working in Italy, the interference of her new in-laws almost precluded her from achieving her dream of joining him in Italy.

Saida

Saida is thirty-nine, divorced with two teenage children. The girl is thirteen and the boy is fifteen. She is illiterate and comes from a rural town in Morocco. Both her parents are now dead. Her mother died in 1992 when Saida had already come to Italy. She arrived in Italy in 1990 as a clandestine migrant, after having worked – illegally – for six months in the south of Spain. After six years of marriage she decided to run away from her husband who was violent and regularly beat her up. She left her house and took refuge at her mother's place with her two young children. She then decided to leave the children there and go abroad in search of a job. When I asked her how she came to that decision she told me that she followed the example of a woman in her family who had done the same in the past.

Saida returned to Morocco from Spain six months later to give some money to her children. She found a letter informing her that her husband had divorced her, and she was relieved. She then left again, this time for Italy. On the train to Italy she heard from fellow-Moroccans that Bologna was a good place to find employment and so she decided to go there. When she arrived in Bologna she realised that it was very difficult to obtain a 'permit to stay' there and so she left for Sicily:

> Down in Sicily it's very easy to obtain a permit to stay… Here in Bologna they want a lot of things – they want the house, a job with a legal contract – in Sicily they don't want all these things – they just do it.

Getting a permit in Sicily turned out to be relatively simple but there were hardly any jobs there and therefore Saida decided to go back to Bologna.
Saida did not know anybody in Italy when she arrived and therefore had to do everything by herself. She even had to sleep in empty train carriages before she got her first job which also included an accommodation. During that time she felt like a soldier who had to fight for everything.

Many people went to school but they don't have the courage to come here, you need courage to come not education, it's like a war – a soldier needs to be smart (*in gamba*), he has to do things otherwise he dies, he does not fear for his life, he doesn't fear anything, his job is like that. ... Also my job is like that.

Saida's initial days were also difficult because she could not read or write let alone speak Italian. Yet she managed.

The first time I came to Bologna I only knew two addresses: my home one and my work one. The work one was written with a red pen, the home one with a blue pen. When I left work I used to show the blue address to someone: 'You go this way' and so I went to my house. When in the morning I left the house I look for the red address – because I only knew red and blue.

Saida admits that it is easier for the women who are in her position (i.e., alone) and arrive in Italy today since they can rely on a wider network of support constituted by relatives or fellow townspeople. She gives the example of her cousin who also escaped from Morocco from a man but who, unlike Saida, did not have to struggle since Saida was there to help her.

She came to stay with me, she didn't suffer how I suffered. She came and everything went well, she found me, she found a hot bath, she found a bed, she found food to eat, everything, you know. ... I came and I slept in a cold train – she came and she slept in a clean bed.

Fatima

Fatima is twenty-nine, she is married and had just arrived in Italy when I met her for the first time. She came legally under the legislation on family reunion. She comes from Casablanca. Her father was an employee in an insurance company but he is now dead. She has six brothers and sisters. One of her sisters, who is divorced and has a daughter, is living in Genoa; one of her brothers lives in Kuwait; the other brothers and sisters are all living in Morocco. Two of her brothers are still living with her mother; one of them is unemployed and the other a train driver. All her brothers have studied and she too has been to university where she read chemistry and physics for two years. She then had to stop when her father died and instead completed a course for becoming a model-maker for clothes which allowed her to find employment in various factories in Casablanca. During the period between the death of her father and her marriage she had to sacrifice her studies and help her family. She not only contributed economically through her work in the factory but also – because her mother had fallen ill – by carrying out most of the domestic chores.

She had arrived in Italy two months before I met her for the first time, three years after she got married. During this period she continued to live with her family of origin and her husband continued to send remittances and presents to his mother and sister. Fatima believes that it is because of the money and the presents that her in-laws did not want her joining her husband in Italy since this would have meant an increase in expenditures incurred by him in Bologna and consequently a decrease in remittances.

When Mustapha wrote the telex to tell me that he had the documents for doing the family reunion his mother told him that I cast him a magic spell in order to get an Italian permit to stay and to become rich.

It took a lot of time for Fatima to convince her husband that this accusation was false. Her argument for coming to Italy with him was that she could also work in Bologna and in so doing they could save faster for the money they needed to fulfil one of their projects, to build a house in Morocco.

The worse time for Fatima was the three months before she could finally move to Italy. During this time her husband went back to Morocco and helped to do the paperwork for the visa. They were both living with Mustapha's family and, as Fatima recalls, 'It was like living on fire' since her mother and sister-in-law were trying their best to convince Mustapha that Fatima should not join him in Italy. In spite of all their effort, he did not give in to family pressures and brought back Fatima with him to Bologna.

The Reasons for Leaving

This section has presented some of the women migrating to Bologna and their reasons for doing so. What has emerged from this analysis is the heterogeneity of backgrounds and of motivations pushing women to leave their countries. Having said this, there seems to be an element uniting the reasons for migrating given by these women: their gender-specificity, that is to say, their being related to women's (gendered) roles and positions within their families and societies of origin. Among these reasons I identify the following. First, we can note the frequent absence from the household of a male figure (dead or disappeared). A high proportion of my respondents – both Moroccan and Filipino – come from female-headed households. The reasons for this can be twofold: greater independence of the women belonging to this type of household, or greater necessity (forcing them to move further) on the part of these women to earn high wages. Second, the need for a well-paid job in order to help financially other members of their families is important, more so for Filipino women but also found for poor working-class Moroccan women (see also Chell 1997, 2000; Escrivà 2000a; Lazaridis 2000; Ribas 2000a; Tacoli 1999; Zlotnik 1995). Third, there is the desire to escape from oppressive familial situations, often masked with the 'excuse' of good job opportunities abroad (see Phizacklea 1998; Tacoli 1999). Finally, women migrate for family reunion and within this category Moroccan women often migrate as a result of marriage with co-nationals already resident in Italy. Family migration – the reason most commonly associated with female migration – does not preclude other reasons, which may include economic ones and even the desire to escape from oppressive situations at home.

As regards the ways in which women manage to migrate, the existence of networks (both those made of kinship ties and wider networks) seems crucial. Most of the international migrants seem to have lived in urban centres before migration, since it is there that they can get better information and access to those networks that will take them abroad. In the Philippines, as we have seen, there are specialised agencies that help migrants to go to Europe illegally. Within these illegal networks to Italy women seem to be a majority, since it is women who – through their well-paid jobs as domestic helpers – will be able to raise the money to pay back the agency. Family and kin already abroad are extremely important in this context (Boyd 1989), both for initially paying the agency's fees and for providing help upon arrival, particularly important if the migrant is clandestine and therefore reliant on informal contacts in order to find jobs and housing (Staring 1998). To conclude, it is already evident from this section how families – and more specifically women's roles and responsibilities in them – as well as kinship ties and networks play a key role in facilitating, constraining or simply shaping female migration.

Settling Families, Supporting Families: The Hardship of Settlement

Whereas the previous section has dealt with the reasons for moving, this section will centre on the issue of settling down, paying special attention to women's strategies to secure housing and to their participation in the local labour market.

Filipino Women

Filipinas in Bologna, as many authors have noted as regards Filipinas elsewhere in Southern Europe (Chell 1997, 2000; Lazaridis 2000; Ribas 2000), seem to be at the top of the hierarchy of domestic workers. In fact, they appear to have few problems in securing jobs as both domestics and carers. They are generally considered 'hardworking, honest, clean and educated' and to provide a better quality service than other immigrant groups (Parreñas 2001a: 176). As one of the staff of ACLI confessed, Filipinas are indeed the most requested group in town, and she lamented that now they are becoming too expensive for many families.[4] She told me that over the years Filipinas have become choosier, also as a consequence of the fact that they seem to be very aware of their rights and press to have them implemented. For instance if they are employed as a carer for an elderly person they will generally refuse to clean and cook, whereas other immigrant women will accept doing everything. Although she herself seems to agree with the common view that Filipinas are the best domestics (she told me that she looked in vain for months for a Filipina to take care of her grandmother), she also resents the fact that they are becoming too 'difficult' and expensive.

I encountered a similar attitude at another charity which centres around a much discussed priest. It is known in town that Filipinas get privileged treatment by Padre Franco. Many immigrant women I met elsewhere told me that this was the case and that I could see this in practice if I went along on one of the days dedicated to job requests. I was warned to notice that Filipinas queue separately from the other immigrants, as was in fact the case. Moreover, when I interviewed Padre Franco he openly admitted that he preferred Filipinas whom he thought were more reliable than other groups, for instance the Moroccans, whom he described as 'liars' and 'thieves'. He then added that sometimes he had to place women of other nationalities because Filipinas are becoming too expensive. Like the woman at ACLI, he too lamented the fact that Filipinas in Bologna have changed over the years, referring in particular to the fact that they are more aware of their rights and that they ask high wages.

The combination of high demand for domestic workers, the high educational levels of Filipinas, and their presence in Italy and in Bologna over a number of years results in the fact that a proportion of Filipinas is getting established in the city and after many years in employment they are starting to reach the top of the domestic worker career. That is to say, they are able to secure for themselves legal contracts (with the concomitant rights, i.e., one and a half free days per week, paid holidays, maternity leave and so on), live-out work, and high levels of pay (L 20,000 to 30,000 for those who are paid hourly, up to L 2,000,000 per month for those who work full-time). This is, though, only a minority and many of the women I met had not reached that position yet. If they had, they did so only after many years of hard, underpaid and exploitative work.

Some of the more established Filipinas, on the other hand, lamented the job segregation to which they are condemned. In spite of their high levels of education (often they have university degrees), they cannot access any other type of employment except care and domestic work. This gender and ethnic stereotyping of Filipinas – equating Filipinas with domestic work – obviously sets limits on their full socioeconomic integration and amounts to a negative discrimination in the labour market.

Many Filipinas at the beginning of their careers work as live-in maids. This is the easiest job to find and it provides additional advantages for the newly-arrived migrant, solving both the work and the housing problem in one go. This solution also presents an important economic benefit since all living expenses are paid for by the employer. In spite of these advantages, living with one's employer is not so easy. The daily life of a live-in domestic maid revolves around the rhythm and the times of the employers. The domestic has her own room, and often also her own bathroom, but having to live within her employers' house means that she cannot use freely and fully her living space. For a live-in domestic the house is therefore not only the private space but also and above all the work space. At any moment the domestic can be called on to perform some task and therefore her needs, such as eating and resting, have to follow those of the other members of the household. Her only private space is her bedroom but she has a very limited amount of time to spend there; besides if the need arises she can be called by her employers at any time. The other rooms of the house, including the kitchen, are essentially work spaces. Below is how Maria described this experience during a focus group:

> It wasn't like when you are in your own house or in a little flat far away from them [the employers], it is different because you can't move in a comfortable way because the master is there! That's how it is.

As far as the live-in job is concerned, most of my interviewees (who had since moved to live-out work) expressed their dissatisfaction with that type of employment. Both in the focus group and in the individual interviews, they lamented having to be workers 'night and day' (De Filippo 1994), that is to say to be on duty theoretically for twenty-four hours. The job is particularly hard when there are young children, since it is normally the domestic who has to look after them throughout the day and often also at night. This is why Maria left that kind of job:

> Particularly when there are children – they take advantage when they go out on Saturday night – because the children stay with us. Where I was working before every Saturday night they went out for a meal and so the three children stayed with me, particularly the little one who used to stay with me until 1 A.M. So I said to myself I don't want to work as live-in any more because now all the hours are theirs! As a part-timer, after you finish working that's it.

The fact that the domestics are in many cases the only ones responsible for the care of the children, as was the case for Maria, creates another set of problems in addition to the stretching of the domestic's timetable. It can happen that the children get closer to the domestic than to their parents and this – as in Rita's experience – can result in jealousy and envy on the part of the employer:

> I was working there all day with the baby, we were going to Margherita gardens, then we were playing, and then I was doing the cooking, cleaning, and ironing.

... Then at night they were coming back and then sometimes they were going out again, then after a while the *signora* started to be – a bit jealous because the baby was closer to me than to her, so she was looking for a way of expressing her envy by making me work too much.

After a period spent as live-in workers, most of the Filipinas in Bologna found that they could not continue indefinitely with that type of arrangement, and so moved to live-out work. Live-in work is considered as an initial strategy in order to get inserted in the local labour market but it is rarely, at least in Bologna, a long-term perspective. Ceasing to live at the employer's home, however, means having to enter the city's competitive and exclusionary housing market.

The first step towards independent housing for Filipinas in Bologna was the renting of flats for their free days. Small groups of women got together to rent flats where they spent holidays and their weekly days off. Here the women could keep warm and cook their favourite dishes together with their friends during the cold winter afternoons without being bothered by their employer's presence. Jessica found her flat through a Filipino friend who was married to an Italian. It was this woman who initially rented the house and then gave it to Jessica and her seven or eight friends as a 'second' house. At first none of the women was living or sleeping there on a regular basis; all of them were working as live-in domestics and were using the flat only to rest and cook on Wednesdays and Sundays instead of spending this time hanging around in Piazza Maggiore, as they used to do previously. Stasiulis and Bakan (1997) note similar housing arrangements for Filipinas in Toronto and Decimo (1996) for Somalian women in Naples.

Gradually several Filipinas decided that they could share flats not only for recreational uses but also as stable residences. At that point the problem became how to get access to new flats. The possibilities for these women were the following: seeking help from an employer, going to an estate agent, or answering a newspaper advertisement. As far as the estate agents are concerned, Jessica pointed out in the focus group that:

To the estate agent only the Filipinos who are factory workers go, those who are domestics don't go there. ... They don't give houses to domestics, maybe because they think that domestics don't get a regular income – that they can't pay the rent.

Estate agents seem therefore to have prejudices against domestic workers whom they think are not able to meet the costs of a rented flat. Actually, Filipino domestic workers tend to earn more on average than factory workers. The problem is that their 'official wage' is lower since their employers declare only a part of their real wage for tax purposes. This is why Filipino maids find themselves with an official wage that is inadequate according to the requirements of the estate agents. Moreover, this does not mean that Filipinos (men) who are factory workers do not face obstacles in finding a flat. In their case they can be accepted by the agencies but there is no guarantee that they will be able to find a landlord willing to let property to foreigners. As Teresa explained to me, there are a lot of Italians who, 'if they know that they have to deal with foreigners, say no, no, no'.

The best method of finding a flat for Filipinas is to use the help of their friends, relatives and employers. Since rents in Bologna are extremely high, Filipinos can rarely afford a flat either on their own or with their nuclear family. Thus they usually share flats with other families or groups of friends in order to be able to afford the rent. Teresa, for instance, shares a two-bedroom flat with six people: 'I live with my sister, my brother, my sister-in-law, her son, and also another sister-in-law and her husband'.

Having to share a flat with other people is not very easy, due to frequent quarrels and disagreements. Having to share with members of one's own family is seen by Edna as a preferred option to sharing with non-kin:

Even if we argue and fight a bit with my mother – it's fine like that because one washes the dirty linen within the family, you know, because if we take flatmates who are not our relatives – well with your own mother, father and family things stay there and don't go out – with friends who share the house with you this is not the case.

In order to be able to meet all their expenses, some Filipinos have started to apply for council housing, now open also to the immigrant residents of Bologna. Remarkably, no Filipino has been so far allocated one of these flats. This can be explained by analysing the rules by which points are given to people who will gain access to the flats (see Bernardotti and Mottura 1999). An enormous weight is given to the condition of having lived in a Centre of First Shelter (CPA), but no Filipino lives there. Other conditions are low income (women who are in Bologna on their own and who receive a regular wage will never qualify for that), and large number of children (another condition uncommon for Filipinas due to their type of employment, which makes it impossible for them to be able to keep any of their children with them).

Zeni (who is married and has a son) did try to obtain a council flat but with little success:

We applied for a council flat but – nothing. No Filipino ever gets to the top of the council's list – there is no Filipino in council housing, they are all Moroccans, and other nationalities … I don't know why – what I got to know is that the council said that Filipinos can cope by themselves, they are good guys, but we also need a house! They don't make laws that are the same for everybody!

As regards the current job situation of my Filipino informants, at the time of fieldwork nineteen out of twenty were in employment. Only one, Judith, was unemployed. She had worked for five years as a live-in maid for an elderly woman, but after she got married and had her two daughters she only managed to find occasional work. She told me that several employers had refused to employ her because she had small children who would need to be looked after when sick.

Of the other nineteen, fifteen work as domestics or carers and four have other occupations: Mina who works as a sample maker for a fashion designer; Ester who works as telephone operator in a 'phone centre' that caters mainly for immigrants; Rebecca who is a clerk at one of the two Filipino banks in Bologna; and Melissa who works as a cultural mediator at one of Bologna's hospitals. Melissa also teaches Italian to Filipinos and volunteers both at the CGIL trade union and at the Association of Filipino Women. Her position is somewhat different from the other women since, having married an Italian, Melissa is effectively an Italian citizen. In the past, however, she too worked as both live-in and live-out domestic.

Another occupation outside the domestic sphere in which we encounter Filipinos in Bologna is as factory workers. Many Filipino men are moving to this sector which, although it does not necessarily offer better wages than those commanded by established domestic workers, does guarantee higher levels of job stability, security and pension entitlements. Two of the women I met also said that they had previously worked in factories: Melissa and Lori. Lori had a long experience of factory work also in the Philippines, where she reached the level of manager in the quality control sector of a factory producing plastic bottles. She also worked in two factories in small towns outside Bologna but she gave up these jobs because they were too far out from the city.

Of the fifteen women who are working in the domestic sector, thirteen are live-out domestics; two, Tita and Maria, are live-in carer/domestics. Among those who are live-out domestics there are variations concerning the type of job performed, the hours worked, the conditions of employment and the salary received. As regards the type of job, some women have to take care of children as well as cleaning the house and cooking; others have only to clean and iron; whilst some have to care for elderly people while cleaning and housekeeping. As far as the hours are concerned some do what is called *lungo orario* which means full-time (eight hours) live-out work for one employer; others work part-time, sometimes every day for the same employer (this can be from three to six hours per day), or weekly or twice weekly for several employers. Also the conditions vary. Some women are satisfied with their employers, who have complete trust in them and they are therefore free to organise their work independently. Others are unhappy with their employers whom they perceive as too strict or demanding. The rates of pay also vary – according to the particular type of domestic work performed, the experience of the worker and also her legal condition.

As confirmed also by the officer at ACLI, few Filipinas seem to turn to agencies such as hers in search of employment. Even at Padre Franco the separate queue reserved for Filipinos on the day of my visit was rather thin compared to the main one and was comprised mostly by Filipino men (who seem to find it harder to get employment as domestic helpers, probably due to gender stereotyping in this sector in Bologna). Most of my interviewees told me that they found their current or past jobs through personal contacts given to them by relatives or former employers. Often Filipinas take up the job left vacant by one of their relatives who has moved on to another job or has left to go back to the Philippines (on holiday or permanently). Rita, for instance, was helped by her older sister to find her first job and subsequently, once she became more established, she herself helped several relatives to get inserted in the local labour market thanks to the contacts she had with her employers and their friends. What emerged from Rita's account is that Filipinas suggest only names of fellow-nationals whom they trust (that is why they are usually relatives) since if there are any problems with the new worker the employer will go back and complain to the person who had introduced the worker to them.

When my interviewees were asked to talk about their employers, only Gina had good words for her *signora*. Today she works as a part-time maid. She works for four hours per day and earns L 1,300,000 per month. She has been with this employer for eleven years. She considers herself really lucky because she has had two employers who are 'human' and who helped her on different occasions.

The others chose to focus on peculiar aspects of their employer's behaviour which they considered to be odd. Edna said that she left her former employer because she was 'crazy'. She worked for this elderly woman for six years but as her employer became older and more ill, she was becoming more 'suspicious', 'nervous' and 'neurotic'. Edna felt a mixture of compassion for this elderly woman who 'taught her a lot' about how to clean and do things in the house, etc., but also resentment for the way she was treating her. Rita too felt that her former employer was not completely 'normal'. Both Edna and Rita spent a lot of time explaining to me the strange relationships they noticed between the members of the families they were working for (between older parents and their children or between husband and wife) and they both attributed to these tensions some of the negative behaviour of their employers towards them. Both Edna and Rita tolerated what they perceived to be difficult working conditions for a while but eventually turned to the trade unions for help and left.

Although many Filipinas complained about the degrading conditions related to their job, most of them did not consider domestic work as a negative or humiliating profession as such. What is positive for them about their job experience is the wage, since through domestic work abroad they can achieve goals for themselves and their families which are inconceivable for the majority of Filipinos, including those in good jobs. In Jenny's words: 'In Italy it is much easier to live. With domestic work you can earn enough to buy many things. We earn more than a professional in the Philippines, this is why we are here'.

The money earned in Bologna is generally sent back to the Philippines. Two Filipino banks in Bologna cater exclusively for the Filipino 'community', their main activity being the transfer of remittances from Italy to the Philippines. Rebecca, who works in one of the banks, told me that generally people remit up to L 500,000 monthly. Nineteen of my twenty interviewees declared that they sent money back home; only Vicky said that she only sends presents and buys things for her relatives when she is in the Philippines. Two others, Melissa and her cousin Lota, send money only occasionally; all the others send money regularly, either monthly or at specific times of the year, for instance (as in the case of Gina) when the school fees are due. The amount sent varies between L 250,000 per month to up to L 1,500,000 in the case of Purita who was helping her children to get through high school and university. At the focus group it was confirmed that mothers with their children back home are the group which remits the highest sums of money; according to Jenny, 'They send everything they earn'.

The main purpose of the remittances is to improve the socioeconomic position of the family of origin of the migrant (Chant and McIlwaine 1995; Tacoli 1999). A large share of earnings is spent on the education of children, brothers, sisters, nephews and nieces. Money is also sent to support elderly parents once they have stopped working, and to brothers and sisters to start an activity or simply to complement their insufficient earnings. Gina, for instance, has helped or is currently helping all her brothers and sisters:

> I sent money to my sister to buy a small car ..., a jeepney, in order to earn some money for her family. Then I sent money to my brother and my sister because they wanted to raise pigs but they didn't have the money. ... Then my other brother asked me to help him to sent his children to school, because over there if you don't have money you can't study, you have to pay for everything!

Sometimes remittances are used to sponsor the emigration of other family members. Rita, for instance, was called to Italy by her older sister, then she started contributing to her family budget and eventually she sponsored the emigration of two cousins and two sisters-in-law:

> When I finished junior school she [her elder sister] made me study midwifery because she said that midwifery was the best course in order to come here in Italy ... then she paid the tourist agency that helped me arrive here as a *clandestina*. ... She used to reproach me ... you have to stay here and work because you have to help the other brothers and sisters – because there are four of them after me. ... I worked as a live-in maid and now little by little I'm sending money to my mother, to my brothers because they are studying – but you know boys don't have the same commitment as girls, it's a bit different and difficult. ... I helped two cousins to come here and now they are independent

– and now I'm trying to help two sisters-in-law – because one was abandoned by my brother who left for another woman. The labour office has already issued the document, I have to sent it to her DHL so that she can sort things out there and then she'll come here and I will not have to support her anymore.

The initial expense of getting a relative to Italy can be high but in the long run it is a worthwhile effort since, once abroad, the beneficiaries will stop being recipients of remittances and become themselves generators of income to be sent back home to those who stayed behind. At that point the original migrant can start investing money in more personal projects such as buying land, building a house in the country of origin, or even buying properties with the view of renting them out.

Contrary to what has been noted by Tacoli (1999) about Filipinos in Rome, in Bologna if a husband and wife live together, it is generally the woman who keeps all the money and decides on what it should be spent – as is apparently the norm in the Philippines (Chant and McIlwaine 1995). Apart from remitting money to help relatives, Filipinas save money in order to buy land and build houses, and if they can they also try to keep some savings in the bank which can be used for emergencies and for when they go back to the Philippines.

This subsection is concluded with the brief accounts of the working experiences of two of my informants, Maria – who performs a typical 'Filipino job' as a live-in carer – and Mina – who has a job that differs from those of her countrywomen, but which is not necessarily seen as an improvement by her.

Maria

Maria was a nurse in the Philippines and now is working as a live-in maid in Bologna for an elderly woman who is eighty-four and suffers from Alzheimer's. She came to Bologna from Florence because, as we noted earlier, she knew that in Bologna it was easier to find employment with elderly women, and she was dissatisfied with her job in a family.

I had to look after the two children and take them to school, I had to wake up at 7 a.m. and prepare their breakfast – then sometimes the parents went on holiday – once they left me alone with the children for two months. Also when the children were ill the parents left them with me, because they knew that I was good at that – that I'm a nurse, also at the seaside house they always left the children with me. They went to the sea. I was fed up with that family, I had to bring the children to school – ah, it was a hard job – and my salary was low, they only gave me L 1,100,000. ... Now it's fine because with this elderly woman is not like with that family that I always had to do something, always cook, always think what to cook.

Her current work consists of cleaning the house of the elderly woman, cooking for her and making sure that she eats, washing her, dressing her and looking after her throughout the day and if anything happens also at night. Although Maria can never leave her alone she says that the job is fine. Looking after one person is less demanding than having to be responsible for four members of a family, particularly if there are young children. At the time of the interview the elderly woman was quietly sitting in front of the television, only stopping from time to time to ask who I was. Maria says that she does not complain about the job but she would like to earn more. She is currently earning L1,400,000 per month. As a live-in maid she does not have to pay rent and food, so she can save a substantial part of her salary. She has total control of the house and the daughter of the elderly woman has complete trust in Maria and only comes to check things out once a week. During the rest of the time Maria is in charge of the house and of the elderly woman, whom she considers as a member of her family; she actually calls her *nonna* (grandma).

Since she does not have to send money to her brother any more – he has finally started to work in Canada – she can now save more for herself. At the time of the interview she was saving for her wedding. Traditionally it is the groom's responsibility to pay for the celebration but since Maria is working she will contribute to half of all the expenses.

Mina

Mina was a therapist in the Philippines and now works as a sample maker for a fashion designer in Bologna. This is her first job in Italy. She met her current employer when she went for an interview to work as a domestic. At that time the sister of the person who interviewed her was starting her own fashion company with her husband. She decided to employ Mina since she had previous experience of sample making in the Philippines. Mina stated that she is happy about her job:[5]

> I'm so lucky because I have found a different job, unlike the other Filipinos, you know, the jobs that Filipinos have here are as domestics, but me, I'm so lucky because I'm an assistant fashion designer.

Later on in the interview she said that she was actually thinking of quitting that job because although she thinks that it is more interesting than a domestic job the pay is not as good. She is also torn about the reasons why she decided to come to Italy (she did so voluntarily and actually against the will of her mother). She has decided that she is doing it basically for the money. Once she has accumulated enough money to buy another house (she already owns a house in Manila) and start some kind of business she will go back, probably in about five years.

Before, I didn't understand, my first year here I always cried, I didn't understand why, why I am away from my family, now, my second year I understand that yeah there is the money!

Her dilemma is that if her reason to be in Italy is to be able to save as much as possible and then have a more comfortable life in the Philippines, then her job as a sample maker is not the best she can have. She earns L 2,500,000 per month but she thinks that domestic workers can make up to L 3,000,000 by combining more than one job and working also during holidays and free days. She has not got much time to take up extra jobs since she works eleven hours per day and she has already 'volunteered' to work also on Saturdays.

Apart from the salary Mina is also getting dissatisfied with the growing amount of work she has to do in the company. In fact, when the employers are away not only does she have to get on with her normal tasks (i.e., making the samples) but she also has to answer the phone, reply to faxes, deal with delivery people, do all the office work. In some parts of the interview Mina seemed very proud of her job, which allows her to learn many new things and be involved with something (fashion) that she is interested in. At other times she seemed less happy about it, not only because of the income but also for the workload. She is a very flexible employee who works until she is needed even doing extra shifts at night if her employer has to meet a deadline.

She justifies what she does (in terms of workload, flexibility and hours worked) by casting it in the light of favours that she does for her employers and framing it in the context of the special relationship she has with them. She is proud of doing more for them than should be required from an employee:

You know one thing Italian people admire about me? I'm not working with the employer like an employee, I act like a friend, I'm like a friend. Like, for example, I'm a sample maker for a fashion designer employer – I colour her hair, I brush her hair, yeah it's true, I cut her hair, I do a lot of things because I like to act as a friend, the relationship – because it's better – employer-employee – it's better.

She thinks that the fact of committing totally to one's job, whatever it is, is a Filipino characteristic and it is something she feels proud of:

This is one thing to be proud of as a Filipino, because we work wholeheartedly, we work with so much dignity – that we are proud of it. ... Our work is like that ... that you dedicate yourself to whatever kind of work you have.

It seems that Mina finds herself in a difficult position as a result of her job, which is different from the jobs done by all my other interviewees. For Filipinas, coming to work as a domestic is the norm and it is an accepted thing to do within the Filipino community. Mina is not quite sure if her job in the fashion industry has the same respectability as a domestic job and if it fully justifies her absence from her family and young son. She told me that normally she does not tell the other Filipinas she meets what she does, 'Because I want to show to them that we are the same'.

At present she was saving money to have her sister come to Italy. Her husband got very upset with this since he also would like to come to Italy. There is no job he could do in her company and Mina does not know how she could explain to him that he would have to work as a domestic help (he is a medical therapist) while she works in a fashion company. She thinks that her sister could help her sewing so she could join her in the company. It has been noted by Tacoli (1999: 657) that often migrant women prefer to favour the immigration of female relatives – seen as more reliable in generating income for remittances – thus contributing to reinforcing the gender-selectivity of Filipino migration. Besides, Mina does not want to reunite her family in Italy since she is aware that then it will be more difficult to go back to the Philippines. She does not approve of the Filipinas who spend their lives in Italy; her plan is to save enough to go back as soon as possible. She does not send large remittances (L 300,000 monthly) because she prefers to accumulate her savings in the bank for her return.

Moroccan Women

As we have seen, Filipinas are equated with domestic work (Chell 2000; Lazaridis, 2000) and have no problems in finding jobs in this sector. The same cannot be said for Moroccans who in Bologna are considered mainly as housewives and dependants of male breadwinners. However, while conducting fieldwork I soon realised that most Moroccan women in the city *were* involved in paid work and those who were not were actively seeking work. Contrary to the Filipinas, who hardly need any help in securing jobs as domestics, Moroccan women do not seem to have access to the same successful networks as their Asian counterparts. From the (stereotyped) perspective of local employers, Moroccan women are not seen as such 'desirable' employees as the Filipinas, who have carved out a niche, and a good reputation, for themselves in the domestic work and care sector. In order to find jobs Moroccan women rely more heavily on agencies and voluntary associations.

The staff at ACLI told me that they have a significant number of Moroccan women who seek employment through them, generally part-time hourly paid work. They admitted that Moroccans do not have a very good reputation in the city and many employers do not want them. When I asked my ACLI informant if employers made explicit distinctions according to nationality when asking for a domestic, she answered that she encountered three types of attitudes. The first group of employers did not make (at least in principle) any distinction. The second group simply refused to take on any foreign woman. The last group made a specific distinction, for instance refusing to employ Muslim women. Some of the excuses for turning down Muslim women that were reported to me were for instance: 'I don't want any Muslims because with all those veils they cannot move properly'; 'I don't want Muslims because they do not eat everything and then they have all those veils!'; 'I don't want Muslims because the children might get scared' or 'My mother is old and she is not used to them'.

The ACLI officer I interviewed seemed to condemn these attitudes although she felt that ultimately the employers are paying a wage and are free to employ who they want. The situation is worse for Moroccan women at the charity of Padre Franco. As already pointed out, the priest overtly favours Filipinas over everyone else and he is particularly vehement against Moroccans. Two of my interviewees mentioned going to his charity but were not prepared to go there again. Zohra explained to me that she does not go there because he is racist:

> When I went there I dressed well and put make-up on. Padre Franco called me inside, making me jump the queue, then he asked me: 'Are you Kosovar?' 'No, I'm Moroccan,' I replied and he reacted furiously saying: 'Ah but for Moroccans there isn't anything here!'

For Moroccan women migrating on their own (either divorcees or working-class women), going to work as a live-in maid is – as for their Filipino counterparts – the easiest and most likely option to solve their housing problem. Saida, when she arrived in Bologna and had nowhere to stay, was eventually helped by Caritas to find a job as a domestic which, although it offered a very low salary, was good insofar it provided her with some accommodation.

But for Moroccan women (like their Filipino counterparts), live-in work is rarely a long-term solution particularly for those who are divorcees, like Saida, and have the problem of getting reunited with their children.

> When I arrived I even slept at the station once and then I found a *signora* who employed me and then I looked for a job at the cooperative because I was tired of – because I was staying with this family also to sleep and everything, I was working doing really everything, then I asked to bring my children but they don't want children. I wasn't here to leave my children behind, I came here in order to find a house, a job, you know.

Another option for vulnerable migrant women on their own, particularly if they have children with them, is that of being hosted by council or charity structures. Such emergency units are however very few and target either men or women with a high number of children (with them in Bologna). Buchra was aware of this situation and was furious about it:

At the Immigration Service they only find houses for families with children, they don't care about a woman without a job, about a woman on her own. Children, children, children, they don't deal with women on their own. If there was a place here where women could sleep when they lose their job until they have found a new house... Without that women become prostitutes – you know, there are a lot of foreign women who become prostitutes, really a lot out in the streets, because if one comes here, she doesn't find a place to stay – you know – when she loses her job, from tomorrow where does she go? If she doesn't find a place to sleep the first night, the second night, then comes a man who tells her all right you can come to stay with me tonight and she goes because she doesn't have any alternatives, already she is taking a bad route.

Among my interviewees only one, Habiba, was a guest of one of these charity structures, namely the hostel of the nuns of Madre Teresa. Although she did not complain about the treatment she was receiving there, she was hoping to be able to leave the hostel soon, probably once she had found a job as a live-in domestic. Her mother and one-year-old sister were also hosted by the nuns in a different hostel. Her mother too was looking for a job as live-in maid but for her – with a young child – that will be much more difficult.

Another possibility for women who come on their own, particularly for those who have arrived more recently, is – as we saw in the case of Saida's cousin – to be hosted by relatives and family friends or to rent rooms in houses with other people, both Italian and foreigners. However, live-in domestic work seems to be still the most likely way in which Moroccan women migrating on their own manage to solve their housing problem.

When Moroccan women are in Bologna with their families they need flats. Moroccan strategies to secure such flats are generally different from those adopted by their Filipino counterparts. The one that has drawn most of the media and public attention in Bologna is their occupation of empty buildings. At the beginning of 1990 about two hundred Moroccans (many of whom were women and children) occupied an empty building (a former school) in Via Gobetti and divided it up in a number of 'flats' that became their home (Bernardotti and Mottura 2000). Saida was among the people who took part in that occupation. She went to the Immigration Service of the City Council to see if they could help her to find accommodation in order to be able to reunite with her children (she was then living in a bed-sit provided by the cooperative where she was working). They were not able to help her but it was there that she heard that some Moroccans were going to occupy an empty building and transform it into temporary housing and so she decided to go along with them.

It wasn't the Council that gave it to me. It was just a group of people who went there like that, you know, I wasn't the only one, there were a lot of people without a house then, without anything.

With a growing number of immigrant families and particularly children without adequate housing, the Council was forced to intervene in the early 1990s and take responsibility for the problem (see Bernardotti and Mottura 2000; Però 1997). The Council intervened by providing temporary solutions for the cases that they considered most urgent. At the top of the list there was solving the problem of the illegal occupations, which were causing high media attention and protests from local residents. Therefore when the first CPA (Centre of First Shelter) for families was opened in 1993 the first immigrants to be housed there were those who had carried out the occupations.

Saida was among them. In 1993 she got a place for herself and her children at the 'Centre of Stalingrado'. Stalingrado – although an improvement on the decrepit squatted buildings such as those in Via Gobetti, where there was no light, water, etc. – is still not a proper and stable solution. The flats had been left empty since it was found out that they could not become council housing because they did not meet the national health and safety regulations, among other things because there is a polluting factory adjacent to the buildings. In 1990 the empty buildings were occupied by single immigrant men. Subsequently, with the emergency of the immigrant families to solve, the Council decided to buy the buildings of Via Stalingrado and, after carrying out minimal repairs, to transform them into a CPA for families.

Some of my Moroccan interviewees were still living there seven years after it was opened. The centre is located in a zone of the city surrounded by industries and facing a busy main road. The exterior of the buildings looks quite run down. Because of the way it was created (to respond to the occupations carried out by Moroccan families), the residents of the centre are in large part Moroccan. Many of my interviewees felt that this was a problem since they feel they have been put in a sort of ghetto, isolated both from the local population and even from other foreigners. Haziza, now in her twenties, told me that when she was at school nobody ever dared to come there to see her, for her friends and classmates were scared to visit such a place. To have anything delivered there (including the post) is still a problem since even the postmen refuse to come.

Numerous tensions arose over the years from this unwanted cohabitation by a large number of co-nationals who often feel that they do not have anything in common with their neighbours and with whom they feel in competition over the scarce resources that are available to them in Bologna (see also Decimo 2001). Sadia, for instance, is very disappointed that when she had to vacate her former flat she was re-housed by the Council at the Stalingrado Centre:

> I have always been among Italian people – it's only a year that I'm here with the Moroccans. I don't like being here but unfortunately the flat they gave me was here. I don't get on with their character because I think that even if a woman is married she can still drive a car, smoke, do what she wants, but

here there are people who say: 'Ah she's too free', which means she is a prostitute, I fight against this, I fought in my own country and I also fight here ..., some people came directly from their village and are not yet open-minded.

The possibility of leaving the CPAs is minimal for many families. Generally Moroccans (as we saw also for Filipinos) find it very difficult to find landlords willing to let properties to them. In Sadia's words:

Now even if you want to take up the phone and rent a flat, they ask you: 'Where are you from?' If you tell them that you are Arab, Algerian or Moroccan they put down the phone and don't give the house to you. We suffer for these things.

This is why at present Moroccan families who want to reunite in Bologna or families that want to leave their inadequate accommodation need to go further and further out from Bologna in order to find affordable housing. But villages in the plain or the mountains where flats are available tend to be poorly linked to the city, with only infrequent public transport. Young Moroccan women tend to feel very isolated in these out-of-town places, with little or no access to work.

During fieldwork I conducted participant observation at a small charity helping immigrant women to find work. Unlike ACLI, they accepted women without a permit to stay. Because of that, the charity had two main groups of Moroccan women 'clients': those who were looking for temporary, hourly paid jobs, generally those with a permit to stay (the same women who also went to ACLI); and those who were looking for live-in work of any kind, usually women without documents and/or in situations of 'emergency'. At this charity the women of the latter group ended up mainly as carers for elderly people. Often the employers were not wealthy people but working people who could not care full-time for elderly or ill relatives. Illegal women represented a solution for their problem since they are more flexible than the other workers (i.e., there is nobody that can guarantee their rights since as clandestine immigrants they do not have any rights) and above all they are cheaper (the monthly salary for a live-in undocumented maid/carer ranged from L 1,000,000 to 1,400,000).

At this charity it seemed that the volunteers tried to strike a difficult balance between the needs of these elderly people and those of immigrant women. This approach – which Andall (2000b) calls that of the Common Victim – was summed up effectively by Saida when talking about a larger charity, Caritas:

The wage was low – L 600,000–500,000 you know, because Caritas wants to help people, but they also want to help the people where you go to work, you know – an old lady, poor thing, does not have the money – poor thing me and poor things both of us – anyway it's fine like that because one goes there four months, six months, three months and that person in the meantime starts to know the country well, the job and everything – then little by little – it doesn't happen that you go to work with full pay immediately, you know.

The people who have an urgent need for a carer and are not prepared or cannot afford to pay the average wage (from L 1,400,000 to 1,800,000) cannot be too choosy as far as the nationality or religious affiliation of their employee is concerned, but they will still try to make known their preference. Initially many employers ask for an Italian maid; when they are told that there are none doing that kind of job, they start listing their preferred nationalities which almost never include Moroccans, and often include white groups such as the Eastern Europeans. At the end, many have to compromise and after some convincing on the part of the volunteers they will eventually employ domestics of other nationalities, including the Moroccans.

Three of my interviewees found jobs through this charity during my period of participant observation there. Ilham, who had all the documents, got some hourly paid work. Samira was without documents and she found a place as live-in carer for an elderly woman. She accepted the job without knowing how much she was going to earn but she needed a place to stay and also to start earning immediately in order to send some money to her mother in Morocco. The three children of the elderly person she was caring for are all professionals but they still decided to employ an undocumented person in order to save money. I was told that it was because they were already paying for a maid who was working at their mother's from 9 to 1 and did not want to pay another full wage. Samira's wage turned out to be L 1,000,000.

Amina was recruited to look after an elderly woman by a social worker. The social worker (a local council employee) turned to the charity to find a live-in carer for an elderly couple she could no longer help. Since the couple had savings, the Council could not provide them with care. Besides, the woman needed twenty-four-hour care and the Council could not have offered it anyway. Amina had papers but she had been forced to leave her brother's house so she did not have anywhere to go. She accepted the job for L 1,500,000 but she resigned before the end of her trial period. She did not have her own bedroom (she was sleeping in the living room) and felt looked at by the elderly man. After a couple of weeks Amina was able to find another job as live-in carer.

At the time of my fieldwork eleven out of my eighteen Moroccan interviewees declared themselves to be in employment. Among the seven who declared themselves unemployed, at least one, Naima, was actually involved in paid work twice a week, as it emerged from an interview I had with her friend. Since she was receiving help from Social Assistance she probably preferred not to mention this work to me. Besides, she was actively looking for more work. Three of the others, Fatima, Buchra and Malika, had arrived in Bologna only a few months previously and did not even speak Italian yet. All three were already looking for a job. Both

Buchra and Fatima had worked in Morocco, Buchra as a secretary and Fatima as a cutter in various clothes factories. Malika was a student. Haziza was unemployed when I first met her (she had just finished high school in Bologna) but had found a job in a tobacconist's when I met her for the second time. Habiba had lost her job as live-in carer when the elderly person she was looking after died, whereas Halima had left her job in a cleaning company working for the hospital because she claimed that she was scared to pass on some disease to her toddler.

Among the eleven who were in employment, five worked for cleaning companies or cooperatives. Ilham complemented her work as a cleaner in a bank (Zohra was working in the same bank) with part-time domestic work. Kalima was doing part-time domestic work. Samira was a live-in carer, Rachida was working full-time as a carer in a nursing home and Aisha was a clerk for a legal firm who dealt with Arab-speaking clients.

As we can see, few of my interviewees were actually working as domestics and this is probably due to the stereotypes that Bolognese employers seem to have against them, as confirmed by my visits to the three major places that offer domestic work in Bologna. It seems easier for them to be employed by cleaning companies who need workers prepared to work hard and at difficult times (the cleaning of the bank, for instance, takes place from 6 a.m.) and with a permit to stay. Contrary to what happens for the Filipinas, live-in work does not seem a point of departure for Moroccan women's insertion in the local labour market. Instead, I would point to two types of Moroccan women's labour market involvement. Those with a permit to stay and a house to live in will never seek live-in work but will normally go for part-time hourly paid work. Those without papers, or those in very precarious situations (divorcees, widows), will seek live-in work, which will normally be as carers of elderly people.

It is instructive to note that only two of my interviewees found jobs outside the care, cleaning and domestic sector – these are Haziza and Aisha, two young women who had completed high school in Bologna. In the next few years it will be interesting to see if young people of immigrant descent, partly or fully educated in Italy, will manage to escape the niches of employment that at present confine their parents and older brothers and sisters.

Moroccan women, unlike their Filipino counterparts, do not seem to help each other in finding employment. None of my interviewees mentioned having had access to a job thanks to a contact given them by relatives or friends. Nezha laments that the women who live with her at Stalingrado, even if they know of places that have jobs to offer, do not share this information with the other women of the centre; on the contrary, they hide it in order to improve their own position vis-à-vis the others.

Another difference between Moroccan and Filipino women's relation to work is that the former do not seem to dedicate themselves 'wholeheartedly' to any job they have. In fact, many complained about current or past jobs. Halima left a job that she found unsatisfactory even though she was the sole earner in her household of six people and three months after quitting that job she was still unemployed. Other women, although they claimed that they were looking for jobs, refused to take up some offers even if they desperately needed an income. The reasons for refusing or quitting an occupation are various. Halima was scared of picking up illnesses from her work as a cleaner in an AIDS ward in the hospital. Nezha tried a full-time cleaning job but then left because she found it too heavy since she still had to be the only one responsible for her house and her family. She decided that she could not fulfil what were effectively two full-time occupations at once. Naima too wants a job that is compatible with her desire to look after her children, that is a job from 9 to 4. She is aware that the only jobs available in Bologna for few hours per day are those in the domestic/care/cleaning sectors, but these are not what she would ideally like:

> I have to work in homes as a carer for elderly people, baby-sitter for a few hours, clean the houses, but I don't want to lose my path because I have a diploma, I feel that I have a potential career that I don't want to lose, the housework I do it already twenty-four hours in my own house. ... I feel blocked here in Italy, really very blocked, sometimes I tell myself that I have to go back to Morocco because I see that there is a big difference, because with the diplomas I acquired in France I can work, the wages are low there but I still could live well...

Nabila cannot give up her job as a cleaner at the hospital because, unlike the others, she does not have a family in Bologna that can function as a safety-net while she finds a new occupation and she has to pay a high monthly rent, unlike those who live in social housing. She also finds her job unsatisfactory and demeaning. Although she has a university degree she is aware that her job possibilities in Italy are few. Nonetheless she hopes to leave her cleaning job in order to become at least a factory worker (this is what motivated her to move from Rome to Bologna).

Almost all the Moroccan women I met want to work in order to earn some money, but most of them are not prepared to dedicate themselves to full-time jobs that are not satisfactory to them and which are not reducing their workload in their own houses as carers of their own families. The money earned by Moroccan families in Bologna seems hardly enough to cover their costs. Among my interviewees ten said that they did not give any financial help to their families in Morocco. Among these there are the women who come from families that do not need economic help and those who do not even earn enough for themselves and their families in Bologna, let alone to remit money.

Contrary to the Filipinas, in general there seems to be a weaker obligation for children (especially daughters) to remit money to their parents. It seems to be the parents (and in case of divorce, the mother) who are those who have an economic responsibility towards their children until they are quite old and even when they are already married. For the daughters, once married, their responsibilities and obligations seem to be mainly towards their newly-formed family, i.e., their husbands and above all their children. Seven of my interviewees affirmed that they were sending remittances but none on a regular basis. Half of them said that they send money when they have it and the other half when their family needs it, for instance for paying unplanned medical expenses. None volunteered to specify how much they sent and how frequently. Only Aisha declared giving L 350,000 monthly to her parents (who are living with her in Bologna) as her contribution to the family budget.

Of the women who have a husband in full-time employment in Bologna, their reason for engaging in paid work was related to their desire to increase their newly-formed family's income. The main and most recurrent goal to which family savings are dedicated was the purchase of a house in Morocco. Contrary to what happens to the Filipinos who buy houses with the hope of going to live in them permanently, Moroccan women's project is to buy or build holiday houses in their country (not necessarily in their village of origin) in order to have a place to spend their annual August holiday and to improve (or demonstrate to have improved) their socioeconomic position back home. Generally Moroccans did not talk in detail about earnings, spending or remittances. Since they rely much more heavily than the Filipinos on Social Security and Council structures, it may be that they are cautious about sharing information relating to their wealth due to fear of jeopardising their possible access to help and resources.

Nabila

Nabila is thirty-five and is single. She has eight brothers and sisters and comes from a provincial town in Morocco where her father had been the director of a school. Nabila went to study in Casablanca where she got a degree in Arab Literature. After completing her studies she stayed in Casablanca where she did several jobs which included two years of voluntary service in a tribunal, a job as a secretary in a legal firm, shop assistant and many more. But she was unable to pass the public exam which would have enabled her to find a more qualified and stable job.

Tired of repeated disappointments, Nabila decided to go abroad in search of better job opportunities. Her preferred option was France where she had spent time as a student but now without a student card and only sporadic employment she did not stand any chance of entering that country legally. A friend who was working at the Italian consulate in Casablanca offered her the possibility of going to Italy. She accepted and he arranged a job as live-in carer for a family near Bari where she arrived in December 1994.

Her first job in Italy did not work out very well but she had to put up with it because she had to pay back the money for the journey and also because she hardly knew any Italian and did not know where else to go.

My job near Bari didn't go well because they didn't let me go out, they were always making problems and nobody wanted to look after the grandmother when I had my free day. So in the end I always had to stay with her. ... I stayed on because I needed the money, I had paid the trip and I had to return the money but they only paid me L 550,000 monthly. They didn't pay me the free days that I worked, nor contributions nor anything. Well, they gave me a bad deal!

She stayed there for a year (the length of her contract) and then moved to Rome where she worked as a domestic until 1998. At this point, tired of domestic service and attracted by the possibility of finding at least a factory job, she decided to go to Bologna. When I met her two years later she had still not managed to fulfill her plans and was working in a hospital as a cleaner. She is quite dissatisfied with how things have turned out for her. Her shifts starts at 6 a.m. and her job consists in cleaning the wards. Nabila finds it hard to cope with this type of occupation:

I would like to be able to use my brain in my work, I can't stand those jobs in which you don't have to think, like the one I have at the moment. But I have to do it because I don't have alternatives. When I wake up in the morning I feel as if I'm going to hell, not to work.

In spite of her negative experiences, Nabila has not given up on the idea of finding a better kind of job, for example as a translator in a legal firm. She is also thinking of convincing her sister to join her in Italy so that they could both work and help each other. In the meantime, when she has enough money, she sends some to this sister in Morocco who has recently divorced.

Aisha

The only one of my Moroccan interviewees who had a job outside the usual domestic/care/cleaning sectors is Aisha. She is twenty and has been living in Bologna (today at Stalingrado) with her family since she was ten. She attended the intermediate school and three years of high school in Bologna. Unlike the other women I met, she is extremely happy and satisfied with her job.

For now I am fine, I like my job very much, because I really get on with the people I'm working with, also my boss he is fantastic and my colleagues too. For now I just want to work and to create for myself a better future.

She is a part-time employee in a legal firm that deals with immigrant clients. Aisha was recruited two years ago because her boss needed a clerk with Arab mother-tongue. At the time of the interview Aisha was dealing mainly with the appeals of those who had not been granted a permit to stay after the new regularisation law and with issues related to the work problems of Moroccan, Tunisian and Algerian clients.

Monday is her free day but, as she says, she does not like to have free time. This is why on Mondays she works as a volunteer at the Foreigners' Centre of the local branch of the CGIL trade union. Here she deals mainly with the work-related problems of Arab women. After she finished school she started with the same type of volunteer work at another trade union branch (CISL). She had a friend working there and she started going there to help him with translations of matrimonial acts, driving licenses and so on. It was there that she met the lawyer who told her about a job possibility in his firm and invited her for an interview. Aisha loves her work and she thinks she will carry on working even when she gets married and has children. To my question as to whether she would carry on working once she has formed her family she replied: 'Are you kidding? I will never be a housewife. Never'.

'Getting a Life' in Bologna

This section has provided a sense of what it is like for Moroccan and Filipino immigrant women to 'get a life' in Bologna, giving special attention to crucial issues such as housing and employment. Housing has emerged as a problem that affects both Moroccan and Filipino women. Live-in work represents the short-term strategy for solving the problem for women of both groups, but in the majority of cases it is rarely a long-term solution. Filipinas and Moroccans have other, and different, strategies for securing accommodation: Filipinas opt to share flats with large numbers of people, and Moroccans have opted for occupations of vacant premises. However, due to lack of institutional support, they all have to rely on their own initiative. In this context the role of networks made up of family, co-nationals, former neighbours and new employers seems crucial to help the settlement of these women.

As regards employment, my research has confirmed the results of other Southern European studies (Chell 1997, 2000; Lazaridis, 2000; Parreñas 2001a; Ribas 2000a; Tacoli 1999) by noting that Filipinas are at the top of the hierarchy of domestic work also in Bologna. And yet (or perhaps because of that) they too suffer from job segregation. My analysis further shows some of the consequences of Filipinas' privileged position within domestic service – such as their increased bargaining power within the sector leading some of them to obtain gains comparable to those enjoyed by Italian domestic workers. I also documented the attempts made by some Filipino women to move to other sectors of employment.

On the Moroccan side, my field results have exposed the myth which regards Moroccan women migrants as generally inactive and passive dependants of male workers. In spite of the common desire of both Moroccan and Filipino women to engage in paid work, these two groups of women seem to have a different attitude towards it. Whereas for Filipino women paid work is always placed before home-care work, Moroccan women were trying to strike a balance between paid and unpaid work, since they often considered the latter as more rewarding than the kind of jobs that they could access in Bologna.

Finally, Filipinas use a network made up of relatives, friends and fellow-countrywomen in order to secure jobs, which proves quite successful. Moroccans, instead, do not seem to have any group solidarity in sharing information concerning employment, rather they are in competition with one another. They tend to rely more heavily on local charities and organisations to seek and locate work.

Transnational Families in Bologna

This final main section of the chapter looks explicitly at the arena of social and family relations of the two groups of migrant women since it is argued that this sphere is vital for a full understanding of immigrant women's lives and their different patterns of incorporation in the context of arrival. But how are family obligations met and how are support networks maintained across physical separation and through the migratory experience? What is the role of women in such transnational networks and families? How do different groups of women strike a balance between the competing demands of paid work, household and family management, and motherhood? We already saw how Filipino and Moroccan women are heavily involved in the care and domestic sectors; but if immigrant women provide care for the local population, who takes up the caring tasks for immigrant families? These are some of the issues addressed in the pages that follow.

Filipino Women

Of the twenty Filipino women I interviewed in Bologna, thirteen were married and seven were single at the time of the interview. Among those who were single only one, Jenny (aged thirty-eight), was not in a relationship. She did not want to talk about anything to do with her present or past relationships. She stated that she wanted to remain single and that she did not plan to have children because she thinks that is a too great a responsibility. The other six all had partners in Bologna. Rebecca (thrity-three) and Maria (twenty-eight) were with Filipino men. Rebecca aimed at getting married to her boyfriend but he had already a girlfriend back home and she feared that he would marry the other woman during his holidays. Maria instead was only few months away from her much-wanted marriage. At the time of the interview she was saving for the wedding. She was really looking forward to the wedding and quite relieved that it was finally going to take place. She confessed to me that in the last few months she had stopped going to Bible studies (a charismatic Catholic group very popular with Filipinos) because she was embarrassed with her current situation. Her fiancé was living with her in the house of the elderly woman she was working for. He had his own job in a cleaning company but was staying with Maria and was paying L 200,000 towards rent. She did not feel at ease about living with her boyfriend before marriage. She will join the group again after she has been to the Philippines and got married. Pressure and fear of losing her reputation with fellow Filipinas seemed very important to Maria. She told me that ten months before the interview she fell pregnant but, although she claims that she wants a baby, she had an abortion; her view was that she preferred to get married first and then have children. According to Chant and McIlwaine (1995), virginity at marriage is still considered extremely important in the Philippines; this is probably why Maria was scared of having the baby before being married since this could have resulted in a break with her family back home.

Other Filipinas explained to me that it is true that in their country of origin women are expected to arrive virgin at their wedding but in Bologna, far away from parental control, many women are having premarital sex and are living with their boyfriends. However, this increased autonomy deriving from migration is limited by the influence of communitarian organisations which exert forms of control on these women. As in the study by Chang and McAllister Groves (2000) in Hong Kong, in Bologna too it seems that Filipino religious organisations take up the parents' role in monitoring the behaviour of Filipino girls and acting as the guardians of the reputation of Filipino women and by extension of the Filipino 'community' abroad.

Vicky (thirty-six) and Ester (twenty-one) have relationships with Italians. At the time of the interview Vicky was confused over what to do. On the one hand, she felt that at her age it was time to form her own family (she felt the pressure from her family of origin to finally settle down) and also that marrying an Italian could carry some advantages (e.g., citizenship). On the other hand, she feared getting stuck in Italy, which had never been her ideal destination. She is an engineer and she left the Philippines first to go to Saudi Arabia and then to Italy in order to 'travel the world'. She would like to end up in the United States where she knows she could get a skilled job matching her qualifications. She jokingly told me that she did not know whether she had to pursue her career (which would entail migrating further) or to form her family (which would mean coming to terms with life in Italy and a job as a domestic).

Lota (thirty-one) and Rita (thirty-three) chose a foreign partner. Lota had just started a relationship with an Egyptian man. Rita lived for six years with a

Nigerian whom she had met through a friend, but in the end she left him when she discovered that he was already married and had children in Nigeria.

Of the thirteen women who are married, eleven have their husbands with them in Bologna and two have them still in the Philippines. We already saw in the previous section the case of Mina who actually does not want to form her family in Italy. Tita (thirty-four) instead would like to reunite with her husband but she does not fulfil the criteria for initiating the procedure for family reunion, an important one being adequate housing.

Among those who have their husbands with them, four met them and got married in Italy and one couple was formed (they are not officially married) in Paris where both partners were working as illegal domestics. In my sample there are only two women who managed to bring their husbands from the Philippines to Bologna. Cristina married her boyfriend who she had met at university on a holiday back in the Philippines and subsequently helped him financially to join her in Italy as a *clandestino*. Only Judith (thirty-seven) was able to call her husband to Italy under the legislation that protects family reunion, thanks to the help of her employer who gave her a flat and acted as a guarantor for her, confirming Kofman's (1999: 289) observation that it is more difficult for women to amass the resources necessary to sponsor family members. The other four women came to Italy together with their Filipino husbands, three of them leaving their children behind.

Of the four women who met their partners in Italy, one married an Italian and one an Egyptian. Melissa met her Italian husband on her first day in Bologna while still at the train station. He was the only person who could speak some English and this is how they started chatting. Gloria met her Egyptian husband while hanging out on her free day in a bar in Piazza Maggiore, the central square of Bologna and a gathering place for tourists and immigrants. Gina and Susan met their Filipino husbands through friends.

Eleven of the women I interviewed had children, ten of the married ones and one among the singles. They were mothers of twenty-three children. Most of them had either one (four cases) or two (also four) children. But of the older Filipinas, one had three and ther other two both had four children. Among these twenty-three children, twelve were born in the Philippines and eleven were born in Italy; seventeen of them are living in Bologna today. At the time of the interviews, eight women had all their children with them in Bologna; one woman, Mina, had her only child in the Philippines being looked after by her mother; and two women had some children with them in Italy and some back in the Philippines.

The older women in my sample migrated to improve the socioeconomic situation of their newly formed families. They had jobs in the Philippines but felt that their income was not going to be sufficient to send their children to school and guarantee a good future for them. Their migration was a family strategy and they left together with their husbands to work as live-in couples in Italy. Flora (fifty-three) left when she was thirty-one, leaving her three children behind; Lori (fifty-three) left aged forty, leaving four children behind; Purita (fifty-two) left at forty-four, also leaving her four children in the Philippines. Their migration was intended to be a temporary measure, necessary only to generate enough savings to fulfil family plans. In reality all three of these women are still in Bologna and generally few Filipinas seem to go back before retiring age. Instead of going back to their children they seem to favour the eventual migration of their grown-up children to Bologna.

The children of Flora did study with the money she and her husband remitted. The eldest son studied engineering but did not finish his course, the older daughter obtained a diploma as a teacher and the youngest one trained as a secretary. Today they are all in Bologna; the boy is working in a factory and the two girls are domestics. Of the four children of Purita only the youngest boy is in Bologna where he is attending school, the other three preferred to study in the Philippines but two of them were shortly going to arrive in Bologna. Two of the children of Lori stayed in the Philippines where they got married and two came to Bologna: the oldest one is a part-time cleaner and the youngest one works at McDonald's.

Although these women managed to fulfil their plans in terms of acquiring land and sending their children to school, the disparity between wages in the Philippines and in Italy meant that in spite of their diplomas their children had to follow in their parents' footsteps and come to Italy to perform unskilled jobs. Chell (2000) has named this type of migration – typical of the Filipinos – 'intergenerational, sequential migration'. These women did not talk about the suffering involved in being separated from their children. They focused their accounts on their working lives and on their economic success. Mina, who has been separated for two years from her four-year-old son, explained to me that not thinking about the family left behind is a strategy to cope with the pain produced by these long-term separations from beloved ones (see Parreñas 2001a).

> Before, I always thought of home during Sunday but now I think I'm not only here for two years – for three years – I need to – I need to relax – to meet some people. I know it helps a lot because I don't feel sad... I don't want to listen to music, I don't want because it's pain for me, I feel sad, it's not so good. I don't have a picture of my son, I don't have any picture of my family, my mother, my father, my husband – I don't want to remember always that... I like to close my eyes and live where I am.

The daughters of these migrants did talk about their sufferings.[6] Edna is Flora's second child. She is now thiry and she arrived aged twenty after having been left since the age of eight in the care of her aunt, together with her brother and sister. She seemed happy to be able to discuss at length the hardship of her childhood and adolescence back in the Philippines. While we were talking, Flora, her mother, was in the room listening impassively. Edna's account was probably directed partly at me and partly at her mother. I asked her to tell me about her childhood:

Oh this is the most dramatic part! Well, when we were little she left us, she abandoned us with our aunt – her sister and her four children – I was only eight, my brother was about nine and the youngest sister was six so we were really young – the first time they left we cried – we cried, then they asked us: 'Do you want your life to improve – our life? Yes? Then we are all happy'. But the day of the departure when we saw the plane going up – our drama started.

It's not easy to live with your aunt and uncle – well, maybe at the beginning things went fine – there were times when the relationship with my aunt and even with her four children was good. But the first child of my aunt is my age but the second one was eight years younger – so we even had to be baby-sitters. My mother was sending money regularly but it was never enough – we also had someone who helped us cleaning but there was always work to do because we were seven children – one domestic on her own could not do everything. The youngest daughter of my aunt was a baby and I saw her growing up. We had to be baby-sitters – we had to work.

Then little by little when we wanted something we would write to my mother and she sent the money. But then my aunt didn't buy the things that my mother told her to buy – she was saying that the money wasn't enough, she was saying that she couldn't – to wait for the next time. I wanted to take guitar lessons, but my aunt didn't pay for that course, my mother was sending her the money but… My brother wanted a bicycle – my aunt said no because she said that the money wasn't enough because the money that my mother was sending for three children, she was using it for seven.

I learned how to wash and iron, when I was twelve I was already very good at ironing – I had already learned how to cook at that age – so we grew up quickly. We had some difficult times, yes I'm grateful to my aunt but it wasn't nice – having to live with your relatives. You know that sometimes I think about it and I'm scared now – because of what I lived through – I can't forget it. My little sister was going to throw away the rubbish – she was going to the rubbish van since the van didn't come to our little street – she was going there early in the morning when she was only nine, my brother who was eleven was going to the market on his own to buy things for the house, I was staying at home and I was helping with the house chores.

…

Then we started to live even worse because my aunt started – because we had grown up and so we had asked our mother to send us the money directly – we grow up quickly – my brother was fifteen then and our parents built us a house, we were settled. But then my aunt started to become more jealous, more gossipy, nastier towards us because she wasn't keeping the money anymore.

...

What makes me feel very sorry is that leaving your children in the Philippines is not right, it's not right. We suffered a lot because of the fact that they are far away – it's not easy to live like that, that's why we started early to have boyfriends and girlfriends. It was like a way to substitute our parents – because when we have problems, we can't discuss them with them – by letter it takes twenty days to arrive – at that point the problem is already gone... so we looked for affection in other people – maybe in boyfriends – that's why we all married so early!

My brother got married when he was twenty – his first girlfriend was also the last one, the one he married – his only love – he never courted anybody else. ... I was twenty when I got married and I still needed my parents' signature; Tommy was already twenty-eight. At that time also his parents were abroad, his sister had taken them to the US – so we were both without parents. We got married in the Council Office like that – without anyone – we didn't even have the witnesses. We got two people there – the officer registered us and it was done. I took the wedding certificate – outside it was raining, we hid the certificate under the shirt because it was raining hard – we were dressed normally just like now – then we came here.

Susan is also a daughter of a migrant. Unlike Edna she was not left behind but forced to accompany her mother in emigration. She was seventeen when she left and was still studying. She did not want to go because she wanted to finish her course and she did not want to leave her boyfriend, but her mother left her no choice. They went to Milan where some relatives were already working but almost immediately Susan met her future husband. He was older than she was and he already had a partner, so Susan's mother decided to move to Bologna to prevent her daughter getting into trouble. Nevertheless he followed her to Bologna and the following year they got married in the Philippines. After having married and had her first daughter it became impossible for Susan to go back to the Philippines. She is now aware that she will be in a position to go only once she retires and her children are grown up. Her mother in the meantime, after having retired, went back to the Philippines and is currently living on the money that is sent regularly to her by her daughter and her other children whom Susan and her husband helped to bring to Bologna over the years.

The majority of Filipinas in my sample migrated when they were still single after having completed their studies. Like the older women who left their families behind, the younger women also had originally planned to stay away only temporarily. In many cases they wanted to combine their filial duty to help members of their families of origin with the possibility of gaining new experiences and earning some money before settling down. Most of them, after several years of hard work in Bologna, are still there today. Many realised that, after having married and above all having had children, going back to the Philippines becomes a difficult plan to realise. Some of them have non-Filipino husbands who will never go to a country – especially to an 'underdeveloped country' – that is not their own and where jobs are few and wages extremely low. Even those who have Filipino partners find it difficult to leave Italy. Many women, as we will see below in the case of Gina, have children who were born and are growing up in Italy and who therefore feel Italian.

At some stage Filipinas start to realise that their temporary migration is starting to acquire a more long-term character. When they were alone in Bologna they could work extremely hard, spend very little and save substantial sums of money. Once they have created their own family in Bologna, life for them changes. First of all, it starts to become more difficult for them to find jobs. In the majority of cases employers do not accept live-in couples with children. This means that for many Filipinos the arrival of a baby has meant changing job. Nurseries in Bologna do not take very young babies. Few Filipino mothers are prepared not to be in employment even when they have very young children. Some have solved the problem by making use of relatives and Filipino baby-sitters; those who do not have a support network in Bologna are in some cases forced to keep their children in the Philippines (usually in the care of their mothers) at least until their babies are one year old and can therefore start to go to nursery in Bologna; others, such as Susan, have found employers who do not mind if they go to work with their baby, but these are few.

The two stories reported below provide good biographical examples of the issues presented above. In the case of Gina we will see how she managed to acquire a certain degree of stability in Italy by marrying and creating her own family. At the same time marriage and children also brought new responsibilities that are conditioning the choices she can make and changing the plans she had made for herself. I will then conclude this section with the story of Rita whose difficult life shows some of the other problematic issues discussed in this chapter.

Gina

Gina had met her husband in 1983 when she was still working as a live-in maid in Salerno and went to visit a friend in Florence. It was he who told her about the possibility of finding employment in Bologna. They got married in Milan in 1985 at the Filipino Embassy. Their son was born in 1986.

> Paolo was born in '86… life was difficult for us then – there was a baby. I left my employment as live-in maid immediately before he was born, I asked a friend of mine if I could stay at her place until the baby was born, so I went to live with her – I asked her to stay there only for two months because also there one couldn't keep babies – then he was born, we baptised him and when he was one month old I took him back to the Philippines because I didn't have a house. In Italy this is problem number one: housing.

One year and a half later Gina and her husband managed to find a house and they brought Paolo back to Italy. When I met them he was finishing the intermediate school and was about to enrol at high school. He has been back to the Philippines only once since he came back to Italy, when he was six. He considers himself Italian, all his friends are Italian and he has no intention of going back to a country that he does not consider his own.

He told me 'You are Filipina, I'm Italian'... then – well then I left things as they were, he has his own friends, he can choose who they are... he is settled very well here.

Gina now feels she is trapped in Italy. She never thought that she would stay in Italy forever but she is now realising that this is becoming a very distinct possibility. She initially was hoping that her aunt (the one who called her to Italy) would get her to the US where she is now living, but now she is aware that without the relevant documents this is almost impossible and above all she would have to abandon her son.

She (the aunt) asked me if I still want to go (to the US) but I said – leave it – it doesn't matter because I have a son now and I can't leave him – I'm stuck here in Italy.

Gina's husband, like her son, does not want to go back to the Philippines. All his family are now abroad and they have already sold everything they had back home. Only one of his brothers is still there but he is also planning to go to Italy to work. On the contrary, all of Gina's relatives are still in the Philippines and she suffers from the fact of not having anybody from the family around. It is particularly hard, she says, at times when you are in difficulty because you do not have anybody to turn to. That was the case when Paolo was little and she had to cope with everything on her own. That is why she did not want to have other children. If she cannot go to the States, once she retires she would like to go back to the Philippines. The problem is that her son will not follow her.

I'm thinking of going back one day, when I'm old, but now my son does not want to go there, he has already told me that if I go I have to leave him here, to cut it short – he was born here, he grew up here, so I have to leave him here.

Gina tried to convince one of her sisters to join her in Bologna but she refused, saying that she could not survive away from her five children. Gina understands her position but was slightly complaining about the fact that since she is the only one abroad everybody expects money from her.

Rita

Rita is working as a full-time maid for a wealthy Italian couple. The husband is in business and the wife works in the stock market. She has been working for them since 1993. At first she was working there only in the mornings (she was then still living and working for another employer) but subsequently took up also the afternoon job which consists of ironing and doing the 'thorough' cleaning (*pulizia a fondo*). Rita complains that her employer is very strict but she does not want to change because she says that she does not want to 'learn the character and the habits of another employer'. Another reason is that after many years she has reached a good level of pay. She now earns L 2,000,000, which is slightly above the monthly average for that kind of employment.

I visited Rita twice on a Sunday, the only day in the week when she is at home and has a bit of time. Before I arrived at 10 a.m. she had already done her part in the weekly cleaning of the flat and while we were talking she was also doing her laundry and cooking the daily meal. We were also playing with the baby, Claudine, and later on Rita was breast-feeding her.

Claudine's father does not live with them anymore. Rita and he broke up when she was still pregnant. He was a Nigerian man whom she had met through a friend. Apparently he told the common friend that he was looking for a Filipina. Rita explained to me that this was because everybody knows that: 'Filipinas are patient with men – you know – they are a bit martyrs'. They stayed together six years but the relationship did not work out.

> That was a mistake in my life... I always do mistakes with men, my sister told me that all men are the same – Filipinos are always drunk and then you have to do all the work on your own, everything – then I said, 'What do you have to get then?' Some of the Italians are also bad, then you take the blacks, with them also it does not work, what shall I do then? Then in the end do you know what I did? I had a baby and that was it!

Rita's reasons for leaving him were the following:

> I was tired – you know – to always look after a man, you have to do everything for them, they are never happy, they are never satisfied, you have to shop, cook and feed, you have to wash, iron – I was tired.

An important reason for leaving him that Rita did not mention in the interview was that in 1999 she found out that her boyfriend was already married in Nigeria and had children there. He had no intention of marrying Rita, although she had hoped that with the arrival of their baby he would.

At the time of the interview Rita was a single-parent working mother who also had familial responsibilities back in the Philippines. She was still economically responsible for a number of relatives back home. Her daily life in Bologna was hard and required a lot of juggling skills.

> I get up at 6.20 a.m., I wash myself, I get ready, I have breakfast and when I'm done I wake her (the baby) up around 6.40 a.m., at 6.45 I dress her – because you have to allow a bit of time for her – so when we are ready at 7.10 we go out and we walk to the crèche, it takes 15 minutes, so we get there at 7.25 and then we wait until 7.30 when the teacher comes, at 7.30 I leave her with the teacher and I run to catch the bus, at 7.37. If I miss that bus the next would come at 7.45 and this will be a little late for me because my *signora* counts every minute.

Rita has to start working at 7.45 so as to be allowed to leave at 4.45 and be at the crèche at 5 before they close. If she arrives late at work in the morning she would have to leave later in the afternoon and this means that the teacher at the crèche would have to wait for her and when this happens she will tell her off. Rita keeps this timetable from Monday to Friday. She usually works also on Saturdays for different employers in order to have some extra income. The crèche is closed on this day so if she is allowed she takes her baby with her to work; if not she leaves her with her sister, if she is available. On Sundays she rests, plays with the baby and, as she told me, gathers the strength to last for another week. She told me that it is really hard to raise a child all on her own but she feels that her life was much worse before she had her baby.

> It's hard but you know – I can cope. When I didn't have the baby yet – you know – when you are all alone it's the loneliness that kills you.

Today Rita is terrified that her baby will be taken away from her. She fears that Claudine's father will take her back to Nigeria and this is why on Saturdays she does not leave her with him any more when she has to work. She is also scared that Social Services would take Claudine away from her. Although she earns L 2,000,000 monthly (a good wage for a domestic) her employer only declares giving her a wage of L 1,400,000 for tax purposes. She pays L 550,000 towards rent and she therefore fears that if the authorities take into consideration her 'official' wage, the amount of time that her daughter is left in the care of other people and her inadequate housing, she could be seen as incapable of providing for her daughter.

Rita's short-term plans for the future are to help her two sisters-in-law to come to Italy so she will not have to support them any more. At that point she will have to send money 'only' to her mother and brothers. In the long run she intends to go back to the Philippines after she has saved enough in order to start an economic activity over there, maybe a restaurant. She told me that her plans are to have a better life in the future and above all to secure a better future than hers for her daughter.

Moroccan Women

Among the eighteen Moroccan women I interviewed in Bologna, eight were single, eight were married and two were divorced. Among the eight who were single, four were young women still living with their parents. Aisha (twenty) was officially engaged to a Moroccan man but she had no intention of marrying him soon, and in the meantime she was flirting with other young Moroccan men. Haziza (twenty) is not in a relationship at the moment. Her father is very strict and does not want her to have boyfriends. Malika (eighteen) too does not have a boyfriend. Habiba (twenty) has an Albanian boyfriend whom she met in Piazza Maggiore – she is freer to go out than the other Moroccan women of her age because she lives in a hostel and therefore has no parental control.

Two of the single women are university-educated women who came to Bologna on their own. Rachida (thirty-two) has an Italian boyfriend whom she met in 1997 through mutual friends. Nabila (thirty-five) would like to meet someone and get married but she finds it difficult to meet somebody suitable. She wants a Muslim (and preferably a Moroccan) partner because she is not prepared to go against her religion, but she finds it difficult to meet Moroccan men in Bologna who are educated and above all who share her liberal ideas about family and husband-and-wife relationships. Kalima (thirty-nine) and Samira (twenty-nine) are both single because they had to help their family of origin and contribute to their household's income. Both of them now would like to find a partner but both feel that it might be too late.

All of the eight women who are married are living in Bologna with their husbands. Four of them (Nezha, Fatima, Naima, Nadia) married Moroccan men who were living in Italy and who went back to Morocco on holiday with the idea of finding a wife. Nezha (twenty-nine) was able to come to Italy almost immediately after her wedding. The other three had to wait for some time before arriving in Italy. Fatima (twenty-nine) got married in 1996 but arrived in 1999; Naima (thirty-four) got married in 1994 but arrived in 1997; Zohra (twenty-five) got married in 1996 and arrived in 1997.

Two other women, Ilham (twenty-eight) and Halima (thirty-two), came to Italy after having divorced their first husbands and then remarried. Ilham divorced her husband after he ended up in prison for the second time; after a few years in Bologna she married a Tunisian man whom she met through a friend. Halima's first husband left her for another woman. A few years later she married a Moroccan man on a holiday back home. She proudly told me that she got him to Italy through family reunion legislation. He now lives between Bologna and Casablanca because he has another wife who is living in Morocco.

Saida (thirty-nine) and Buchra (twenty-three) are divorcees. Saida left her abusive husband and came to Italy in the hope of finding a way to support herself and her two children. After having had a relationship with her cousin in Bologna, which did not work out, she is not thinking of remarrying any more. Buchra instead, who is only twenty-three, is hoping to be able to find a new partner. She is even prepared to enter into a relationship with a non-Muslim, ideally an Italian.

Nine of the women interviewed had children: seven among the married ones and the two divorcees. They were mothers of fourteen children. All had either one or two children; none had more than two. Among these fourteen children, nine were born in Italy and six in Morocco; twelve of them are living in Bologna today. The two children left in Morocco are the sons of Ilham and Samira. In Morocco a woman cannot take the children from a previous relationship into a new marriage (Maher 1984). This is why these two women had to leave their children in the care of their families of origin.

In order to be able to assess the role and status of Moroccan women in Italy, how their agency is constrained or enhanced by their position in a so-called transnational family, or what are the new familial arrangements brought about by the migration experience and the encounter with the local context of arrival, we have to take into account the stage in the women's life-course and the developmental stage of her household (of origin and newly-formed). Older women who married in Morocco have little in common both with their daughters and with the new generation of imported spouses, as we will see below.

Older women arrived in Bologna to reunite with their husbands after having lived part of their adult life in Morocco, where their children were born and the oldest ones among them grew up. These women are used to traditional forms of life in Morocco and for the most part found it difficult to adapt to life in Bologna. Many of the older occupants of Stalingrado came from rural areas and had little education. Once in Bologna they found it very difficult to learn the new language and way of life. Although their income would have been vital for the survival of their large families, they often lacked the skills or the confidence to find any jobs. These women tended to retreat within the 'safe' boundaries of their family and rarely venture out in the city. Almost never do they go out alone and they tend to rely on other members of their families (particularly their daughters) when they do need to go out or get something done.

Their daughters chose to focus on the effects of the migratory experience undertaken by their parents on them. Haziza and Aisha arrived around the same time, aged ten, when their parents decided to reunite and settle their families in Bologna. They remember their past ten years as very difficult. Both have particularly bad memories about their first years at school. Haziza recalls that she was excluded not only by the other pupils but also by the teachers. At the beginning everybody at school ignored her. She thinks that the school did everything possible to make her feel different from the others, including sending her constantly to see some psychologists who were meant to help her 'integrate' but who she felt were making her look even more odd in the eyes of the other children. Aisha too remembers her first months in Italy as a nightmare. She did not understand why her life was so different from everybody else's and why she had to suffer like that.

Here below is an entry from Haziza's diary entitled 'First day of school' which could sum up the experience of the first days of many immigrant children:

He left me at the gate and went.

The building is very big; the dark doorway is open. I have to cross an immense courtyard in order to reach it.

Inside there are many classrooms. I enter the first one I see: it is a V. I find a desk and I sit down.

I don't know the language, how will I be able to explain myself?

I have a white uniform with a blue collar and short hair. I'm sitting down but nobody notices my presence. Teachers come and go and call the register. Everyone replies present when their names are mentioned. My name is not on the register.

I raise my hand and say my name and everybody laughs. At the exit the older girls push me. I do not react and I run home to cry.

Two days later they put me in the first grade.

Both Haziza and Aisha, after their difficult starts, eventually achieved good results at school. As they grew older new problems started to emerge, mostly due to the clash between their Italian education outside the home and their Moroccan education within it, which exacerbated the inevitable generational clashes that most teenagers have to face whether they are in Morocco or in Italy. From the extract that follows we can see how Aisha tries to reconcile what she thinks should be right for young women like her and what she would like to do with her desire not to contradict her parents and their traditions:

The majority of (Moroccan) parents want their children to live with them until they get married, they don't want them go to live on their own, it is like that. I think it's bullshit. I think I should live on my own but I also respect their choices. For me it's fine because I get on well with them but there are girls who don't get on with their parents and would like to live on their own but they can't do it and they have to stay there until they get married. This is something I never liked and I will continue to dislike.

Haziza's diary entry entitled 'Growing up: prohibitions and responsibilities' summaries very well what it means to grow up as an immigrant girl.

People who come and go, happy people, this is what I see from my window. It's dark and once again I'm alone with the music.

My classmates are out having fun.

I can't go out with them, I prefer not to ask, I already know my father's answer.

I look out from my window and I try to invent a world that does not exist, a world that I can imagine only with my fantasy.

In here is like being in a cage. Out there everything is beautiful and positive.
…
I talked to my mother.
She says that these are our customs, the customs of our people; she says that it has always been like that and it will always be. She adds that it will surely not be me changing the world.
I asked her why she does not allow me to live what she did not enjoy, why she does not try to understand me.
'I have been like that', she answers, 'and you will be the same'.
…
I have my homework to do but before there are the house chores, my father's food and my brother to collect from school.
They say that this is my duty, the duty of a woman.

Both Haziza and Aisha feel that they have to do more within their household than their brothers do and think that this situation is unjust.

My mother doesn't speak Italian very well, when she needs something I go and do it or if they have to do the shopping I'll do it, I do everything, they count on me more than on my brother – yeah because he's almost never at home so they can never find him.

Yet their family is very important to them and they are not prepared to push the boundaries of what is expected from them too far. Rather than engaging in an open conflict with their parents they are trying to improve their life by small steps through work and ideally by meeting a (Moroccan) partner who will understand them and with whom they can create a different type of Moroccan family. As Haziza says:

On the choice of my partner I will not accept any influence on the part of my father but he'll have to be a Moroccan. If I have daughters I'll leave them all the freedom they want, I don't want to impose on them the same prohibitions I had; if I have boys it doesn't matter because also in the traditional Moroccan family they already do what they want.

The types of problems and issues that concern these young Moroccan women living in Italy with their family differ from those of the young wives who are currently arriving in Italy for family reunion. The main problem for the latter is first of all being able to enter Italy. The reasons for their delayed arrivals are both practical and ideological. On the practical side, as we have seen, the main obstacle is housing. Husbands have to demonstrate to the satisfaction of the police that they have adequate housing before being able to initiate the procedures for uniting with their spouses. At present, with the CPA for families completely full and a block on any new 'illegal' occupations, these husbands have to go further and further out from the city in order to be able to rent flats at affordable prices.

According to my interviewees, practical reasons are only part of the story, which they think sometimes are used to hide other issues. In Buchra's view, Moroccan men in Italy do not want to bring their wives over immediately for two reasons. First of all, because they want to carry on looking for Italian women. Secondly, she feels that husbands are scared that they will not be able to control their wives once they are in Italy. She explained to me that in Morocco if the wife betrays the husband she will be put in prison but in Italy this cannot happen. Fatima provided a third reason for wives' delayed arrivals: the pressure of the mother-in-law. Traditionally the new bride joins the husband's household where she is expected to submit to the mother-in-law and carry out part of the house chores under her direction. Losing this precious help due to emigration does not go down well with mothers-in-law. In addition to this Fatima felt that in her case economic reasons also played a role. Her sister-in-law and mother-in-law feared that if Fatima had joined her husband in Italy he would have stopped sending large remittances and expensive presents, as we saw in earlier extracts from Fatima's biography.

In spite of all the obstacles, many young wives like Fatima do arrive in Bologna. Once there they have to start dealing with different sorts of problems. The first one mentioned by all of them is that of housing. Nezha complains about the unsuitability of her accommodation in the CPA at Stalingrado; Fatima lives in a place in a mountain village that is both unhealthy and too far from Bologna. She is upset because she does not think that her husband is doing enough to try to secure better accommodation but she is putting pressure on him to do so. Zohra managed to achieve her objective of moving from Porretta Terme, where her husband had rented a flat, to the centre of Bologna. She felt too isolated in Porretta where she was spending entire days alone in the house without talking to anyone. She told me that she spent lots of money during her first year in Italy phoning home to Morocco every day. The problem is that the flat they can afford in the city is much smaller and more expensive than the one they had before.

Another concern of these women is work. They all want to work and contribute to their new household's income but they have to strike a difficult balance between the time they are prepared to spend doing paid work versus the time they have to spend on looking after their families. Young Moroccan married women in Bologna are entering the labour market because their income is necessary for the household's budget; at the same time they are expected to do all the work of a full-time mother and housewife, without the help of kin they would have had in Morocco. This has proved difficult for some of my interviewees. Zohra complained that she is constantly exhausted; in Morocco she never had to deal with household chores since her mother was doing everything for her. She just had to go to work in the office (she was a secretary). It is here in Bologna that she had to learn to bake the Arab bread and clean while at the same time going out and cleaning for a company very early in the morning. Nezha, Naima and Fatima explained to me that, since their work in the house is not negotiable (the only tasks carried out by their husbands are to occasionally pick up the children from the nursery and take their wives by car to do the weekly shopping), they have to reduce the amount of time they are prepared to do paid work. Nezha recounted:

> Once I found a full-time job (as a domestic) but after a few days of trial I gave it up – you know my husband does not do anything in the house and I had to go back home and take care of the child and the house. Today for instance my husband was at home and I was working, I came back and he hadn't done anything – really nothing – not even prepared the lunch. It was good that I'd taken two pizzas with me so at least we could eat.

Apart from taking care of the house and their husband, an important role of a Moroccan wife is that of giving birth and taking care of children. New Moroccan wives, though, do not seem to be prepared to have a large number of children (unlike their mothers). All of my interviewees said that they do not want to have more than two children and, as we saw earlier, none of them had. Ironically the City Council has not realised this and in its plans to re-house immigrant families there is the idea that they will take up the council flats for large families which were built in the 1960s for Southern internal migrants and today are vacant due the decrease in family size of the Italian population. Having to work both inside and outside the house without any help from kin means that for my interviewees it seems inconceivable to have more than two children (actually due to the same problems faced by Italian women).

Not wanting too many children seem to be accepted also by Moroccan men. Nadia's husband, for instance, suggested to her that she could have an abortion if she did not feel ready to have her second child so soon after the first one. She eventually decided to have the baby but he left the decision entirely to her. The problem for Moroccan men seems to be that of not having any children at all. A volunteer at a charity told me that Nezha's husband had another wife before her whom he repudiated because she could not become pregnant. He tore up her papers and sent her back to Morocco. Nezha, when she saw that she was not getting pregnant and anticipating what might be her fate, decided to take an active role. She consulted a specialist and convinced her husband to go to see him with her. She managed to have a baby girl through artificial insemination and she is now hoping to have another baby.

Married women with a place to live and a husband in employment are considered by the other Moroccan women as the luckiest. Those who are not in that position (divorcees and single women) have to work harder and their position in Bologna is much more vulnerable. Some married women therefore fear that if they do not perform their wifely role conscientiously their husbands will abandon them and therefore they will be left in a vulnerable position. But this does not mean that these women are passive subjects. On the contrary, as we have seen in the case of Nezha, they are resourceful and are trying to improve or protect their position as best as they can.

All the women I met, whether single, married, or divorced, were involved in trying to negotiate and reconcile certain traditional roles (as daughters, wives, mothers) with new ones; they try to acknowledge tradition while at the same time introducing elements of change and greater equality between them and the men of their families. This is not easy, given the precarious situation of immigrant women in Bologna. Below, Saida's and Ilham's stories highlight some of the issues introduced in this chapter. Both Saida and Ilham are divorcees but the former was unable to remarry whereas the latter could. The former enjoys probably more freedom and independence than the other Moroccan women I met, but Ilham and the other married women generally prefer to have the security and stability that marriage gives to them since they feel that, outside the family, they simply could not find support and protection anywhere else in Bologna.

Saida

Saida is a divorcee who came alone to Bologna and subsequently brought over her two children. Today, almost ten years after her arrival, Saida has a stable job in a cleaning cooperative, both her children are living with her, the boy has completed the compulsory cycle of education and the girl is about to complete it, and they are all living in a council flat.

In spite of her low rent, Saida has to work really hard at the cooperative in order to pay for all the expenses and for everything her children need. She does a lot of extra time and she also works on Saturdays. She says that it is really hard to raise two children without economic – or any other kind of – support from anybody else. This is why she thinks that many women stay in unhappy or abusive marriages. She thinks that it takes a lot of courage for a woman with children to decide to leave a husband and start a new life independently.

> It is a problem if she has children, where does she go? It is better to shut up, isn't it? These children, where do you send them? They have to go to school, they need books, they need clothes – it is better to leave them with their father and shut up. This is a real problem. ... Now I'm fine, I work, I don't need him. Now I don't. Because the problem of my children – now I'm lucky that they have grown up – now that the problem is not there anymore.

Saida has always had to work full-time in order to be able to support her children. Her mother looked after them for two years but then she fell ill and eventually died. She hopes that the worst part of her life is now over. She has a job, a house and above all her children are growing up. She says that they are very well integrated in Italy, all their friends are Italian and they are used to living there. She says – with a slight sense of sadness – that they speak excellent Italian because they have always spent very little time with her since she has been working all the time.

> They only come to my house to sleep – all day they are in school – in the morning they leave at 8 and they stay there until 4, I come back from work at 7, I prepare the dinner then they go to bed straight away. They never stayed up with me and chat with me – that's why they only speak Italian.

Sunday is the only free day for Saida. She says that she uses it to do things in the house since during the week she does not have any time. She never goes out on Sundays, normally she stays at home and, after she has done her domestic chores, she rests. Often people come to visit her so she spends some time chatting with them. When I visited her on a Sunday her Italian neighbour was there drinking coffee and chatting with her. Both her children were out visiting friends. Her cousin was also out with a Moroccan boyfriend she had recently met in Bologna. Saida told me that they are going to get married. She sadly commented that it is easier for her cousin to find a new partner because she has not got any children. Saida feels that if she did not have the children she would have also been able to remarry. She sees her future and that of her children in Italy:

> Now I'm used to being here. I want to go to Morocco only to have a look, to go as a tourist and that is enough, yes I like it here. Before I didn't like it but now it is already ten years that I'm here – day after day now I like it here – when somebody does something for the first time it's hard but now I'm happy here.

Ilham

Ilham is twenty-eight, she is married and has two sons. She arrived in Italy in 1991 as a *clandestina* after her first marriage collapsed. She comes from a middle-class family, her father is a policeman and her mother a hairdresser working in her own shop with one of Ilham's sisters. They are six brothers and sisters. Two of her brothers and one sister are living in Italy. In Morocco there are still the youngest sister who is thirteen and another sister who is working with her mother.

Today, Ilham lives in a one-bedroom flat in Casalecchio, half an hour from Bologna. She pays L 800,000 monthly. Her husband works in a factory and earns L 1,500,000. The first time I interviewed her this was the only income of the family. On top of the expenses related to the flat she also had to pay L 300,000 monthly towards the crèche fee for her two-year-old son.

Until ten months before the interview Ilham was working looking after an old person. This person eventually died and so she lost her job. I met her the first time at a charity where she went to look for a job. She told me that at first she was only looking for a couple of hours of work per day, only 'to help out', but now, because their debt has increased, she is prepared to work much more. She also told me that because of their financial situation at present she was unable to send money to her nine-year-old son whom she had with her first husband and who is now in Morocco living with Ilham's parents. When we had our first interview she told me that she was hoping to get a job so that she could get her son to Italy.

When I had the second interview with Ilham she had managed to find a job. She was working as a cleaner for a bank. She told me that her life was really hard at the moment. She had to get up at 5.45 a.m. to go to the centre of Bologna to clean the bank, and then she had to go back to Casalecchio to take Mustapha – her son – to the crèche. After that she went to do a couple of hours of cleaning for a family who lived nearby. She has not told her husband about this second job because she uses this income to send money to her other son. She does not want her husband to find out about it, so she has to keep her own flat perfectly clean otherwise he will become suspicious and he will make a big scene.

On the day of my second visit to her house she had just come back from her second job after having worked in the bank early in the morning. At 4 p.m. we went together to pick up Mustapha from the crèche. We went by moped, which is the means of transport that allows her to commute between Casalecchio and Bologna in a limited time. She was then in a rush to feed her son and finish tidying up the flat before her husband would arrive at 6.30 p.m.

The first time I visited Ilham there were five people and the child living in her one-bedroom place. Apart from her husband they were her brother – who had just arrived from Morocco – and two women, Khadija and Amina, who were not related to Ilham. She had met them while visiting the usual places in Bologna that offer jobs to immigrant women. They both had terrible stories and did not know where to go to stay since they had had disagreements with the few relatives they had in Bologna. Ilham decided to host both of them in her flat and spent a month taking them around Bologna in search of a job or at least a place to sleep. Finding a bed for them turned out to be more difficult than finding a job.

The presence of these two guests provoked endless quarrels between Ilham and her husband. The situation degenerated week after week; at first he was only complaining, later on he stopped talking to Ilham altogether and was refusing to eat at home. But she was determined not to give in and be forced to tell them to leave.

I did that because before I had also been without a husband, without a house, without a job. If an elderly person dies, people cry for her – I cry because I don't know where I'm going to go. From tomorrow they send me away, but where shall I go? I had already been through these things, you know? This is why I always used to say if one day I get married and have my own house, if I find one woman outside I'll take her to my place.

Ilham had these experiences when she came to Italy to find a way of supporting her first son after divorcing from her previous husband. She worked in several places in the north of Italy before meeting him while she was in Pordenone working as a live-in maid.

Although Ilham has another son in Morocco whom she cannot manage to bring to Italy, she told me that she was thinking of having another baby. When I asked her if a baby at that particular time would not have complicated her situation further, she replied that she had the feeling that if she did not have another baby her husband would leave her. She had consulted with her mother who shared her fears. Her mother offered to help her if she decides to have another baby; she volunteered to keep him in Morocco for a while. Ilham confessed to me that the reason why she does not bring her other son to Bologna is not only economic. It has to do with the fact that he is not the son of her husband. Although she misses him a lot, sometimes she is happy that he is not there because she fears that her husband would make his life too difficult. She thinks that he is happier with his grandparents. The only thing she regrets is that one day he might hate her for having abandoned him, but she feels she has no choice.

Ilham too sees her future in Italy. She is happy to go back to Morocco once or twice a year on holidays to see her family but she has no desire to go back there for good – 'I don't think I have a life there anymore, never again. My life is here'. Her husband is expecting a large some of money from his insurance for a work-related incident he had a few years ago. Ilham was hoping that with this money they would be able to pay the deposit on a house. Having her own house will mean stopping to worry about the possibility of finding herself on the street again without anywhere to go.

Families across Borders

This section has explored how immigrant women's agency is constrained or enhanced by their position in so-called transnational families; what are the new familial arrangements brought about by the migration experience; and the role played by the local context in influencing such processes. What has emerged is considerable heterogeneity and diversity of experiences, which are partly the result of a variety of factors such as the socioeconomic position of the migrant and her education levels (cf. Ribas 2000a); the stage in her life-course and also the stage in the developmental course of her household (cf. Bjéren 1997).

As far as the Filipinas are concerned, we have seen that migration has brought changes in family formation patterns. They are marrying later than their parents, having fewer children, sometimes they are living together with their partners before marriage, and they are often seeking non-Filipino partners. Their motives for doing so seem to be less linked to the desire to acquire Italian citizenship and more to their wish to establish less abusive relationships. Chant and McIlwaine (1995: 271) report that it is commonly stated by women in the Philippines that 'finding a "good man" is difficult, since several treat their wives badly, whether through drinking, infidelity or domestic violence', a view shared by my interviewees in Bologna. Filipinas are involved in creating and maintaining transnational families in which members move to different countries according to different possibilities offered at different stages of both their productive and reproductive life-courses. Workers stay in Italy where wages for domestic service seem to be among the best world-wide (but if possible they try to reach the US, where they know they can find jobs matching their qualifications), whereas retired people, students and babies commute between Italy and the Philippines. These transnational arrangements, although they have benefits in maximising resources and possibilities, also have consequences for some of the individuals who have to endure long-term separation from their loved ones, as we saw in the account given by Edna (see Hondagneu-Sotelo and Avila 1997; LARG 2005; Parreñas 2001a, 2005). The local context (particularly in relation to labour market demands, poor housing provision, inadequate child care for small babies) clearly determines some of these choices and shapes such processes.

As for the Moroccan women, they often see the Italian context (considered European and therefore advanced) as one that is potentially favourable to them and where they can improve their status (by working, having legal protection, by distancing themselves from the extended family and their role assigned within it), but their aspirations are often frustrated by the reality they find in Bologna, characterised by racism, stereotyping and lack of rights. Like their Filipino counterparts, Moroccan women are also having fewer children than the average in their country, partly as a choice reflecting changed attitudes to family formation and partly due to the difficulty of raising children in Bologna.

By virtue of their 'multiple presence' (Ribas 2000a), both Moroccan and Filipino women are key actors in the maintenance of transnational networks.[7] They manage to be present and contribute to different families and different markets. Their continued involvement with home areas is achieved in a number of ways, such as by sending remittances, presents, helping relatives to initiate the migratory adventure, keeping contacts and communication, contributing with their work to invest in the country of origin, and so on.

Conclusions

The first section explored the reasons why immigrant women arrive in Bologna. What emerges from this analysis is the heterogeneity of the motives behind migration, which can only be partly explained in economic terms. 'Family reasons' (broadly conceived) seem to play a very important role for immigrant women, whether it is to emigrate to help the family of origin (as is the case for the majority of Filipinas and for some poor Moroccan women); to marry; to save in order to create a new family in the country of origin; or to escape an abusive partner or parental control. This section also revealed some of the hardships and adventures involved in such journeys and the emotional strains involved in separation. Some of the (illegal) mechanisms that are in place to facilitate the arrival of potential migrants in spite of tighter border controls were also been briefly documented, dispelling common and increasingly also institutional views that associate illegal migration with criminal activities.

The second section explored the local context of arrival, paying particular attention to housing and work. My analysis showed how the lack of adequate and affordable accommodation represents a crucial problem for immigrant women shaping their settlement process. As regards work, it demonstrated how both Moroccan and Filipino women are inserted in broadly the same sector – the care and domestic sector – but differently. Filipinas are at the top of this sector (in terms of pay, rights, ease of finding employment), whereas Moroccan women seem to be in a much more vulnerable position. This is partly due to racism and stereotyping in Bologna, but also to different attitudes of the two groups towards work (in particular towards the desired balance between paid and care work).

The final section looked at the wider sphere of family relations. This section demonstrated the centrality of women in so-called transnational families and networks. It also showed that the role women have within such families can at times enhance and at times constrain their agency, depending on the interplay of a number of factors. Another important aspect highlighted in this section is how familial arrangements and cultural norms are not static but change as a result of migration and of particular conditions encountered in the local context of arrival (such as entry requirements, labour market demands, housing and welfare prevision, etc.). Women of both groups have been shown to be actively engaged in the difficult attempt to improve their status and position both within their families and groups and within the receiving society. The next chapter will explore similar questions in relation to Barcelona.

Notes

1. This is taken from Haziza Naciri's diary and school project given to me by the author during our interview; the translation from Italian is mine.
2. Sex-work is another possibility for those who remain in the Philippines: 79 per cent of sex workers in the study conducted by Chant and McIlwaine (1995) belonged to female-headed households.
3. One of my interviewees told me that she paid L 14,000,000; according to Tacoli (1999) the average in 1993–94 was $6,700 but in some cases was as high as $10,000.
4. ACLI (Associazioni Cristiane dei Lavoratori Italiani) is a Christian organisation. For an analysis of its evolution and activity in the sphere of domestic work, see Andall (1998).
5. This interview was carried out in English.
6. For an in depth account of the experiences of the children left behind in the Philippines see Parreñas 2005.
7. For similar experiences in other immigrant groups see Mand 2006; Reynolds 2004, 2006; Zontini 2004a and b, 2006).

4

IMMIGRATION, WORK AND FAMILY IN BARCELONA

I prefer my job here because in the Philippines the pay was very low. My job there [as a police officer] was also very hard but I was earning very little. All of my children couldn't study with that money, nor could they buy enough food. It's much better to work here so that all of my children can study because one earns more!
(Maricel, 50, Filipina)

This chapter takes Barcelona as the second case-study for my analysis of the social and family relations of Moroccan and Filipino immigrant women in Southern Europe. By taking into account the experiences of the same national groups of women in a different setting (that of Barcelona), I hope to shed some light on the role of the receiving context in shaping processes of migration and also, as Parreñas (2001: 9) has done, provide 'a tool to study how similarities emerge in two different contexts'. The account that follows, together with the one on Bologna presented in Chapter 4, will provide the basis for the comparative analysis presented in Chapter 5.

The Routes to Barcelona

Filipino Women

Filipino immigration in Barcelona started in the 1960s. One of the first Filipinas who arrived in the city did so in 1966 as an employee of a Filipino diplomatic family. In the late 1970s more women started to arrive, getting employment as live-in maids for wealthy families in the city. During the 1980s many more

Filipinos (this time including men and children) came thanks to family reunion. At present according to Clara - the president of the Filipino women's association AMISTAD - the majority of Filipinos are arriving thanks to entry quotas reserved for domestic workers by the immigration law. In order to be able to enter Spain this way the potential migrant has to have a job offer signed in the country of destination; only then can she or he apply through the national consulate for a visa and residency permit. In spite of their entry mode, Clara sees a diversification of activities in which Filipinos currently engage. According to Clara, Filipinos are migrating to Barcelona from the three main islands of the archipelago (Luzon, Visayas and Mindanao), and she thinks that there is a large majority coming from Luzon (see map on page 131).

The majority of Filipino women I interviewed in Barcelona (see Table 4.1) came from large families ranging between three and fourteen children (an average of seven children per family). All of my respondents came from Luzon island (confirming Clara's impression), both from provincial cities and villages. The socioeconomic background of my respondents tends to be – for the most part – quite poor. Several of them were living in what they called a 'chalet' – basically a bamboo hut – and several stated that the family income was hardly enough to cover subsistence costs. Five of my respondents come from female-headed households. For Lola's mother the death of her husband meant that she had to start working in a coconut factory to support her four children. Cori's husband left her for another woman and she too had to start working in order to support her young daughter.

Half of the fathers of my respondents were farmers. The other occupations of their families of origin include: restaurant owner (mother) and apartments administrator (father) in the case of Vivian; teacher (father) in the case of Priscilla; jeepney driver (father) in the case of Mirna; wood carver (father) in the case of Margarita; factory worker (mother) in the case of Lola; weaver (mother) and construction worker (father) in the case of Vicky. In the cases in which the mother did not have an occupation, she often contributed to the family's budget by buying and selling things in the markets or by going to the cities to sell agricultural products. The majority of my respondents were born in the countryside, and then they left for Manila or the nearest city to study and/or work, usually hosted by an aunt or another close relative. This is in line with the feminisation of the rural Filipino exodus noted by other authors (Chant and McIlwaine 1995; Ribas 2000a).

In the majority of the cases the decision to go was taken independently by the migrant, but the true 'autonomous' nature of this is open to debate – often the decision was taken in order to help financially other members of the family. Married women migrated because they were not earning enough to send all their children to school. Both Priscilla and Basilio – a former teacher and a former local councillor respectively – left their jobs and their families behind as a necessary strategy to ensure their children's future. They took the decision supported by

Table 4.1 Basic biographic data on Filipino women interviewed in Barcelona

Filipino women	Age	Place of origin	Internal migration before emigration?	Number of siblings	Household head	Marital status upon migration	Number of children upon migration
Anneline	27	Batangas	Yes	7	M	single	0
Mirna	30	Batangas	Yes	14	M	single	0
Margarita	35	Batangas	Yes	6	M	single	0
Annie	36	Rizal	No	3	M	single	0
Victoria	37	Batangas	No	7	M	single	0
Vivian	38	Batangas	Yes	8	M	single	0
Eleanor	41	Baguio	No	1	F	single	0
Rosa	42	Pangasinan	Yes	7	F	single	0
Rosevilla	43	Batangas	No	5	F	widowed	4
Feli	46	Laos	No	3	M	married	3
Beatrice	46	Paniki-Tarlog	No	6	M	single	0
Natalia	48	Buni	Yes	7	M	single	0
Maricel	50	Village (Luzon)	Yes	13	M	married	5
Clara	51	Batangas	Yes	3	M	single	0
Priscilla	52	Village (Luzon)	No	7	M	married	3
Zeni	54	Luzon	Yes	7	M	single	0
Basilio	55	Village (Luzon)	No	6	M	married	4
Necitas	56	Village (Luzon)	Yes	7	M	married	0
Cori	58	Baguio	Yes	7	F	separated	1
Lola	60	S. Cruz	No	4	F	married	3

their husbands, who eventually followed them to Barcelona. Maricel did the same but without her husband's support. He was an alcoholic who was not contributing at all to the family welfare.

Some of the young adult children are 'forced' to migrate by their sense of duty towards their family of origin. Severe economic hardship was at the root of many departures. Margarita, for instance, came to Catalonia aged seventeen 'because the money was not enough'. Rosa left her home and went to Manila for the same reason. She was not able to find a job there, but after a while she saw an advertisement for becoming a domestic in Spain in the window of an agency and she decided to apply. Also Mirna, Victoria, Annalyn and many others left to try to improve the deprived situation of their families and give some chances to their many brothers and sisters. In these cases often the potential migrant does not have the economic means to realise her project and therefore she has to consult with and convince other family members to help her to find the resources necessary to leave. Victoria, for instance, was helped by her mother. Her father objected to the project due to the risk of failure and its impact on the survival of the family. The female members of Victoria's household – as in other cases studied – were the most proactive and adventurous in trying to solve a situation of poverty.

> My father did not approve of my plan to leave but my mother had more courage. My father was scared because since we are poor he was thinking where were we going to get the money from, how were we going to pay? It's that we had to borrow money from the bank and my father was saying: then when I'll have to pay, let's see if you got there or not, and if not what are we going to do? He was scared but my mother had faith.

Whereas some women decided on their own to migrate – even if pushed by a sense of responsibility towards their families – others were told or influenced to migrate by other relatives or friends. When the motivator of migration is a relative the reason is usually to share the burden of work abroad with other members of the family. Lola, for instance, was called to Barcelona by her sister in order to replace another sister who had migrated on to Canada. Lola, in turn, some years later, initiated the migration of her eldest daughter, Annie. In other cases, when the one asking the migrant to come is a friend or a colleague, she does so in order to alleviate the loneliness of living in a foreign country, or perhaps to share the risks of the adventure of illegal migration.

As we saw in the previous chapter, the options for a potential migrant are two – legal and illegal emigration. In the case of Barcelona, ten of my twenty Filipino respondents migrated legally and ten illegally. Those who arrived legally did so in various ways. One possibility that applied to the women who came at the beginning of the Filipino migration to Spain was that of finding a job abroad through a recruitment agency, as we saw in the case of Rosa. Priscilla and Beatrice arrived in the same way. Beatrice also had an application for Italy but since the

Spanish contract arrived first, she left for Barcelona. The other women came to Spain through the mechanism of the 'direct call', having job offers which had been found for them by relatives or friends. Some women, such as Eleanor, arrived through family reunion as daughters of naturalised migrants.

The majority of those who arrived without having a job contract did so as 'tourists' and then got regularised through subsequent amnesty laws. Four of my interviewees paid an agency to help them to arrive as illegal immigrants. As was the case in Italy, these organisations provide plane tickets and a tourist visa towards countries neighbouring the destination – in the Spanish case, this appears to be mainly Portugal – and then transfer across the border by various means (trucks, taxis). The payment – in contrast to what was reported by my interviewees in Italy – generally happens in advance.

Victoria described her experience of illegal immigration as follows. What is interesting to note is the sudden passage from legality to illegality, a shift dictated by rules which the migrant has little knowledge of and little control over:

> I was scared because we were travelling without knowing were we were going, where we were going to end up, yes, I knew that my cousins were waiting for me here but... I think that until Portugal we were legal, what happens is that after Portugal we were already illegal. We arrived here by lorry, from Portugal to Madrid and then from Madrid to here by taxi.

None of my interviewees had moved within Spain before settling in Barcelona. They all arrived directly there and then stayed on. The main reason for staying is perhaps linked to the local labour market which provides abundant jobs in the domestic sphere, as we will see later on. Another reason is the existence of a strong and well-organised Filipino community in the city. The community revolves around the parish of Saint Augustì, the first in Spain headed by a Filipino priest. The presence of relatives and friends in the districts close to the centre of the city and the support provided by the Centro Filipino (Filipino Centre) works as an incentive to other Filipinos to come and settle there.

To the question 'Why did you come to Spain?' nine women replied that they came to work and earn more than in their country of origin. Priscilla explained very clearly that when she left, in 1980, she was earning only 5,000 ptas monthly working as a teacher in the Philippines; whereas later in the same year she was earning 19,000 ptas as a domestic in Barcelona. Victoria too needed a better-paid job:

> We were poor, we are seven brothers and sisters, and I was thinking over and over how are we going to live, yes I was earning money but it was not enough for everything. My brothers and sisters had to study and also we needed money to buy the daily food. Thank God for the opportunity he gave me and thanks also to my cousin who gave me this opportunity.

Six said they came to work in Barcelona because relatives were already there; one – Eleanor – to study, because her mother was living in Barcelona; others arrived by chance. Feli, for instance, went to Spain because she 'had nowhere else to go'. She did not want to return to the Philippines, the country of her husband (she is originally from Laos), and she did not want to follow him to Liberia where he had been posted (he worked for the US government). She wanted to reach Paris but she could not get a visa so she opted for Spain where she could enter as a tourist. Vivian also arrived in Spain because her application to another country – in her case the USA – did not go through. She had a good job in a company and was active in a trade union in the Philippines, but was eager to change her life. It was one of her colleagues who convinced her to go to Spain by saying that it was easy to find work in Barcelona. Necitas too came on the advice of a colleague (we will see her story later on).

Although wages improved sharply for Filipino women, working in Spain meant a severe deskilling for the majority of my interviewees. Many of them are graduates and several had jobs in the public sector in their country of origin, notably nursing and teaching (Anthias 2000; Chell 1997; Escrivà 2000b; Kofman et al. 2000; Tacoli 1999). During the first weeks and months in Barcelona these women had to learn to adapt to a job – domestic service – that many of them had never done before.

The two stories that follow exemplify some of the issues introduced above. Both Necitas and Maricel came from humble backgrounds and large families but they migrated at different moments of their life-course and for different reasons. Necitas was recently married and had no children whereas Maricel was already thirty-six and had to support five children. For the former, migration was like an adventure which she undertook to satisfy her curiosity; for the latter migration was more a matter of survival. Both eventually stayed on in Spain because their earnings were necessary to support other members of their families. In both cases their gender roles affected their life chances, but both acted on their situation and tried to improve it.

Maricel

Maricel is fifty, now a widow with five children. She is from Batangas where her parents were farmers and petty-traders. She is the youngest of thirteen children. Unlike her, all of her brothers and sisters graduated from college. Several of them are now working abroad and, as she says, 'They have good jobs'. Three of her sisters are nurses in Saudi Arabia; one brother is an architect, also in Saudi Arabia; one brother is the captain of an ocean-going ship; another brother works on a ship as chief cook. She resents not having a degree like the others: 'I'm the only one who hasn't finished college because I got married. I had bad luck.'

When she was young Maricel was working in Manila as a police officer and it was there that she met her husband, whom she married only two months after their first meeting. What she did not know then, but soon discovered, was that he was an alcoholic. In ten years she had five children. Her husband had a job as a bus driver but he did not help her in any way.

> He was working on a bus but he wasn't giving us any money because he was spending everything on alcohol, with his friends. He wasn't giving me or my children anything. I was alone. I was alone fixing my children. He wasn't giving them clothes nor anything else. I was alone, alone.
>
> He was living with me but when he was going to drive the bus then was eating at his mother's and then he was coming to my house all drunk and there wasn't any money, none at all. But I'm strong and every day I prayed to God and in the end he gave me all the benefits.
>
> I was suffering but what was I going to do? I was married and marriage is very sacred in the Philippines. I was suffering but I didn't know what to do – until I decided to come here.

Maricel saw in emigration both an escape route from her obviously unhappy marriage and a viable option for providing independently for her children. It was 1986 when she tried to leave for the first time but reaching Southern Europe did not prove easy. She tried three times to emigrate until she finally succeeded in 1987. It was her mother who helped her raise the money to leave by borrowing money and mortgaging the house. Her first attempt collapsed because the agency proved to be fake. The 'directors' of this agency collected considerable sums of money from Maricel and other Filipinos eager to leave the country, gave them false documents and then disappeared to North America. The second time Maricel tried to leave through an agency based in Barcelona and recommended by one of her sisters who was already working there. Also in this case they gave her false documents and she was apprehended by the police at Barcelona's airport and sent back to the Philippines. After having twice lost her mother's money and under a lot of pressure from her family of origin, she turned again to the same Barcelona agency begging them to give her a second chance. She had to pay more money, but this time she managed to enter the country, arriving through Alicante.

Maricel's problems did not finish there. After having finally reached her destination she realised that she was an illegal immigrant who could potentially be arrested by the police and deported any time. She lived three years in this nightmare, frightened that she would be forced to leave before paying back her considerable debts. Thus, she spent her first years in Barcelona working extremely hard, scared of even walking around the city.

Necitas

Necitas is fifty-six, separated with no children. She comes from Luzon where her father was a farmer. Her mother was a housewife but then started helping her husband doing some petty-trade in order to be able to send her children to school. An old unmarried aunt helped Necitas's mother in raising her seven children. All the boys finished college but Necitas had to leave at the end of her second year. Today one of her brothers works in a public office and the other two are farmers. One of her sisters is a nurse in Saudi Arabia. The other two are housewives in the Philippines; their husbands are working in Saudi Arabia.

> I finished only two years of college because my parents preferred to support the results of my brothers because they said that it's better for the boys to be in school. Well, a little bit of discrimination [laughs], because they said that girls are going to marry and we will stay at home and according to them it was better for the girls to stay at home. During their time it was the men who were the ones working and the girl stays at home, housewife. That was their mentality before. So they preferred that my brothers finished their studies.

At that point Necitas left the countryside – against her parents' will, for they wanted her help in the farm – and went to Manila to look for a job. She became a worker in a cigarette factory where she worked for fourteen years. During that time she got married to one of her fellow-workers.

> I had no intention to come here because we had no children and I also wanted to stay with my husband in Manila, we also had a little house there. ... One day my supervisor in the factory encouraged me to come here. What is the work there? I said. We didn't really know, we just went ahead. I had only a tourist visa and I had no plan to come and stay here. But I was eager to see another place, not only the Philippines, I really didn't expect to stay here for a long time. Now it's sixteen years that I'm here but I told my husband that I was leaving only for one or two years, just to see. That was because I'm adventurous, I wanted to see also – yes, we are reading about Europe, about Spain but I thought that it was better to see the place for myself. So I came here in 1985. It's already seventeen years ago, no?

Necitas did not go back to the Philippines as early as she had planned, because her family situation changed soon after she arrived. Her father became ill and her remittances were suddenly vital for supporting her family and paying for his medical expenses.

By staying here I could help my brothers and sisters, especially when my father got ill. We spent a lot for him and after five years my mother died. After three years she got sick and had a heart attack and for that you also need money. My brothers and sisters could not help because they have their own families, children to send to school, only me have got nothing. Maybe that's my mission. Sometimes I think that that's the will of God because if I had stayed in the Philippines I could not have helped the way I'm helping now, because the salary in the Philippines is not enough.

At first Necitas found it really hard to adapt, her main difficulty being the language. She felt quite isolated in Pineda de Mar (forty-five minutes from Barcelona), not able to communicate with anyone. She too, like Maricel, suffered during her first two years as an undocumented migrant exploited by her new employers, who were taking advantage of her limited ability to understand the language and her complete ignorance about her rights.

Moroccan Women

Moroccan women's current migration destinations are mainly Italy and Spain. This migration signifies a rupture with previous migration flows with respect both to the sending and receiving contexts. With regard to the former, it is the first time that women (attached or not to men) have migrated in order to get inserted in the labour market of the receiving country; with regard to the latter, contrary to earlier Moroccan migrations to Northern Europe, women started to migrate from the beginning without having to wait for the processes of family reunion in order to settle in destination countries (Ramírez 1998: 265). In order to understand the new migrations of Moroccan women I will first look at their situation in the country of origin and what they claimed were their reasons for migrating.

The Moroccan women I interviewed in Barcelona tend to come from large families ranging from the twelve children of Halima's family to the three children of Salwa's family (Table 4.2). On average they had six brothers and sisters, so mean family size was seven, identical to my Filipino sample. The majority of Moroccan women migrating to Spain tend to come from the Rif, the mountain region in the north of the country, but there are several women in my sample (especially those who migrated alone and not for family reunion) who come from Casablanca (see Figure 3.2). Perhaps we can hypothesise the emergence of new female networks of migration originating in this big city. This impression was shared by Mohamed Chaib – President of the Moroccan Immigrant Association Ibn Batuta – who commented that there are now Moroccan women migrating to Barcelona with the idea of engaging in domestic work through contacts and information they received from female friends and relatives who have done the same – similar, in other words, to what happens for Filipinas.

Table 4.2 Basic biographic data on Moroccan women interviewed in Barcelona

Name	Age	Place of origin	Internal migration before emigration?	Number of siblings	Household head	Marital status upon migration	Number of children upon migration
Laila	28	Lorchi	No	9	M	married	2
Salwa	29	Tetuan	No	3	M	divorced	1
Nawal	29	Oujda	Yes	7	F	single	0
Nadira	31	Casablanca	No	8	F	single	0
Latifa	32	Casablanca	No	9	F	single	0
Myriam	33	Tanger	No	10	F	divorced	0
Rhannou	33	Casablanca	No	5	M	single	0
Mbarka	34	Casablanca	No	8	F	single	0
Fathiya	36	Meknes	No	9	M	divorced	1
Batul	37	Tanger	No	5	M	divorced	0
Jasmina	39	Kenitra	No	7	M	married	2
Jamila	42	Kasal-Kebir	No	5	F	divorced	2
Assja	42	Casablanca	Yes	6	F	divorced	0
Halima	42	Rif	Yes	12	F	married	2
Selma	46	Casablanca	Yes	5	M	married	1
Sahar	47	Meknes	No	6	M	married	2
Lubna	48	Kasal-Kebir	Yes	5	F	single	0
Shama	58	Casablanca	No	6	M	divorced	1

The socioeconomic background of my Moroccan respondents in Barcelona varies but none seemed to come from wealthy families. As with my respondents in Italy, and for Filipinos in Barcelona, in the case of Moroccan women in Barcelona too there seems to be a clear link between low socioeconomic status and female-headed households. Nine of my interviewees came from this type of household. All, except Mbarka's family, had a difficult economic situation. In her case her father, who was a nurse, had a house which they rented out and also he received a pension from the hospital. The other fathers – two soldiers, a trader, a farmer, an occasional worker – died leaving very little. Nawal's father – a forest-guard – stopped helping his previous family after divorcing his wife and remarrying. The other women who had fathers in employment and who were living within the household had a generally more stable economic situation. As Laila pointed out, for this type of family, survival is not a problem: what they lack is the possibility of saving and improving their socioeconomic position. They compare themselves with the successes of the emigrants who are going back to Morocco with new cars and money to buy or build properties. Although several of my interviewees could be said to come from the lower middle classes, there are certain differences among them. Some had been able to study until the end of the baccalaureate or even university (although none of them had finished it) and never worked until they left Morocco; others, instead, are illiterate and before marrying had to work to contribute to their families' income, as was the case for Batul, who started working in a factory when she was only ten.

The Moroccan women in my sample did not migrate from the countryside to the big cities in order to study or work, as was often the case for their Filipino counterparts. The majority of them came to Spain directly from their town of origin. However, some of them had moved within Morocco before international migration. The reasons for their internal migration were mainly two: change of residence as a result of the father's job; or marriage migration, i.e., change of residence due to marriage with a man of another place.

Only five of my interviewees came to Spain to reunite with their husbands. As far as this type of migration is concerned, although it is normally described as the prototype of dependent migration (women 'follow' their husbands), the reality is less clear-cut. In fact, even in the cases in which the husband migrates first, the wife is not necessarily passive, since she might have contributed to planning his departure and the eventual migration of the entire family. That was the case of Laila who made a migration project for her family together with her husband, who went ahead to look for work and documents while she took care of the children, joining him later.

The opposite warning has to be made when looking at women migrating on their own in order to seek work, since the description of 'independent migrant' is not always the most appropriate one for their situation. In Jamila's case, for instance, her migration was planned and influenced by her entire family, who needed the remittances she would have to send in order to ensure the household's survival. As the eldest of six brothers and sisters, Nawal too had not many options when her father divorced her mother and stopped supporting them. She was chosen by her family as the one who had to emigrate in order to guarantee the well-being of the rest of the family.

The issue of dependent as against independent migration is somewhat blurred also in the case of divorcees. Some, like Assja, had to migrate after their marriages collapsed because they did not have any other form of subsistence. Others, like Fhatiya, have gone back to work after they separated, but they preferred to emigrate in the hope of earning more or simply of reaching a less stigmatised social position. Some women, like Salwa, simply ran away from difficult situations (in her case an illegitimate pregnancy) in the hope of solving them and having a better life in the 'West'. Two women, Nawal and Mbarka, migrated against the will of their husband/fiancé, defying the norm that sees Moroccan men as sole initiators of migration.

Although at present all but two of my Moroccan respondents have a legal residence status in Spain, only half of them entered the country legally, and of those who arrived legally, only four had a residence permit. Nawal got her papers thanks to a job offer that her brother had obtained for her; Mbarka arrived thanks to a job found for her by a friend; Nadira arrived with a visa to marry her Spanish fiancé; and only Jasmina, of my entire sample, entered the country in what is considered the most typical form of female emigration: with a permit for family reunion. This picture confirms the increasingly stringent requirements for family reunion across Europe (Kofman et al. 2000). The others who entered legally arrived with a three-month tourist visa: in two cases to visit a relative who was already living in Barcelona, and in the remaining cases obtained because the women could demonstrate that they were in full-time employment in Morocco (in order to prove that they are not potential emigrants).

Of those who arrived illegally, two had husbands who were already living in Spain yet were not able to get the family reunion permit. Prolonged delays and criteria which were difficult to meet (a stable job, proper housing) forced Halima and Laila to resort to illegal emigration in order to be able to reunite their families.

> My husband had been here six years on his own without seeing his children. He got his papers but then he lost them again. Then he got them again and now it's a year that I'm here but I didn't arrive thanks to the papers, I arrived because I paid.

As we have just seen in the case of Laila, emigration is in some cases only made possible by paying an agent to get a false visa. This was also the route taken by Jamila. In her case the possibility of reaching Spain as an illegal migrant cost 700,000 ptas, paid for with the help of the entire family. The other women I interviewed entered without any papers, hiding in relatives' cars or eluding the checks in some ways. Myriam for instance:

I arrived here in my brother's car. *Sin papeles*, in the normal way, like everybody else.

Selma's strategy involved resorting to the help of a cousin who was working in a travel agency:

I spoke with my cousin who owns a travel agency. She asked me – which country do you want? I said I only want Spain because its near, I don't want to go far away. She then talked with people from here and a man agreed to write a job offer and so I bought a plane ticket and I came directly from there to here.

Five of my interviewees had lived in other Spanish cities before settling down more permanently in Barcelona. After an initial stay of four months in Barcelona which ended with Assja's decision to go back to Morocco (she was dissatisfied with her job with an Indian family with whom she had come from Morocco), she eventually reentered Spain and went to live in Malaga because 'it is near to the border'. After four years there she decided to move to Barcelona because wages were higher in the Catalan capital. Nawal too left the south of Spain (in her case Almeria) where her brother was and where she had a job in a greenhouse in the hope of a less hard and better paid job. Two women (Jamila and Batul) moved from Madrid to Barcelona. Jamila did so convinced by a friend that it was easier to find jobs there, whereas Batul – who had a job in Madrid as well as a flat – had to move once she got married to a Moroccan man who was living in Catalonia. Also for Rhannou her husband was the one responsible for her transfer to Barcelona from Palma de Majorca. He came from Morocco as an illegal immigrant to reunite with her and decided that it would be easier for him to live as a *sin papeles* in a big city like Barcelona rather than in Palma, where police checks were more regular.

Some women, apart from having moved within Spain, had experiences of living in other countries. Two had spent almost a year in another Arab country: Assja going to stay with a friend in Algeria soon after her father's death, and Lubna by prolonging her trip to visit Mecca by working as a baby-sitter for a Saudi Arabian family. Another two interviewees (Batul and Nawal) had lived in France (which they both did not like) and then left for Spain in the hope of being legalised.

The reasons why Moroccan women decide to migrate to Spain seem, therefore, to be variegated and less clearly linked than was the case in Bologna to their socioeconomic background and their marital status. Moroccan women do migrate to reunite with their husbands (five cases in my sample) but often this is a decision that had been initially taken together by the couple. Even when the husband had decided to go without consulting his wife, this does not mean that she is against the decision and she can have her own reasons to be eager to 'go to

Europe'. Laila, for instance, had always been attracted by Spain even though she never made any explicit plan to go there. Then, when her husband decided to migrate, she supported his decision:

> I'm from Lorchi in the north of Morocco, near Tetuan and Ceuta, that is why I see a lot about Spain. I saw everything on TV, we had channel 1, channel 5, all of them. I knew a lot about Spain and I liked its lifestyle, but I never thought that I would come here, that I would leave my family and my country, never. But when I got married my husband thought that it was better to go to Spain to look for a better life. He is a carpenter and many friends who were in Spain and were coming down for their holidays were saying – look, you can do your job in Spain and earn a lot. So we thought he should come. He told me – I go and you stay here with the two children. He thought that life here [in Spain] was good, easy, he could get a job, money, papers, and in a year everything will be sorted out. But it didn't happen like that.

Selma's reason for migration was also linked to the family, in her case to her desire to ensure a good future for her son and also for herself after her husband had taken a second wife:

> When I came here it was for my son. He didn't want to study in my country, he didn't want to do anything. I was thinking of what to do and finally I thought – better that we go to Europe to look for something.

The majority of my respondents stated that they came to Spain principally in order to work (thirteen of them). Contrary to what I found in Bologna, not all of the women belonging to this group were poor working-class women or divorcees. Six of them were single and among them there are some who decided to emigrate attracted by the possibility of earning more (they were already working in Morocco), enjoying more freedom and improving their life. One woman in my sample chose not to marry and found in the possibility of coming to work in Spain a viable option to support herself without having to rely on her family or having to give in to an unwanted marriage. That was the case of Lubna, who had initially come to Barcelona to visit a sister-in-law and then decided to settle permanently and enjoy her newly-acquired independence.

Divorcees represent a significant fraction of the Moroccan women who come to Spain in search of a job and a new start in life. Five of my interviewees were divorcees. Some of them had severe financial problems once their husbands stopped supporting them, whereas for others economic necessity was not the main push factor. Like some of their single counterparts, they saw in emigration the possibility of enjoying more freedom and gaining a certain degree of independence. Batul's reasons, for instance, were the following:

After I left my husband and went back to my house I thought – What am I doing in the house? It's better that I work – I worked very well in a garments factory and, you already know how it is in Morocco, men came to propose to me but I didn't want. I wanted to travel to Spain or to France. My friends were coming from France and were saying – France is very nice and Spain is also very nice.

In a previous part of the interview Batul explained why Moroccans generally go to Spain:

People from here think that all foreigners from Morocco suffer hunger, but that's not true. People come because they want to change things, everyone has problems in Morocco and they would like to change. People are fine in Morocco, they have their families there and they live well. But people want liberty and things like that, that's why they come here. ... If I go back to Morocco I'm treated by my family like a queen but I don't want to go back. I can suffer here, I don't want to go back to Morocco.

Two of the women in my sample had migrated to Spain to work even though one was already married and the other was engaged, leaving their partners behind. Below is how Mbarka described her reasons for coming:

I came because I had many problems. The problem was that I was working in Morocco and I was earning little. Moroccan people who were living here [in Spain] they were saying, 'We earn a lot of money there'. I wanted to see this country and see if one could earn a lot here. That's why I came. I was thinking of my neighbours. I thought – I can also get to Spain to work, to earn a lot of money, to improve. I worked for eight years in Morocco and didn't earn very much, I couldn't buy anything, no flat, nothing. Well, I thought that I too could change my life – do you understand me?

When these women manage to achieve their objective of reaching Europe and finally arrive in Barcelona, they encounter a less rosy picture from the one described to them by their fellow-Moroccans who have emigrated and are returning to Morocco for the holidays. Apart from difficulties in finding satisfactory jobs and adequate housing (see next section), one major problem is that of 'papers'. Some of the women who arrived in the early 1990s were able to benefit from various amnesty laws, but newcomers find it more difficult to get their residency permit. The situation has deteriorated due to the entry into force of the very restrictive immigration law 8/2000. Two of the women in my sample were still *sin papeles* at the time of the interview. Jamila has been in this situation for two years. She did not manage to regularise because, having bought a false visa in order to reach Spain, she is labelled as an offender and therefore not eligible for legal residence. The situation of illegality to which she has been condemned by the authorities has various negative consequences which go beyond the constant fear of being deported to Morocco. First, she is finding it extremely difficult to get employment. Secondly she cannot see her two daughters whom she left two years ago, because if she went back to Morocco she would not have the documents allowing her back into Spain. Salwa is in the same situation but at least she managed to bring her son with her, and she thinks she is very close to winning her appeal for residency.

Another problem affecting these women is that of everyday racism. Several of my interviewees said they had experienced episodes of intolerance. Nabila was suffering the consequences of intolerance at the time of our meeting. Her family was the victim of bullying by their Catalan neighbours who were insulting her and her children every time they saw them. They arrived at the point of putting a plastic roof on top of her balcony to divide their space from that of a 'despised' Moroccan family. Apparently her Catalan neighbours could not accept the fact that a Moroccan family had got access to council housing, something that in their mind should be reserved for the 'locals'.

Below I present further elements of the stories of Salwa and Batul, two women who migrated after their first marriages collapsed. Gender subordination – both in the form of marginalisation for not producing children and social stigma against having a child outside marriage – was at the origin of these women's migration. Both – as we will see – took a proactive stance and tried to improve their situation, with different degrees of success.

Salwa

Salwa is twenty-eight, she is divorced and has a five-year-old son. She is from Tetuan where she studied until the baccalaureate. She is the eldest of three daughters and her father was a factory worker. She got married in 1994 to a carpenter who was three years older than her. In 1995 they had a son. At that point problems started because he was not coming home every night and often he did not give Salwa any money for herself and the child. She then left their house and went back to her family. She finally obtained a divorce and custody of the child in 1997. After the divorce she started seeing another man who had promised to marry her but then left her when she became pregnant.

For Salwa the only way out of this situation was to try to reach Spain in order to have an abortion:

> With my pregnancy – because in my country you can't be pregnant without the certificate, without being married – I decided to come here [pause] to have an abortion, not even my mother knows that I had an abortion, it's something that I can't reveal.

Here below is how she describes her departure and her arrival in Barcelona, where within a few days she got her abortion:

One day in May 1999 I decided to come here to Spain. I took my son, took out a few things and since I have a passport from Ceuta I could enter without visa .... My father and my family didn't realise anything because I always used to take my son and go for a walk or to see my aunt, so I took a bit of money that my mother gave me – yes, my mother knew that I was going away from Morocco. But she was scared to death that they were going to capture me there, because I'm not legal – I feared that they will send me to prison and then they take away my son from me and give him back to his father and I go to prison.

Well, without thinking about anything I got on the boat with my son. I was scared to death. Then when the boat started to leave the port I started to calm down a bit. When I got off the boat in Spain I started to feel a bit lost – where do I have to go? With whom do I have to speak? What will I do? How will I reach Barcelona?

At that point I met a woman who told me that she was also going to Barcelona. Then I went with her and we eat a little bit since I was starting to feel a bit calmer after I thought that my heart was going to break. Then we eat and we took the bus, on the 23 May 1999. I came up with line 24 and I arrived at 3.15 in the afternoon. I called my neighbour and they sent their son to collect me from the station.

...

I arrived here and on the 31 May I went to the Health and Family Centre [Centro de Salud y Familia] with my friend and I asked them to help me and they sent me to a clinic. My friend had to pay only 8,000 ptas and Salud y Familia paid the rest. So on 9 June I had the abortion. Then I felt a bit bad, imagine how I felt. At that point I started to look for a job but there aren't any jobs without papers, without papers they can't give you any jobs. I went to the social worker and I told her that I wanted to do a course or something to be able to find a job. So she sent me to SURT[1] where I had an interview and was accepted on the course as kitchen helper [*ausilar de cocina*].

After she solved her main problem (the unwanted pregnancy), Salwa's next concern became to find a job. In order to improve her chances – apart from enrolling on the course – she appealed against the decision that denied her the documents. She had a receipt proving that she was in Spain on 9 June but the decree governing the regularisation procedures required proof of entrance before 1 June. Her lawyer assured Salwa that she had a 95 per cent chance of winning her appeal. With the help of her neighbours she has already managed to find a small flat for herself and her son where she pays 40,000 ptas and for the time being she was living with a cheque of 53,000 ptas paid for by Social Services. A few months after our first interview she got her residency permit and a job in a restaurant.

Batul

Batul is illiterate, she has divorced twice, has a seven-year-old daughter and comes from Tangier.

I'm from Tangier. When I was young I was fine, really. My father was a truck driver. When I was very young, when I was ten I went to work in a factory. I was happy, I was fine, when I was a bit older a man from France came and my father wanted me to marry him but I didn't. But in Morocco when your father and mother want you to marry, you have to marry. Then my father forced me to marry and I stayed married for twelve years.

So, at the age of fifteen Batul went to live with her new husband and his family; problems for her started to arise almost immediately:

You know how it is in Morocco that when you marry a man you don't live alone but with his mother. Then I didn't have any children. His mother was waiting for the babies but they didn't come. When I married this man problems started to emerge because he left me in the house with his mother and he was travelling to France, you know? When he came back there were many problems. I stayed married for twelve years and I didn't have any children. Then his mother said: leave her, she hasn't got children, that can't be. I have been to the doctor and he checked me and told her – wait a bit, this girl is young. She didn't want to listen. The he left me. It was over, he left me and got a new wife. I didn't want to stay because I can't live with more wives. He had married me and I can't accept another wife. I left him and I didn't want anything. I went back to my house and started working again.

After three years Batul decided to leave Morocco and join her sister in France, from whom she had heard many positive things about Europe. She found it difficult to live without papers in France and her main desire was to find a job. With a friend she decided to leave France and go to Madrid. There she immediately found a job as live-in. After two months in Spain and with the help of her employer, she managed to regularise her position and obtained the residence permit. She then changed job (to earn more now that she had papers) and rented a flat with her friend. At that point she met a Moroccan man:

I didn't want to marry, I didn't want children. I was modern, now I'm fat but then I wasn't fat at all, I had my hair long to the waist, I was really beautiful! Really, I was really well, without headscarf, without everything, wearing trousers, skirts. I was modern, I was well! I didn't need anything, I didn't have any problems in my head like now, really! Everything was fine. But I thought this man loves me a lot, why shouldn't I marry him?

She finally decided to marry him and because of that she had to leave her life in Madrid and follow him to Barcelona:

We went to Morocco to get married and he told me – look I work in Barcelona not in Madrid. Look, here in Madrid is over for you. You have to leave this friend, leave this flat, leave everything. You come to Barcelona. Fine... When I came back from Morocco I went there to Gava', a small village and that is it.

He had a good job and a flat in Gava' and things went fine at first, but after four months Batul fell pregnant and immediately after problems started to arise because he was seeing other women.

Reasons for Migrating

Both Moroccans and Filipinas in Barcelona seem to have a low socioeconomic background; a large number of Filipinas have experienced rural–urban migration prior to international migration; a high proportion of Moroccan women interviewed came from female-headed households. As I have already reported for the Italian case-study, the reasons pushing women of both groups to migrate are often linked to their role and position within their families and to their gender roles. More specifically, women migrate to help their families of origin; they move because their family has dissolved (e.g., after divorce); they leave their countries to escape from oppressive situations within and outside their families; or they go abroad to reunite with members of their families. What I noted in the Spanish case is that the proximity of Morocco means that a growing number (and variety) of Moroccan women are starting to get access to migration, including women in relationships who become the 'pioneers' of family migration and thus defy the stereotype of Moroccan women as merely 'followers'. As far as access to migration is concerned, I noted the more institutionalised form of Filipino migration and the more spontaneous and informal character of Moroccan female migration. In both types of flows there is the presence or emergence of female-controlled networks of migration. Another element relevant for both flows is the dubious relevance of the categories 'legal' and 'illegal' due to their fluid nature. In fact, most of my interviewees had crossed these categories several times. These changes in status have a fundamental importance for the migrant, but are little controlled or even understood by the individuals involved.

Homemakers and Breadwinners:
The Role of Women in the Settlement Process

In this section I look at women in the context of arrival and at their key role in the settlement process. In the account that follows I will first describe the kinds of jobs the women do in Barcelona, including their experiences, perceptions and working conditions. Second, I will look at how women dispose of the money they earn and what degree of control they have over their money.

Filipino Women

Filipinas in Barcelona, as in Bologna and other Southern European cities, are at the top of the domestic sector niche. They easily get employed in this sector, they tend to be better paid than other national groups (e.g., Moroccans), and in many cases have long-term and stable jobs. In Maricel's view, the fact that Filipinas have rather better working conditions depends on the good reputation Filipinas have built up for themselves over the years:

> Filipinas never enter a job with bad conditions. They always enter with a *señora* with good conditions, as the law says here. They pay every month and twice a year you get the extra pay and during holidays they pay as well, and the salary it's good, the pay is not too low, it's how the law here says. But the work we do is also good, we don't just sit down. When you are in the house you are always doing something because if you don't do that, that's not good and they can fire you. We are dedicated to our work, it's because we are from very far and what are we going to do here if we don't work? If you are not prepared to do the job well what will happen?
>
> If the *señora* is not happy with your work she sends you away but you can't stay here without working so this is our work strategy: we are happy with our bosses and they are happy with us because if they want to send you away you won't have any references nor anything, that's why *las señoras* don't have so much confidence with those of other countries that are nearer. They don't want to work hard, when the *señora* goes out they'll sit down, they relax in the house and when the *señora* comes back they pretend to be working really hard but it's a lie. That can't be, that's my observation. They like us Filipinas a lot, I have talked to many *señoras* and they told me that they prefer Filipinas and also that they are very polite.

Filipinas normally start working as live-in maids, accepting the hardest and most demanding jobs. As they acquire skills and experience (in many cases they never did domestic work before) they move to better-paid jobs and/or jobs with better working conditions. They leave the previous occupation to the newcomers and those starting their 'career'. The ones with more years of experience are normally working as live-out domestics with indefinite contracts and doing the less heavy tasks within the household. As we saw in the previous chapter, Filipinos' specialisation within the domestic sector is not only the result of the attitudes and goals of these women, it is often reinforced and fossilised in the conditions found in the receiving context. Some women I interviewed with high education levels were not keen to engage in domestic work and therefore tried to find other job possibilities, but with little success. Some of my interviewees compared the situation of other countries, such as he UK or the US, where there is a perceived greater chance to deploy their accumulated skills, with the situation in Catalonia, where the Filipino view is that the locals are always put in front of newcomers.

In Barcelona, as in Bologna, live-in work has been used by Filipinas as a way of getting started in the local labour market and as a system to reduce living costs and increase the level of remittances. It appears to be an occupation that women take up in order to solve severe housing problems. However, overall in Barcelona housing did not seem as problematic for Filipinos as it was in Bologna. The settlement of Filipinos in Barcelona is relatively 'old' and they have now consolidated their presence in the central area of Ciutat Vella, especially in the district known as Raval, historically an immigration district (Aramburo and Zegrì 1994).

Some of my Filipino interviewees had arranged their accommodation in Filipino-run pensions (which are effectively large flats whose landlords sublet beds to guests) before leaving the Philippines. Filipinos in Barcelona live concentrated within a few streets in the Raval. Over the years they have leased several properties, some of which were quite run-down, they have refurbished them and are now passing them on within their ethnic network. Most of my interviewees got their present accommodation from friends and relatives who had vacated their flats. Several Filipinos who have acquired Spanish nationality are also buying properties in this part of town, which has the advantage of being centrally located and only a few streets away from the Filipino parish, the community centre, and the Filipino shops, call centres and restaurants which are starting to appear in this area.

At the time of fieldwork every one of my twenty interviewees was in full-time employment: sixteen worked as domestics and four had other jobs. Rosa, for instance, works as a telephone operator in a medical centre. She found the job by replying to an advertisement she found in a local newspaper. She works eight hours daily and earns slightly less (130,000 ptas gross) than her domestic worker counterparts, but she seemed happy to have a different type of job from the majority of Filipinas and to have managed to escape from the domestic sector niche. Her previous job experiences in Barcelona had indeed included domestic work and she had also worked as kitchen assistant.

Necitas is another 'ex-domestic', who now works in an Italian-owned boutique. She had been working as a live-in maid for her current employers and this is how she got the job in the shop. She now works nine hours daily from 8 a.m. to 1 p.m. and from 4 p.m. to 8 p.m. and earns 130,000 ptas monthly.

In the morning I clean the shop until we open at 10. When the boutique opens I do the sewing and pressing of the things to be displayed and that until now is my work. It's nice. I prefer that than working in the house because it's different. In the house you do everything: cooking, cleaning, ironing. In the shop it's different, it's better.

Beatrice and Rosevilla work in restaurants, Rosevilla as an employee and Beatrice as co-owner (with her husband) of a Filipino take-away. Rosevilla is very happy about her job since she gets on well with her boss and fellow-workers but she admits that it is very tiring. Beatrice is ambivalent about her new job in her restaurant. She got away from the boredom of domestic work and she has set up her own business, which represents the dream of many of my interviewees. The earnings are better and she and her husband do not have to depend on anybody. But the hours are long and the work is quite heavy. She now works twelve hours daily from 10 a.m. to 10 p.m. and she has no free day since the shop only closes half-day on Mondays.

The restaurant business is a sector that in Barcelona employs several Filipino immigrants, both men (as waiters and cooks) and women (as assistant cooks, waitresses and kitchen helpers, etc.). Mainly sons and daughters of Filipino migrants work in this sector. Generally their parents did not have access to this type of work, or in some cases they did not choose it because of its incompatibility with their Church and community commitments. Here is Eleanor's opinion about it:

Now it's good for the young ones, the sons of Filipino migrants, because they start working in supermarkets or in restaurants, although it's quite difficult. I can work if I want in a restaurant as a waitress but it's the hours that they have that I don't like. The weekend is very important for me because we sing in the Church for mass and Sunday is the most important day for me. For example, if I'm working in a restaurant I don't have the weekend free, it depends upon the rotation and the salary is just like almost the same. If you have been working for a long time in a family, well your salary is already quite big. It's not like if you are going to start now that the amount of money is quite low. The difference is that they have also the tips, but then if you have to work an extra hour, then it's just the same.

Another occupation mentioned by some of my interviewees was factory work. Mirna, for instance, was sent to work in her employer's factory although he did not change her contract as a domestic worker, which entails lower contributions and fewer rights (no unemployment benefits, no sick leave). Priscilla has worked for a factory producing jackets, sewing jackets with her family from her flat for three years. She was paid by piece until at one point her Spanish employer stopped paying his workers. She then quit the job.

Several of my interviewees, especially those who have suffered the most marked deskilling as a consequence of migration, are now doing volunteering jobs both in the Church and in the *Centro Filipino* which was created by some nuns to give help and support to Filipino migrants. Here former teachers (like Priscilla, Victoria, Zeni and Clara), former nurses (like Annalyn), former councillors (like Basilio), trade unionists (like Vivian), police officers (like Maricel), and various former university students and graduates teach Spanish to other Filipinos; teach religion and Filipino culture to Filipino children; organise the activities of various associations; and give various types of support and advice to their newly-arrived fellow nationals. They all value this type of work highly and are now unwilling to renounce the satisfaction and self-value that it provides to them.

In spite of the involvement of some Filipinas in the professions mentioned above, the majority of my interviewees are still working in the domestic sector; thirteen as live-out domestics and three live-in (Mirna, Annie and Annalyn). Mirna has been working for the last three years for a couple with four children. Annie has also been working for three years, for a couple with three children. She has a permanent contract and earns 120,000 ptas monthly. Annalyn has changed jobs several times, both because she started her career as a 'reliever' (someone who substitutes other Filipinas who are temporarily leaving their jobs for holidays, maternity, sickness, etc.) and because she had some bad experiences of exploitation. The great majority of my interviewees had done live-in work at the beginning of their career as domestic workers, and many had stayed in this mode for several years (more than ten years in many cases and sixteen years in the case of Lola). At some point most Filipinas either choose or are forced (by the arrival of children, for instance) to move to other types of occupation, usually live-out care or domestic work.

Eight of my interviewees opted for full-time live-out work for one employer, whereas five decided to be self-employed and work for different families, offices or restaurants. In the first type of employment the domestic should work eight hours daily, normally from 9 to 5, with Saturday afternoon and Sunday off, and earn approximately 150,000 ptas monthly. But this was not the case for all of my subjects. In this type of job the hours worked by each worker seem to vary. They ranged from the six hours per day worked by Clara to the ten worked by Basilio and the eleven undertaken by Lola. Furthermore several women supplement their earnings from their full-time job by taking up additional hours during their free days, holidays or evening time. Victoria, for instance, has an eight hours per day contract but twice a week she does three additional hours as a baby-sitter for her employers. Pay and conditions also vary, with some women having to do the thorough cleaning plus cooking, looking after children and general housekeeping, whereas others have to carry out only specific tasks, i.e., cooking or general housekeeping. Some of the households for which my interviewees worked had more than one domestic. In these cases the tasks are split and the employee with more experience does the physically less demanding tasks.

Some women prefer to be self-employed, pay their own social security contributions and work for several employers. This type of work may give the woman more flexibility as far as hours worked, although normally my interviewees (like Maricel or Natalia) seemed to work all their available time (on average ten hours) in order to earn the kind of wage they needed. The current hourly rate for a domestic/carer is 750 ptas with social security contribution and 1100 ptas without. The task normally carried out in this type of occupation is that of general cleaning (both of houses and offices), but it can also include caring for elderly people.

Filipinas normally rely on their own networks to find jobs in Barcelona. They usually help each other by sharing information with friends and relatives about job openings. Current and past employers are also a source of help for finding additional work or placing a friend or relative in the local labour market. The Church and the Centro Filipino are also involved in helping Filipinos find jobs both in domestic service and in various firms. Because of the above-mentioned channels (friends and relatives, current and past employers and the Church), Filipinas normally do not have to turn to recruitment agencies, which they consider less reliable; although there are a few Filipino agencies who place both Filipinos already resident in Barcelona and those who have not yet arrived.

When they were asked to talk about their employers, some Filipinas had good words for them, saying that they had been treated very well. As was the case in Bologna, although Filipinas in Barcelona complain about particular employers and might not enjoy domestic work, they do not consider it as a negative or humiliating profession as such. In many cases they find it an easier and more dignified way to earn substantially more income than they could with their jobs in their country of origin. In Clara's words:

> I don't mind doing it because I do it pim pum, pim pum [laughs]. Sometimes I get bored because I love very much going around. When someone needs something then I'm very happy with what I'm doing, but work in the house? No. I'm not a house person. The thing is that here the money is higher.

Only Vivian, among my interviewees, still finds it difficult to accept what she considers an unbearable decline in terms of employment status. She regrets having left her job in a computer firm and as a trade union delegate, but she now feels that she has no way back because she has a Spanish husband and a daughter in Barcelona.

Defying the stereotype that see them as passive, some of my interviewees had tried to improve their work situation by going to check other markets in different countries of the world. Priscilla and Eleanor both went to try to work in the US (more on their stories below). Natalia tried working as a domestic helper in London. She got a job through a friend who was working there but in the end she decided that she was better off in Barcelona and so she came back.

A large part of the money earned in Barcelona is sent back as remittances to the Philippines. Indeed, nineteen out of my twenty interviewees said that they sent money back home. Only Vivian never does so since her family does not need it. All the others are sending money either regularly or on certain occasions (such as Christmas, or when some payments – such as school fees – are due). The amount of money currently sent by the women in my sample ranges from 10,000 ptas to US $ 300 monthly but several explained how, when they were still single or when their children were still in the Philippines, they were sending much more, almost their entire salary. The women in my sample who are currently sending more are Beatrice ($ 200), Lola ($ 100–300), Annie (30,000 ptas) and Zeni ($ 300). [2] The first three have sons and daughters in the Philippines whereas Zeni – who at fifty-one is still single – took up the responsibility of supporting her nephews and nieces through school and university. Additionally, several women declared sending various presents, books, clothes, medicines and even food.

Like the Filipino women in Bologna, the reasons why Filipinas in Barcelona send money are usually related to improving the socioeconomic position of their family. One frequent goal is that of helping children (as well as nephews, younger brothers, sisters and cousins) to get through what in local Filipino terms is quite an expensive education system. Necitas, for instance, helps her nephews through college:

> Sometimes my nieces and nephews – who are studying at college in Manila – need my help. Normally they have their parents [who are working in Saudi Arabia] helping them but last semester one of my brothers-in-law went home to the Philippines because his contract had already finished and they found it hard to support the boy who is already at college, so they asked me to help.

Other purposes of Filipinas' remittances are to support elderly parents in a country where there is no welfare system. Clara for instance has a ninety-year-old mother who lives alone since one of Clara's brothers has recently died and the other lives in London. Between her and her brother they are now paying for the carers (local young girls) who look after their mother and for her medicines. Also the children of her brother send money to the grandmother.

Money is also sent to help the family to become more economically independent and to achieve various goals, as was the case for Victoria:

> I had a lot of dreams like having a house, help my brothers and sister to live well and to finish their studies, help my parents . Working together [with her sister] we saved everybody. We got a house – well we already had a house but what we built then was a proper house, one that when it rains it doesn't rain inside. Then we could buy a means of transport and thank God because that was an opportunity that they gave us that we couldn't forget because it saved our life.

Many migrants, like Victoria, buy houses for their families to live in, and also as a form of investment to rent out. Having a property is also seen an insurance policy for when the migrants retire back home. Necitas, for instance:

> I built a house in Manila, a two-door apartment, one door is the one were I stay when I go home and where my youngest sister now stays, and the other one is for rent. That's my souvenir from Barcelona.

As in Bologna, money earned abroad is also used to sponsor the emigration of relatives who will in turn become producers of remittances. Victoria's case is very interesting in this respect since she is the initiator of the migration of more than eighty people!

> I brought here all my family and also their relatives, for example the sisters of my sister-in-law also came after me. I was the first to arrive and then I helped to get my sisters and then all the brothers. After me also came my cousins, my relatives and also another family.

But Filipinas also invest in Barcelona. Many of them have bought their own houses, both with the idea of leaving them to their Barcelona-resident children when they themselves retire back to the Philippines, but also as an investment. Priscilla, for instance, bought two: she lives with her family in one of them and is renting out (to Filipinos) the other one. Some women managed to save in order to invest in economic enterprises, like Beatrice who opened a take-away restaurant with her husband.

As in Bologna, in Barcelona too the woman seems to be the one managing the family budget. Maricel keeps the money of her sons and daughter and it is she who decides on the family investments (they are currently building a large house in the Philippines). But in some cases the husband has a say. Mirna has to negotiate with her husband in order to be able to send the large sums of remittances her family needs.

Here now are two stories – those of Eleanor and Priscilla – that defy the stereotypes about the passivity of Filipino women in their submission to domestic work. Both women are engaged in this sector and both suffered a severe deskilling through migration, but both have tried hard to escape this market niche.

Eleanor

Eleanor was a student in the Philippines and now works as full-time live-out maid for a family of four. She feels she had a happy childhood as the only daughter of a separated woman. When she was nineteen her mother told her to join her in

Spain, promising Eleanor that she would be able to carry on studying. Although Eleanor found it very difficult to learn the new languages (Spanish and Catalan), she took and passed a computer course in Barcelona. Then she went for several job interviews but was unable to find any job matching her newly-acquired qualifications.

> Just after I finished the course I applied for a job and I passed the examination and then I think I was the first but then, of course, there were Spanish people, Catalan people, and they didn't give the job to me. It is quite difficult to work here, especially for a migrant, because they choose the people from here first. You know, even if you are capable of the work they don't give you the job, there is too much discrimination.

After a few months of repeated lack of success she decided to put aside her aspirations and enter domestic service:

> I said OK, I have finished studying computing but what am I going to do here? My mother was working already in the domestic sector so I said – I better work because if not I have to go home. Since then I started to work as domestic and it's already twenty-two years ago now.

For ten years – from 1979 to 1989 – Eleanor worked as a live-in maid. Then she decided that she had had enough of that type of job and looked for hourly paid work and a flat. She found a small flat in the city centre and bought it together with her mother. In her twenty-two years career as a domestic she only worked for five families, and she said that she only had positive experiences with her employers. What she appreciates is the fact that she has always been treated like a member of the family by them.

For the last eleven years she has been working full-time as a live-out maid for the same family, composed of parents and four children. At present she is working just for the parents since all the children have left home. The hardest part of the job for Eleanor is the repetitive routine.

In 1998 Eleanor went to the US, where she had an aunt, to see if she could find a better kind of job. Through a Filipino contact she found a job as a cashier in a shop. She did not dislike the job but her earnings were low due to the fact that she did not have a work permit. She stayed in Los Angeles three months and then decided to return to Barcelona.

She went back to the same job she had before and now plans to stay with that family for at least another two years. She is thinking of the possibility of going back to the US, but this time with a work permit. She has another aunt in Las Vegas who could help her in finding someone to sign a contract for her so that she can work legally, perhaps in a casino. She has also thought several times of going to the UK, another country where she knows she could work outside the domestic service sector, but eventually she always changed her mind:

> Sometimes I say, 'Yeah I would like to go there', but all the times I think that, I meet people from London and change my mind. I have met so many Filipinas who have been there and then come back here. I have many friends there who say that in London you have the advantage that you can use what you have studied. The only disadvantage is that everything is so expensive.

A recent plan Eleanor is developing is that of establishing a business in the Philippines. On a seven-month break in the Philippines she just had before the interview, she had seen an unspoiled island where she would like to build a house to rent out to European tourists. At present she is back in her old job and is thinking of possible ways to save enough money that will allow her to buy the property, build the house and establish the business.

Priscilla

Priscilla was a teacher in the Philippines who now works as an hourly paid cleaner. She arrived in 1980; her reason for migrating was the necessity to earn a higher wage in order to be able to send her children to school. When she left her country she thought that she could work as a teacher also in Spain, but she soon realised that this was not the case. She found it particularly hard to adapt to her new job as a domestic since it was something she had never done. She was a professional in her country and she herself had a domestic helper there. During the first years she regretted having migrated, but with the years she accepted her new life and at present she is broadly happy with her decision.

The hardest years were the early ones when she was working as live-in maid and was far away from her family. She did not see her husband and her three children for five years. Finally, in 1985, her husband arrived in Barcelona with their eldest son and one year later the other two children followed. With the savings of her job, in 1986 she bought her first flat in the barrio del Raval where she went to live with her reunited family and where she still lives today. In 1988 she bought another flat a few streets away, which she rents out to Filipinos.

At present she has several jobs. During the week she cleans offices, several houses and a restaurant. Her daily schedule is from 10 a.m. to 1 p.m., from 4 p.m. to 6 p.m., and from 8 p.m. to 10 p.m. During the weekend – as well as volunteer work in the Filipino centre – she has her own businesses. She sells home-made cakes at Filipino gatherings and every other Sunday she organises excursions. That is to say, she rents a van and takes Filipinos to visit places such as Andorra or the Pyrenees in exchange for a fee. By combining these various activities she can earn monthly up to 300,000 ptas (well above an average Spanish salary). Apart from money (she remits 25,000 ptas monthly), she also sends food and medicines to parents, sisters, nephews and in-laws in the Philippines.

Like Eleanor, Priscilla tried to see if she could escape the domestic service niche by exploring working opportunities in other countries. First, she went to Japan with the help of a brother. There she worked in a factory and as a baby-sitter. She thought that the work possibilities were better in Japan but she finally decided to go back to Catalonia because it was where her family was. Subsequently she went to San Diego (US) to open up a business with the help of another brother who was living there. She tried to open a video rental and a Filipino food shop with the capital her brother lent her (he had the same type of business). However, she stayed only five weeks and then returned the money and went back to Barcelona because she did not manage to convince her youngest daughter to stay there. She has now decided that she will stay in Barcelona until she retires and then she will perhaps start travelling.

Moroccan Women

Finding a job and accommodation are the first priorities of newly arrived immigrants, and my findings amongst Moroccan women in Barcelona certainly confirm this. As was the case in Italy, there seem to be two types of Moroccan involvement in the local labour market: single women, widows and divorcees engage in live-in domestic work or, in fewer cases, full-time live-out work; whilst married women with families in Barcelona tend to engage primarily in hourly paid work.

As for Moroccan women's ways to find employment in Barcelona, it seems that they rely less heavily on charities than was the case in Bologna. In Barcelona, charities are used mainly by the city's large South American immigrant population. In Barcelona, Moroccan women rely mainly on temporary work agencies of which there are several in the city. Here the woman goes to file her job request in exchange for a fee that can range from 500 to 2000 ptas. Afterwards the agency links the petitioner with a potential employer and receives part of her salary for a given period. For some of the Moroccan women I met it has been relatively easy to find a job this way. Those who find it more difficult are the women wearing the veil, who tend to be rejected or less frequently chosen by employers who have often at their disposal a large number of applicants. Lubna experienced this type of discrimination directly when she went to several agencies to look for a job.

> When I left my job and went to look for another one I didn't find anything because nobody wants a woman who wears the veil, who is religious. One day they sent me for an interview with a family that needed a domestic but when they saw me with the veil they told me that they had to think about it, that they would call me back. Of course they didn't.

Some of these women find it easier at times to locate employment opportunities through information passed on by friends and relatives. Contrary to what was happening in Bologna, in Barcelona there seems to be some level of cooperation among co-nationals although the networks of Moroccan women are still quite weak compared to those of their Filipino counterparts. They normally work in very specific situations and, according to the women of Al-Wafa (the Association of Moroccan Women), Moroccan women would pass on information only to very good friends.

As regards the occupations of Moroccan women in Barcelona, apart from the dominant domestic service niche, we can find them employed also as kitchen assistants in the restaurant sector. A very small number of Moroccan women have managed to escape these two niches of employment. Some of the most qualified women work in administrative positions, as teachers or as cultural mediators. However, all three of these last-named occupations are directly related to the immigrant population. Apart from the obvious case of the cultural mediator, those who work as Arabic teachers or administrative staff do so in immigrant associations, NGOs and other types of organisations dealing with the immigrant population. It is still very difficult – if not impossible – for Moroccan first-generation immigrants (as is the case with their Filipino counterparts) to escape the domestic service/restaurant sectors and find better jobs which are not related specifically to 'servicing' other immigrants.

As far as housing is concerned, the situation for newly arrived immigrants is deteriorating fast. Those who arrived a few years ago could still find reasonably priced flats and thus several Moroccan families and groups of women were able to settle in Ciutat Vella (as did the Filipinos). At present, however, the local administration has decided to embark on important projects of inner-city regeneration. Old and delapidated buildings are being demolished, new squares and streets are being created and new modern apartment blocks are being built. If on the one hand the neighbourhood is improving its image, on the other hand immigrants and other marginal categories seem to be losing out in this process.[3]

A report of the Xenofilia project noted that there is a very strong correlation between the blocks that are currently being demolished and those where immigrants used to live (Proyecto Xenofilia 1996).

The Council is re-housing or compensating those who reside in the buildings due for demolition. However, as Bergalli (2001) notes, those who do not have a legal tenancy agreement, those who are subletting or who are temporarily accomodated in such flats do not have any rights. Many of these are likely to be immigrants. Several of my interviewees were indeed affected by the regeneration programs. Five of them, who are currently living in a block now bought by a construction company, had an order to vacate their flats as soon as their contracts expired. Selma's contract was the first one due to end. She came to the charity where I was working as a volunteer to find help, but eventually she managed to find a new accommodation by herself. It was an attic which would not have met any health and safety requirements, but it was the only thing she could find.

Nowadays prices are going up in the entire city and especially in Ciutat Vella which is well on its way to becoming a 'trendy' neighbourhood. What makes the situation worse for immigrants in general, and Arabs in particular, are the prejudices and racism of both landlords and letting agencies. I personally followed Laila's search for a flat for her family that lasted over two months. Both she and her husband were legal residents and her husband had a regular job with a contract and his boss was willing to write references for him. In spite of the fact that they met all the requirements asked for by letting agencies, and that they could afford the market rent (55,000 ptas) for a flat, they were not able to rent anything. I personally accompanied Laila to visit a flat (worth 45,000 ptas) and to present all her papers to the agency. The clerk took the documents and told us that she would be in touch: a few days later she returned the documents saying that Laila's husband's contract was not indefinite and therefore they could not rent him a flat. We accompanied Laila to visit several agencies, wrote reference letters, and sent her to her district social worker; all with no success. Eventually she managed to solve the problem herself through a contact she obtained from a neighbour. She rented a flat that would not meet any 'liveability' criteria and that nobody who was not in her desperate situation would have rented. But at least it was a flat and a way out from the pension were she and her husband had spent the past two months and which was starting to become too expensive for them.

Nabila was the only one of my interviewees who benefited from a re-housing scheme. When the block where she and her family were living was bought and demolished they were offered the possibility of choosing between an indemnity of 1,200,000 ptas or a council flat. Nabila rightly calculated than she would not have been able to do much with that sum of money, and since her family of five needed a place to live, she opted for the flat. They now have a modern flat in the city centre but their problems have not ended. They are constantly bullied by their neighbours who do not accept that council housing is allocated to 'immigrants', as we noted earlier.

Going back to the issue of work, at the time of fieldwork ten out of eighteen of my interviewees were in employment. Of the eight who were not, two (Salwa and Batul) were doing a full-time course of job training and because of that were receiving a PIRMI (a kind of unemployment benefit amounting to 53,000 ptas monthly) from the provincial government. Salwa was taking a cooking course with the aim of finding a job in a restaurant, and Batul was taking a sewing course. Batul had worked in a restaurant previously but for health reasons cannot do that type of job any more; her wish is to find a cleaning job, ideally in a hotel. Although her course is not related directly to the job she wants to do, by going to the training centre she is able to qualify for the PIRMI; and she can also benefit from the teacher's contacts in order to access other types of jobs. Nabila had completed the same course that Salwa was doing but she was still unemployed (except for three hours weekly of cleaning). Two of my Moroccan interviewees were out of work at the time of the interview but normally are in employment. Latifa had just left her live-in job due to the arrival of her first baby and Assja left a job in a restaurant after she broke a toe – since she had no contract she could not take sick leave. Jamila was desperately looking for any kind of work but thus far unsuccessfully, due partly to the fact that she has no papers. Only two of the eight unemployed women I interviewed were not looking for a job. Both Jasmina and Laila have arrived recently and have husbands in employment (they are both carpenters). However, Laila said that as soon as she has finished sorting out her flat she will start looking for cleaning jobs in her area of the city in order to contribute to her family's budget.

Among the ten who were in employment, four worked as live-in maids, three (Lubna, Selma and Fhatiya) had full-time live-out domestic jobs, and two (Halima and Nadira) had hourly paid jobs which included a combination of house and office cleaning, looking after children and cooking Moroccan food. Mbarka was working as an assistant cook in a restaurant and Salwa – who was unemployed the first time I interviewed her – had a similar type of job the second time I met her (in the meantime she had also managed to get a work and residency permit).

Contrary to what I found in Bologna, few women were employed in cleaning companies in Barcelona and several Moroccan women work as domestics. Prejudice against them does exist, as in Bologna, but they are still employed in houses (especially those who do not wear the veil), partly because they are cheaper than, for instance, Filipino women. As in Bologna, live-in work does not seem to be a point of departure for Moroccan women's insertion in the local labour market. Live-in work seems to be the type of work performed by single, divorcee or widowed women. Women with husbands and children rarely opt for this type of work and normally perform hourly paid domestic work, although I noted some exceptions. Rhannou, for instance, had worked as live-in in the Canary Islands when her husband was still in Morocco and Latifa – who also was married – remained in this occupation until her first baby was born.

Only Mbarka (subsequently also Salwa) among the women of my Barcelona Moroccan sample worked outside the domestic sector. Both worked as kitchen assistants in restaurants, a sector where there are several immigrant women currently employed in Barcelona. Although the work is hard and involves spending long hours standing in the heat of often very small kitchens, Moroccan women tend to see this type of work as preferable to domestic work. In Mbarka's words:

I work in a restaurant as an assistant cook and now I'm fine. I'm working there for two years and I have a permanent contract. I work ten hours daily, which is a lot. But the truth is that I like it, there is a lot of work and by the evening I'm very tired – but my problem is that I don't like working in a house. You know? Live-in maid, sleeping in a house that's not yours, I don't like that. It's better to work during the day and then come back to my flat in the evening. I like to sleep in my own flat.

Domestic work is seen by most of the Moroccan women I met as demeaning and below what they would like to do. As the women of Al-Wafa explained:

Domestic work isn't good. It's dirty and it's no good but Moroccan women cannot find anything else. When Moroccan women are looking for a job they always give them cleaning jobs. They give always the hardest jobs to the immigrants because they know that they are the ones who are going to cope.

For women with degrees and those belonging to higher or middle classes in Morocco, this situation is particularly difficult to accept. One woman whose grandfather had been mayor of her town explained to me how, although she needed the money, she could not bring herself to accept domestic work. She had arrived in Barcelona ten years before in order to cure an eye illness. During that time she met a Moroccan man, married him and settled in the city. At first her parents were sending her money as 'reverse remittances' but after a while they stopped doing so. A family friend suggested she start doing domestic service since there was a lot of this type of work on offer and her economic situation was precarious. She refused, reminding the friend that she came from a family where they themselves had two maids, that she had a philosophy degree and that she did not come to Spain to work. The friend apparently told her that in Spain it is not shameful to work as a domestic; besides she could just tell her family that she was working in a office. This woman explained that some Moroccan women – particularly those who had studied and/or had better jobs in Morocco – lie to their families because they feel embarrassed to perform a job that in their view corresponds to women from the lower classes with low education levels. Domestic work in Morocco is the exclusive domain of women of the lower classes and is not considered as a dignified job but rather as a heavy burden that all women wish to abandon upon marriage. However Gregorio and Ramírez (2000) have found that the perception of domestic work changes somewhat through emigration, when it starts to lose its wholly negative connotations as a burden, an obligation and a class position. My fieldwork suggests that the two perceptions of domestic work – the negative one and a more positive one – coexist.

Another element which makes domestic work undesirable for Moroccan women is the limited range of rights that this type of occupation has in relation to other jobs. Batul would like a job as a cleaning lady in a hotel rather than work as a domestic maid in a house:

I can work in houses but to have a contract is very difficult, you have to work without rights, without anything. I can work really hard and then when I'm sick, ill, or I cut myself or something like that I don't receive anything, I'm left with nothing. Restaurants, factories, hotels, these kinds of jobs have rights, firms give you rights, but in the houses you don't have any rights, you know?

In spite of this low opinion of domestic work, many Moroccan women are left with no option but to take it up. The reasons are several. Some of my interviewees have had jobs in restaurants in Barcelona but at some point had to leave them due either to illness or to incompatibility with their domestic role. Assja, for instance, after having worked in several houses as a live-in, managed to find a job in a restaurant. After three months there she had an accident with a hot water pan and was forced to leave (she had no contract and therefore no sick leave). She found another job in a restaurant but here again she had to quit after injuring herself. She is now looking for any kind of job and after her unfortunate experiences is prepared to go back to domestic work. Nadira had managed to find a job as a clerk in a phone centre but she had to leave it in order to be able to look after her daughter. She found it unacceptable to have to work during weekends. She now works as a cleaner in an office from 6 a.m. to 9 a.m. which allows her to be back in time to take her daughter to school in the morning. She does eight additional hours during the week while her daughter is at school.

The work and pay conditions of my interviewees who were involved in domestic work at the time of the interview varied. Nadira, for instance, earns 750 ptas an hour or 1100 without insurance, depending on the agreement she makes with her employers. Fhatiya, Lubna and Selma have full-time live-out work from Monday to Saturday morning. They have been in their jobs for a while and have got accustomed to them. All three have contracts and a good relationship with their employers, so at present they are relatively happy with their work situation. Myriam does live-in work and she too is happy with her employers, but would not mind having the possibility of moving to live-out work.

Nawal had a much worse experience of live-in domestic work. She is the only employee of a rich Italian family of five who live in a large three-story house. Nawal complained that she finds it hard to manage to complete the daily cleaning of the entire house. Her pay is lower than average because her employer considers that she lacks experience. Nawal's day starts at 7 a.m. with preparing the family breakfast and she does not get any rest until 10 p.m., but only when there are no guests. If there are people for dinner (and this happens quite often) Nawal's working day may finish at 2 a.m.

The relationship of Moroccan women with paid work in Barcelona is complex and is linked to the changes and differences in perception of domestic work in emigration mentioned above. There are women who have never worked in their country of origin and might enjoy (or not) the possibility/necessity of working once in Spain. There are women who are not happy about the fact of having to engage in paid work since this adds further burdens on them, particularly if they alone are responsible for their flats and families in Barcelona, without the help of other female members of the family as would be the case in their country.

According to one of the women of Al-Wafa, women work out of necessity and not out of choice:

> Women here have to work because with only one wage it's impossible to survive to the end of the month. The majority of women work here because they have to work. For men to work is their job but for women this is different.

Many Moroccan women in Barcelona aspire to the model of the woman, mother and wife maintained by her husband. On the other hand, there are women who have never been allowed to work (first by their fathers and subsequently by their husbands), and once in Barcelona enjoy the possibility of earning a wage and attaining a modicum of economic independence. There are also women who had to/could work in Morocco and for them a job in Barcelona can be either an improvement of the working conditions they were accustomed to (hours, pay, etc.) or a sharp decline involving a significant degree of deskilling. All this means that it is very difficult to generalise. These women's need or desire to work is linked with other elements of their migration experience, which will appear more clearly in the last section of this chapter.

For Moroccan women the obligation to send remittances is not as strong as for Filipinas (or for other female groups such as Dominicans). As Gregorio and Ramírez (2000: 268) have noted, in the case of Moroccan migration the responsibility for the maintenance of the family is shared. However there are exceptions. The sending of remittances seems to be particularly important for women who have widowed mothers, separated sisters with children, or who have left their own children behind to be cared for by their parents. Nawal, Nadira and Fhatiya send money monthly, ranging from 10,000 to 40,000 ptas depending on availability. Assja too, when she is in employment, sends money regularly. She said that she is the only one in her family who has helped her mother. Her husband does not want her to send money home since he has to support his own family and children from a previous wife, but Assja does it anyway. Other women of my sample send money on a less regular basis, generally to their sisters. Lubna for instance was sending money to her sister and her children to help them to study but currently she finds it more difficult to spare any money. Other women want to remit money but are in precarious circumstances; in some cases they are the recipients of help from their family in Morocco (Salwa, Jamila) or other countries (Batul is receiving help from her sister who lives in France). When Moroccan women manage to save any money their main goal is to buy a house back home, either for holidays or to return to live there.

The stories of Fhatiya and Assja – two women who were already engaged in paid work before migration – provide specific examples of Moroccan women's involvement in Barcelona's labour market.

Fhatiya

Fhatiya is thirty-six, she was a factory worker in Morocco and now is a full-time live-out domestic maid. She studied until she was seventeen in Meknes and once she left school she went to work in a garment factory were she stayed until she came to Spain. When she was eighteen she was forced to marry by her father and eight years later she initiated the divorce. Contrary to what happens generally, she paid all the costs of the divorce thanks to her job. She remained a while at her parents' house and then decided with a friend to try and improve her life by going abroad.

Fhatiya's first job in Barcelona was in a garment workshop. She had to sew clothes and was paid by piece. After this she had several jobs as a domestic until, through asking around, she found her current job. At present she works nine hours daily from Monday to Friday for a wealthy Catalan family. Although she does not like domestic work as such, Fhatiya is happy about her current work since she thinks that her employers treat her fairly. Here below is a typical day in Fhatiya's work:

> I get up at 7, I take a shower then I prepare breakfast for the child and prepare her clothes, washed and ironed to go to school. Then I go to work. I start at 9. I have to prepare breakfast, do the housework and shop. Then I have to prepare lunch and serve it at 2 o'clock. I eat in the kitchen with the guy who works as a waiter. Then I have to clear the table, wash and tidy up. If there are things to iron, I iron. I finish at 6. A lady goes and collects my child from school at 4.30 and stays with her until 6.30 when I arrive at home. When I'm home there is more work to do: clean, prepare dinner, wash the child...

Fhatiya keeps the money she earns for herself. She does not have a joint account with her new husband:

> He pays the rent and things like water, electricity and gas. I help him with the things that I like for the house. I use my money for the things I need. For instance, if I'm with a friend I can go to a bar to have a coffee, or shop for the child, these kind of things.

Another of Fhatiya's expenses is that of the baby-sitter. It has been her responsibility to sort out this arrangement that allows her to keep her job and also to pay for it. Her husband is free at the time when his daughter finishes school but, according to Fhatiya, he does not like to stay at home and look after the child, which he does not see as his responsibility. Fhatiya has also to send money back to Morocco to contribute to the expenses of the child she had from her first husband and who is now left in the care of her parents. She sends between 10,000 and 20,000 ptas (but not every month). When I asked her if her second husband minds about this, she replied that he cannot say anything since that is her own money.

Assja

Assja is illiterate and in Morocco had only temporary jobs in houses or hotels. She went to Barcelona for the first time thirteen years ago arriving with an Indian family she was working for in Morocco. She stayed only four months and then decided to go back home. She was working as live-in maid for a family of six and earning only 30,000 ptas monthly. Two years later she went back to Spain, this time alone, and found a job as a live-in maid in Malaga. She worked four years as live-in maid there but then changed that job because she was not getting on well with the other domestic, who was Spanish, employed in the house. Her new job in Malaga was fine but she was earning only 45,000 ptas which was not enough for her.

She then decided to move to Barcelona because she heard that wages were higher there. After three months in the city she found a job as domestic for a Jewish family. She was earning 65,000 ptas. She then left her job to get married to a fellow-national and for eight months she did not work. Since she could not find any live-out work and her family in Morocco was depending on her remittances, she decided to go back to work as live-in maid. She found a live-in job where they paid her well (120,000 ptas) but after fourteen months she left it because she only had one free day every two weeks and her marriage was starting to be strained. She then found another job as live-in where they paid her less (80,000 ptas) to look after a woman with cancer and her two sons. She did that until she decided that she wanted to stop doing live-in work and finally managed to find a job in a restaurant. As I said previously, both times Assja worked in a restaurant she did so without a contract and both times she was forced to resign after an accident. At the time of the interview she was looking for any kind of job although she was not prepared to do live-in work. The second time I met her she was working once more in a restaurant, again without a contract.

Settling in Barcelona

This section has looked at immigrant women as economic actors and at their various, though constrained, activities within Barcelona's labour market. The emergence of a housing problem for immigrants has also been explored, showing women's strategies to solve it. What has emerged in the arena of work is that Filipinas – thanks to their experience and reputation built over thirty years of specialisation – are at the top of the domestic service niche, as also happens in several other countries (see Chell 1997, 2000 and Tacoli 1999 on Italy and Lazaridis 2000 on Greece). Yet we can detect some changes, with younger women now obtaining jobs in other sectors, such as restaurants and also some low-level administrative jobs. Furthermore, some women are starting their own businesses, both as a full-time activity (e.g., shops, restaurants, hair-dressing salons) or as ways of complementing their income (as women do also in the Philippines).

Moroccan women, as I have repeatedly stated, are increasingly involved in paid work, although their participation is often influenced by their responsibilities for care work within their own families and a widespread low opinion among them of domestic work – one of the few sectors where they manage to find work. However there are changes here too, notably a decrease in the negative evaluation of domestic work if done in the migration setting, and an increased interest on the part of younger women to be engaged in paid work. Female-only migration flows based on the availability of jobs in the care and domestic sectors – similar to the ones pioneered by the Filipinas – seem to be developing also among Moroccan women, showing the importance of pull factors in shaping migration.

The money earned is used somewhat differently by the women belonging to the two groups. Filipinas are the main ones who are economically responsible for their transnational families and who manage the family budget. For Moroccans it is usually the man who is in charge of the family, with women's work seen merely as a help towards the family's budget. However, in spite of the ideal of the male breadwinner, many Moroccan women have found themselves as the economic pillar of their families – a role that gives them both new prestige and further burdens.

Transnational Families in Barcelona

This section considers the arena of the social and family relations of the two migrant groups. My objectives are to show the role and position of immigrant women within the transnational families they are forming or to which they belong, and to explore the consequences that their changing positionality and functions have for their life choices.

Filipino Women

At the time of the interview six of the women in my Filipino sample were married, four were separated, five were widowed and five were single. Among the single respondents, none was in a relationship at the time of the interview. The youngest of the single women is Annalyn, twenty-seven. She has not married yet, mainly because she had to work hard in order to help her family back home, but also because she wanted to postpone marriage in order to avoid making the wrong choice, something which she thinks is quite common in the Philippines:

> There was a friend and I had a feeling for him but you really have to suppress that feeling, you really have to think first – is he going to be responsible to raise a family?

I want a simple family, I want to settle in the Philippines, I want my house in the Philippines, I want three kids and I want somebody who can raise the family on his own, who can deal with life and be able to rise financially. I don't want somebody who drinks, some people are drinking and gambling, that's normal in the Philippines.

Victoria is thirty-seven, has never been in a relationship and is not sure whether she would like to marry in the future:

There have been several men who have courted me but I didn't give them any chance. When I was in the Philippines I was always thinking about helping my parents and to have a boyfriend is quite different, with a boyfriend many things can change and that's why I decided to leave it. Then when I came here my life was spent between work and home, work and home... I didn't have time to think about boyfriends. Besides now I'm already old...

Victoria dedicates her life to work, church activities and above all to help her family of origin for whom it seems that she has totally sacrificed herself.

Eleanor (forty) has had boyfriends in the past, but unlike Victoria she is constantly thinking about marriage. She feels ambivalent about her desire to have a partner and children and her fear of losing her freedom.

I had boyfriends but, I don't know, I'm having this problem of – you know – my independence, this is very important for me. One thing more, at my age, right now, I'm looking for – I'm thinking of the stability of a marriage, not like when I was twenty that I wasn't thinking about the future.

…

You know sometimes – it's not that I'm looking for the perfect man because the perfect man doesn't exist but there are things that I want to renounce and there are things that I don't want to renounce, that's the problem… What don't I want to renounce? My freedom. That's why I always tell my mum that I think I would prefer to have just a kid (without a husband), because, for example, if I want to go out I just tell my mum if she can take care of my son or my daughter and that's no problem. But if I'm married I can't tell my mum, 'Oh can you take care of my daughter and my husband because I want to go out'. It's quite different.

Right now my friends will call to go out to get a cup of coffee and talk and I'll go. But if I'm married I have to tell my husband, 'Can I go out?'!? You know – I am prepared to have a child but then the problem is also that if I'm going to have a child with a man I have to love him! Then it's quite difficult, so there are lot's of problems, oh my God! It's complicated, this is the problem of the women who are my age right now. It's a dilemma. You know, because women are very independent and it's not like before that you are educated to get married, to take care of your husband, to take care of your kids, not like now. That's why now I think that if your husband says that he wants to separate, you just say OK, I have my work, it's not like before.

Five women among my interviewees were widows and two of them had found new partners in Spain. Rosevilla and Feli have entered new relationships and these brought to them new problems. Rosevilla found a Gambian partner with whom she went to live and had a child (she already had four in the Philippines). The problems started as soon as she got pregnant because the two partners apparently did not have the same ideas about the relationship. Rosevilla was looking for a new companion and possibly a new husband but he did not seem to share her ideas and showed no interest either in her or in the child. In the last few years the relationship had stopped, although they are still living together, partly for the child and partly because neither of them can afford a flat on their own. Feli found a Spanish partner when her husband was still alive (they had effectively separated when Feli took her six children and left for Spain rather than following him to his new post in Liberia). With her new Spanish partner – whom she met at a party organised by her local supermarket – she had her seventh child. The problem for Feli is that her second daughter never accepted her mother's new partner and even less her new brother. After several arguments with her mother she left Spain and went to join her father in Liberia. In 1997 he died but the daughter has not came back to Spain and is still refusing to talk to her mother.

None of the women who were separated was in a relationship at the time of the interview. Many quoted their negative previous experiences in order to justify their decisions to discard the possibility of finding a new partner. In three of these four cases we are talking about separation instead of divorce because, as we saw in the previous chapter, divorce does not exist in the Philippines. However, the fact that divorce is illegal does not mean that there is no marital disruption. Men deserting the family and forming new ones seem to be quite common, according to the accounts of Filipinas I interviewed. Cori was left by her husband when her daughter was only three years old; he went off to form a new family with another woman. Necitas's husband did the same while she was already working in Spain and did not even tell her: she found out through her sister that he also had three children.

Even at the Church celebrations of the Filipino religious groups, I found this to be an issue which is often mentioned and debated. In one instance, I listened to the moving account of Manuela, whose husband had left her for another woman while she was in Barcelona working for the family; finally he repented and came to Spain to join his wife. While Manuela was talking several women in the audience were crying, possibly identifying with her experience.

Of the six women who are married, all have their husbands with them in Barcelona. Three met their husbands in the Philippines, and three couples were formed in Barcelona. Beatrice met her future husband in a religious group in the

Philippines, marrying him ten years later when he managed to emigrate to Barcelona by himself. Mirna sponsored the emigration of her husband to Barcelona. She had met him also in the Church and then had left for Spain to work temporarily to save enough money to form her new family. In the meantime her father died and she felt that she had to stay on in order to help her family of origin. Her employers helped her to get her husband to Barcelona through family reunion. The couple still do not live together because Mirna works as live-in maid. She stays with her husband only on Saturday nights.

Of the three women who met their partners in Spain, one married a Spaniard and two married Filipinos. Vivian met her Spanish husband at a birthday party of a friend and two years later they got married in the Philippines. Rosa met her Filipino husband through friends and Margarita met hers through his sister who was the owner of the flat were she was staying during her first period in Barcelona. Both couples got married in Barcelona because – having just arrived – they could not afford yet to travel back to the Philippines.

Thirteen of the women I interviewed had children, thirty-nine between them. Four of them had one child, one had two, four had three, one had four, two had five and one had seven. Of these thirty-nine, eighteen were born in the Philippines, fifteen were born in Spain, three in Laos, one in Iran and two in Sudan (the latter six are the children of Feli who had lived in several countries); thirty-one are living in Barcelona today. At the time of the interviews, eight women had all their children with them in Barcelona; one woman, Annie, had her only child in the Philippines being looked after by her brother and sister-in-law; and four women had some children with them and some in the Philippines.

Some women in my sample migrated when they were already married, leaving their children behind. As we saw in the case of Bologna, they did so because the family income was not enough to cover all the costs, in particular those related to children's education. Lola left when her three children were eighteen, eleven and five. With her remittances all three went to college and got degrees. Today her eldest daughter still lives in the Philippines and is currently a housewife; she takes care of her three small children while her husband is working in Spain. The two youngest ones are in Barcelona working as domestics. Priscilla left when her three children were ten, nine, and one. She then brought them to Spain when the oldest was fifteen and the youngest six. The oldest ones found it difficult to adapt in school, their major problem being the Catalan language which they had never studied before and which nobody in their household was speaking. They soon left school and are currently working as domestics. The youngest one (who did almost the entire school cycle in Barcelona) excelled at school and today is enrolled in English Literature at the university. She is paying her course by working as a part-time domestic helper.

Basilio went away when her youngest daughter was two years old and she reunited with her four daughters only after they finished their studies in the Philippines.

It was difficult to be far from them, for a mother like me that was very difficult. During the night I almost couldn't sleep thinking about them. I knew that they were fine with my mother-in-law but I couldn't stop always thinking of them. It's really very difficult.

The first two daughters did not actually complete their degrees in tourism and medical technology, the third got a diploma as a professional secretary and the fourth graduated as a nutritionist. Currently they are in Barcelona working respectively in an office, in a money-exchange shop, in a restaurant, and the fourth as a domestic.

The irony of this situation should not be lost: these women make incredible sacrifices for educating their children who, however, very often have no other option than repeating their parents' cycle and becoming trapped in the domestic work/service sector. My Filipino interlocutors in Barcelona were quite aware of this paradox. Here below is how Eleanor saw this problem:

Education is very important for Filipino parents. They want their children to finish college, to be somebody, the problem is that when they come here they can't choose. That's the disadvantage. That's why there are parents who are here right now and are saying, 'I don't know if I should send my daughter or my son to college because if I'm going to bring them here then they can't choose to follow what they have studied in the Philippines'. It's like a waste of time and waste of money and – I don't know, this is quite a dilemma.

I think that studying sometimes can be an advantage because if they have finished something they can go to another country where they can work with their studies. It's not just thinking as a waste of time and waste of money. That's why my friend who has a daughter was telling her, 'You have to study, that's the only thing I can give you, that's what we Filipino parents can give, education.'

Although they are aware of the fact that their children's studies will most likely not be of any direct use to them, Filipino mothers still prefer to invest in their children's education and give them tools that they hope will be useful to them, if not in Spain, then perhaps in another country were their English-based education can be recognised. Apart from the wastage of skills, another problem for these mothers is the relationship with their children. Not only have they had to endure long-term separation from their young children, but when they finally manage to reunite with them they find that their bond has weakened and mother and children have to start knowing each other again almost from scratch.

How to educate and keep a relationship with one's children at a great distance is another highly debated issue within the Filipino community. According to Eleanor, parents often try to compensate their absence by spoiling the children who in some cases, rather than studying, waste their parents' money:

Sometimes the problem is that parents try to give their children more money because they are not there, to supplement something that they cannot give, the caring and everything. And so they send the money. It's so easy to be giving the money because they are not there to guide them, they cannot say, 'Oh, no you cannot have that', because the children can say, 'Then what are you there for?' So they are being spoiled in the wrong way, that's the problem with the majority of these children.

If there comes a time when they are very conflictive the parents bring them here and that creates new problems because they have too much freedom here. So there is more conflict, because they grow up with their grandparents and with their aunties and so there is no more connection between parents and children, it's lost. Then they have to start all over again, both the parents and the children, it's quite difficult.

These are some of the reasons why the women who have married and had children in Barcelona try to keep them with them rather than sending them to be raised in the Philippines. Natalia for instance had only one daughter; she said that was a planned choice since she did not want to be obliged to send her children to the Philippines. All the women acknowledged that it is very difficult to raise children in Spain, having to work full-time and not having anybody to leave the children with (all Filipinos in Barcelona are involved in paid work). Beatrice and Annie could not cope with this situation and preferred to send their children to the Philippines. Annie, who is now separated from her husband, sent her daughter to the Philippines when she was six months in order to meet her father. Since Annie works as live-in maid she had no alternative than sending her daughter there to be cared for by her brother's family. She is planning to bring her to Barcelona when she is between ten and twelve, that is to say when she can look after herself. Annie sees her daughter for a month every two years.

Beatrice, who has three children, sent her eldest one with a friend back to the Philippines to be raised by her grandparents. She said that in Barcelona it was very difficult to look after her and she had no other option. Her daughter is still in the Philippines because she has started to study and does not want to interrupt her course of physiotherapy. She was due to come for a period in Barcelona in order to do the paperwork for getting Spanish nationality (Beatrice has acquired it and can now pass it on to her children) and then will go back to the Philippines to finish college. Once she gets her qualification, and with her new passport, she is planning to go to the US.

Other mothers managed to keep their children in Barcelona. However, this strategy implies higher expenses and different sacrifices. Margarita's employers allowed her to take her children to work when they were little, whereas Rosa made use of the kindergarten, relatives and baby-sitters. According to Clara, who is President of the Association of Filipino Women of Barcelona, there is a new trend in Filipino families that allows working mothers to keep their children with them:

Before when a baby was born here they would take him to the Philippines to be looked after by the grandparents, but now they bring over the grandparents to look after the kids here so that the mothers can carry on working. Grandparents stay at home, go and collect the children from school and feed them. When the woman comes back to the flat she is so tired that she can only eat and rest. Now she has her parents here to do all the house work and so she is more comfortable. It's a new trend.

Forming a family in Barcelona and keeping it united has obvious advantages for Filipino women, such as avoiding the pain of separation and having the possibility of raising their own children. However, as we already saw in the previous chapter, having children who are born in Spain and feel Spanish brings new complications. For instance, the migrant mothers cannot migrate further as easily as their single counterparts or those women who left their children in the Philippines. As we saw with the case of Priscilla, she tried on two occasions to settle in other countries but both times she had to come back because her family was not willing to follow her. Vivian is totally dissatisfied with the possibilities that Catalonia offers to her but cannot leave because she has a Spanish husband and a daughter. She is hoping to be able to go to the Philippines when her husband retires (but he is only forty-two!). Rosa's children made it clear to her that they do not want to go to the Philippines. She has decided that she will go there when she retires (she too is only forty two), leaving them behind. She says that she does not want to be a burden for her children and therefore when she will no longer work she prefers to go away and stay in her small house that she bought in the Philippines for this purpose. Margarita too wants to go back; her children have no intention of following her. Her plan is to wait until they finish their studies or get married and then go.

Rosevilla's and Maricel's stories (below) show some of the challenges Filipino women have had to face in trying to support their families back home. Rosevilla tried to create a new family in the context of arrival, whereas Maricel's efforts have been dedicated to reuniting and recreating hers in Barcelona. Both had to face incredible difficulties and are struggling to cope with the consequences of their transnational lives.

Maricel

Maricel now lives with her grown-up children in Barcelona. Her husband died seven years ago when she was already in Barcelona. During her first four years in Spain she was without 'papers' and because of that and because she had to pay back her considerable debts she was not able to go back to the Philippines and see her children. She had left them with her mother and it was to her that Maricel sent, every month for ten years, virtually her entire wage.

Maricel came to Barcelona when her children were aged between five and thirteen. Through her hard work as a live-in domestic she managed to support them all in their studies. Two of them graduated, the eldest one in the nautical institute, and the youngest one in architecture. After finishing his studies the older one worked for two years on a ship but then Maricel convinced him to come to Spain with the rest of the family. After getting her residency permit in Spain, Maricel started the paperwork for Spanish nationality. In 1997 she received her new passport and this allowed her to get her children to Spain. Maricel's youngest son is currently spending his holidays in the Philippines, where he is drafting his first project as an architect: the family house, which is being built with Maricel's savings and remittances.

In spite of Maricel's efforts to invest in her children's education, the possibilities for them to use their degrees and diplomas in Barcelona are scarce. When I asked her about this she replied:

At the beginning I wanted them to study here. The problem is that the language is very different and they would have had to start from the beginning. If they had to start from the beginning it's a lot of money. Here college is more expensive than in the Philippines and with my wage here I cannot afford it. Here I couldn't have made it but there I could pay for them, then if they want they can look for a job in the US or in London because their studies are in English.

Maricel is now happy that she has managed to reunite with her children but she is currently suffering for what she perceives as lack of closeness with them, caused by ten years of living apart:

I left my children with my mother because my mother didn't have children in the house anymore because they all went to other countries. My children know my mother very well but don't know me. I suffer a lot for this, they like my mother a lot and they love only her. But for me it's good because she's my mother. I'm waiting, one day – one day they will love me... But my children are good because they behave very well with me, the only thing is they love my mother more. Yes, sometimes they also love me but not like a mother, just like a friend. Since they lived with my mother everything is different.

At present Maricel's hopes for the future are to see her children fixed up. She says that she will continue to work and dedicate her energies to their well-being. She does not have plans for herself. After her bad experience with her first husband she is not interested in having a new partner and prefers to enjoy some years of peace and tranquillity.

Rosevilla

Rosevilla works full-time in a restaurant in a seaside resort twenty minutes from Barcelona. She also lives nearby. She got married in the Philippines when she was sixteen and had four children there. When her youngest son was one year old her husband died. She then started to do all sorts of jobs in order to provide for her family. Her last job before leaving the Philippines was to make Venetian blinds for a factory from her house. She then decided to try to improve her family's situation by migrating to Spain. She paid an 'agency' with money lent by her brothers.

She worked for two years as a live-in maid and during that period repaid her debts and sent substantial remittances. Then things started to change. One day when she was going to the centre of town to phone her family she met her Gambian partner. Rosevilla needed some help and he was the only person there who spoke English and could understand her. From that day on he was waiting for her every Saturday near the station when she was going to Barcelona to join in church activities. They started a relationship and soon after Rosevilla went to live with him. She was flattered by receiving so much attention after spending two years alone working extremely hard in the house of her employer. Rosevilla thought she had found a companion with whom to form a new partnership and family, but things did not go quite like that.

They were sharing the flat with one of his friends and often Rosevilla was the only one working and paying the flat's expenses. Then, she became pregnant and problems started to arise. Her partner wanted Rosevilla to have an abortion but she decided to go ahead with the pregnancy. He did not take any interest in the child nor did he help Rosevilla in any way. Often he was out of work, spending his time out with his friends and leaving all the responsibilities to Rosevilla. When I visited them for the interview they did not have any running water because he had promised Rosevilla that he would pay the outstanding bill but had not done so.

Soon after the baby (who is now six) was born, Rosevilla decided to end the relationship. But she is still living with her former partner.

> The relationship has finished but we are still living together but each of us goes his own way. At the beginning it was difficult but now I got used to it and also for me it's better because each of us has his own freedom. The truth is that if I had another place to go, a flat, I would take all my things and go away with my child. Look, now I'm really tired because I'm working a lot and I have got many problems.

All these tensions within the household have affected Rosevilla's health and she is now suffering form hypertension caused by stress. She had a period out of work prescribed to her by the doctor. An additional strain for Rosevilla is that she cannot share her suffering with anybody since she feels too embarrassed to explain her situation to her family in the Philippines, to her sister who is in Italy, or to her cousins in Barcelona.

> I cannot tell them what I'm going through because in the Philippines you don't do what I did, that you meet a man like that... They would tell me that I cannot say that I made a mistake because I'm not a child, I should know what I'm doing.

Rosevilla is now paying quite dearly for her 'mistake', since she has to work very hard to make ends meet without any help from her former partner who, even when he is working, hardly contributes to the flat expenses and does not give anything for the child. She works as an assistant cook from 9.30 a.m. to 4 p.m. and from 8 p.m. until 12 or 1 a.m., depending on the work. Although it is very tiring, Rosevilla is happy with her work and she would rather stay at work than in her flat. She has only one free day a week – Mondays – but often spends it working in houses to raise some more money.

Rosevilla finds it difficult to educate Johnny, her child, the way she would like due, in her view, to his father's bad influence:

> There are differences also in the way to educate children. I want Johnny to respect his parents and I also want him to be tidy but he copies from his father who doesn't do anything. In this situation how can I tell the child to be tidy? His father should give him an example.

Another reason why Rosevilla finds it difficult to transmit her values to her child is that she can hardly spend any time with him. She takes him to school in the morning, but when she goes again to work in the afternoon Johnny has not came back yet. When she returns home at night the child is already sleeping. Rosevilla works during weekends when the child is not going to school. To obviate what she perceives as a problem but which she cannot avoid, a couple of times each month she keeps Johnny home from school on a Monday and they spend the day together in Barcelona. One of their typical treats is to go and have lunch on the top-floor terrace of the department store El Corte Ingles, or go to McDonald's.

Rosevilla suffers because she feels that she is neglecting both her son in Barcelona and her four children in the Philippines, whom she had been able to visit only twice in ten years. Besides, she is not even sending large remittances as do most of the Filipino 'distant parents'. In spite of these problems Rosevilla says that her children in the Philippines are very supportive to her.

> Now my children are worried for me because before they don't have a father and I was both the father and the mother for them and they don't forget what I did for them. That's why my oldest son is now telling me that when he's

coming to Spain he's going to work and I can go back to the Philippines and he will support me. But I said that I don't want that. I have to work, while I can.

Rosevilla is currently doing the paperwork to take Spanish nationality so that she will be able to get all her children to Barcelona, although one of them is not enthusiastic about this since he is at college with a government scholarship.

Getting Spanish nationality will also be useful for Rosevilla's other son, Johnny. Although he was born in Spain, as a child of foreigners he is classified as a foreigner. What is worse from Rosevilla's point of view is that he is considered Gambian and not Filipino; for this reason he can travel alone with his father but could not travel to the Philippines alone with Rosevilla.

Rosevilla's hope for the future is that her eldest son will come to Barcelona and through his work will contribute to the family income. With two salaries Rosevilla hopes to be able to leave her current flat and partner and go to live somewhere else with her sons. Little by little she hopes that also the other ones will join them. She also hopes that her eldest son can provide a better role model for Johnny and that he can help her raise the child according to what she considers Filipino values.

Moroccan Women

Among the eighteen Moroccan women I interviewed in Barcelona, two were single, ten were married and six were divorced. The two single women are Nawal (thirty-two) and Lubna (forty-eight). The former had delayed marriage initially because she was studying at university and then, when her mother died, she had to leave her studies and start working to help her family of origin (her father had formed a new family and therefore had new responsibilities) and take up what had been her mother's role. At present she is engaged to an Iranian man whom she met on the doorstep of her friend's flat on her first day in Barcelona. He has already proposed to her and wants to get married soon. Nawal would prefer to take things more slowly but said she was happy about the idea of marriage as long as it does not imply going to Iran, something she is not prepared to do. Lubna has decided to remain single after her fiancé married another woman after three years of engagement to her.

> I thought that if I came here I could leave my mother in peace with her new family and I could live on my own, because I couldn't live on my own in my city because people talk badly about a woman who is not married. For us it's not like here that when a girl is eighteen she can go and live on her own, we can't do that, we always have to live with the family. So I thought that for me it was better to go out of the country than to stay within the family.

Of the ten women who are married, three have their husbands in Morocco. Selma, as we have seen, came to Barcelona when her husband took a second wife. He did so because Selma was not able to have more children. Although officially still married, Selma has little contact with her husband who now has the numerous family he wanted. Latifa and Mbarka married recently in Morocco when they were already living and working in Barcelona; rather like their Filipino counterparts – and countering common assumptions that see Muslim women only as followers of male breadwinners – they are the ones with jobs abroad and the ones who are planning to get their husbands to Spain through family reunion. This seems to be a new trend among young Moroccan women who, like their Filipino counterparts, migrated when they were still single. After a few years abroad they either marry the boyfriends they had before migration or find new partners during their annual holidays back home. None of my interviewees had married a compatriot already living in Spain, but this is clearly another possibility. Rhannou's husband was also the dependent who entered Spain for marriage. Often, as with many Filipino couples, the requirements for family reunion are so difficult to meet that the partners (both male and female) decide to give up waiting and enter Spain as illegal immigrants, hoping to regularise later.

The number of Moroccan women who initiated the immigration of their husbands to Spain is the same (three) as that of the women in my sample who arrived to reunite with their husbands. Nabila, Jasmina and Laila joined their husbands several years after these had settled in Barcelona. Jasmina (and her two children) had to wait more than two years before being able to join her husband in Barcelona, but she managed to do it legally through family reunion. Nabila, instead, lived for seven years with her family away from her husband while he was working in various European countries. When he finally settled in Spain, she joined him there with her first two sons, but had to do so illegally. Also Laila waited six years while her husband tried to sort out the papers for family reunion, but finally decided to pay and come as an illegal immigrant.

Nadira married a Spaniard she had met when he was on holiday in Morocco. She entered Spain with a special visa for marriage and the wedding took place at the Moroccan consulate in Madrid. In order for Nadira to marry him he had to convert to Islam. Nadira says she comes from a family that is very open and that she did not have any problems in marrying a foreigner, but she was not prepared to go against her religion and marry a non-Muslim.

The other two women in my sample who are married came to Spain after having divorced their first husbands in Morocco. Once in Spain, they decided to get married again, in both cases to other Moroccans. Assja (forty-two) got married for the first time when she was twelve and went to live with her husband's family. Problems started to arise mainly because her mother-in-law was reproaching her for not having any children. After seven years of marriage she decided to grant him the divorce and went back to her family. Assja was not thinking about getting married again; she had her job and a flat she was sharing with a friend. Her second husband started to follow her until he proposed to her and Assja accepted. They got married in Barcelona five years ago. After several years in which Assja continued to work as live-in domestic (she says she could not find anything else) they are now finally living together and Assja is satisfied with her new relationship.

Fhatiya (thirty-six) got married for the first time when she was eighteen, forced by her father. She had a son. After eight years she initiated a divorce. Once in Spain, like Assja, she was not thinking about getting married again but finally met a new partner and changed her mind. Her husband is a Moroccan with Spanish nationality who has been living in Barcelona for thirty years and now works as a waiter. Six women in my sample are divorcees who at least up to now have decided not to remarry. All of them were abandoned by their husbands, who left them for other women. Five of them had divorced in Morocco and came to Spain in order to make a fresh start. Myriam was married for only one year and did not have any children. She took advantage of the possibility of reaching Spain by travelling with her brother and now she is satisfied to have a job and her own money. She does not discard the possibility of marrying again but she is not looking for a partner at present. She will marry again only to a man who suits her, she said.

Jamila (forty-two) married very young (at fifteen) and at thirty she found herself alone with two daughters to support and no job. She is now in Barcelona hoping to be able to find a job and support herself and her children. Amina (fifty-eight) also married very young (thirteen), had a daughter and had never worked in her life. She decided to leave in order not to be a burden for her daughter, who now has her own family in Morocco. In Barcelona she started a new life. Salwa (twenty-nine) divorced soon after having her son. As we saw previously, she started a relationship with another man with whom she fell pregnant. Batul divorced twice, the first time in Morocco and the second time in Barcelona when she was pregnant with her first daughter. Now she has no intention of marrying again. Halima (forty-two) divorced nine years ago when she was already in Spain because her husband had an affair with a Spanish woman. She has three children.

Twelve of the women interviewed had children – twenty in all. The majority of these women had only one child (six); four of them had two and two had three. Among these twenty children, five were born in Spain and fifteen in Morocco; fourteen of them are living in Barcelona today. The children left in Morocco comprise: the sons of Laila, who left them in the care of her mother while she was looking for a flat where she could reunite her family; the daughters of Jamila, whom she also left in the care of her mother and sister while she came to Spain in order to look for a way of supporting them and possibly bringing them to Spain; the son whom Fhatiya had with her first husband who is being looked after by her parents; and Amina's daughter, who is already an adult woman and has formed her own family in Morocco.

As already evidenced in Chapter 3, in order to understand women's position and role within transnational families, we have to take into account various factors, such as the stage in the woman's life course and the stage in the development of her household. Older or 'traditional' women who arrived in Spain in order to reunite with their husbands often find it difficult to accept that in addition to being responsible for the domestic realm they now have to involve themselves in paid work, since their husbands' wage is generally not enough to live on. According to Farida, of Al-Wafa, Moroccan women's role should not be that of engaging in paid work, which she sees essentially as men's job. Not all women see the issue of paid work in this way. Nabila, for instance, who is now doing a few hours per week of cleaning, said that she would like to work more. However, in line with Farida's comment, she is not prepared to work full-time since this will mean undermining her domestic role and her responsibilities towards her three children, her husband and her house.

As was the case for some of the Moroccan women of the older generation like Nabila, younger wives too often have the problem of not being able to reunite with their husbands as soon as they would like. Both Laila and Sakira were left several years with their families in Morocco waiting for their husbands to get them to Spain. During this time, remittances can be sporadic or non-existent. Sakira could cope only with the help of relatives she had in other European countries, whereas Laila had to invent her own survival strategies:

It was very hard for me to be there alone with two children but I was working – he [the husband] didn't like that I went out, it was worse than when he was in Morocco… Every week he called asking were I was and what I was doing – so I didn't tell him about my job. I opened a small nursery, I rented a place and set up a nursery. On top of this during July and August, the months when people celebrate weddings, I was doing the drawings with henna for the brides. With this I was earning very well but he didn't like the fact that I was doing it because at the parties there are both men and women and he didn't want me to go. When he called I would lie to him.

When these young wives finally manage to arrive in Spain and reunite with their husbands, things often start to appear less rosy than in their plans. On the one hand there are the problems connected with the context of arrival, which can be less receptive than these women had thought. One major problem of the last few years, as we have seen in the previous section, is that of housing.

On the other hand there are the problems connected with rejoining a spouse after several years in a totally different context. An additional factor is that these young women are less prepared to accommodate and give in than their older counterparts, so some marriages end in separation. Here is how Sakira describes the problems she encountered when she joined her husband in Spain, and how all of a sudden her life changed:

I separated from him but I still don't have a divorce. Many problems – I'm suffering a lot because I didn't come to work, I came to stay with my husband, and then everything changed. I wanted to carry on studying but I had to get my papers, and my child was with my mother, I had to get her here, she came, he didn't see the child, I had to work for the child.

Things that we imagine, they are not that way, I have to work, obviously, but I had never worked, not even in my house. Many things happened here in Spain, people think that when we come here we improve our situation, but this is not an improvement, it's suffering.

Laila too had great expectations on her arrival in Spain. She never had a good relationship with her husband and her life had already changed for the worse when her family convinced her to marry him. But she hoped that things would change in Spain and that she would start all over again with her family reunited in Barcelona. At first things started to go well with her husband:

Since I came here he started to change a bit, he's changing – for instance, now he doesn't want me to wear the veil, he tells me, 'Take off the veil', and he takes me to the restaurant to get something to eat. He has changed a bit. It's better now. He lets me go out, if I need to go and buy something he lets me do it, it's better. Now it's better and it's quite good.

Unfortunately things then started to deteriorate again for Laila. After she managed to find a flat, her husband started to shut her in there when he went to work. He checks on her, gets extremely jealous and at times prevents her from going out even to do the shopping, which has meant that on some occasions she was locked in the house without food. He also keeps the mobile phone, which prevented me from being able to get in contact with Laila and means that she can not communicate with anybody. During the two months that she was in charge of looking for a flat, Laila acquired a good knowledge of the city and also of the services available in it. This became an element that frightened her husband, who probably feared her skills and the possibility that she would abuse them and became 'too independent'. With the collaboration of her brother-in-law – who had been given the task by his brother of 'escorting' Laila when she went around town – she went for help at the NGO where I worked as a volunteer and where I had met her for the first time when she came to look for a flat. The head of the service told me that Laila was desperate when she saw her. She listened to her story and subsequently put her in contact with the social worker that ran a centre for abused women. Laila had to decide whether she saw ways of improving her current situation in order to carry on with her marriage, or leave her husband. If she opted for the latter course, the social workers would accommodate her in a protected flat until she was able to restart a new life independently. Laila was faced with a difficult choice: breaking a marriage can be difficult for any woman but for a recently immigrated woman it is even more so. First of all, because Laila has a residency permit that depends on that of her husband, and secondly because without the economic help of her husband it would be extremely hard for her to be able to get to a position to earn enough to maintain herself and be able to bring over her two children who are still in Morocco. At the time of writing I do not know what choice Laila has made.

For the (few) women who are the initiators of migration, the arrival of their partner can also signify changes and problems. Rhannou got accustomed to her independence, was happy in her job and had a lot of contacts and friendships in Palma de Majorca where she was living. With the arrival of her husband she had to renounce all of that and move to Barcelona where she did not know anybody. She also got pregnant, something she had not planned and that she was not looking forward to. For sure, not all the reunions turned out to be as problematic as the ones described above; however, the adjustment period can be difficult for both partners since it is often accompanied by additional strains such as the difficulty of getting a flat, lack of papers, or the precariousness of a job.

The families formed by partners who were both living in Barcelona seem to have fewer problems, probably because both partners are aware of the difficulties there are in the city and share the same expectations. Both Assja and Fhatiya said they were satisfied with their relationships. The problems faced by these women who are more settled in the city and in stronger unions are different. The main one is the difficulty of combining productive and reproductive tasks. The challenge of reaching a satisfying balance for these women is exacerbated by the fact that they see as totally unsatisfying the kind of paid jobs they are doing in Barcelona. They feel torn between family and work, but without the compensation that a satisfying job can give. The possibility of earning a wage does not seem to be valued greatly by the women I interviewed, since most of it is dedicated to expenses related to the house and the children.

Moreover, the arrival of children brings these women new commitments and responsibilities which are less easy to meet than in Morocco where they had the support of the extended family and in many cases did not need to engage in paid work. The difficulties of raising children are even greater for divorced women. This is how Lubna explained it:

> The two of us, as you know, don't have children and things are easier. People who are alone without children don't have many problems. If you become unemployed this can be a problem but later you'll find another job, but for women who have children it's much more difficult. For mothers it's very hard.

In order to avoid these difficulties some women are forced to leave their children in Morocco to be cared for by their families until their position in Spain gets more settled and their children grow a bit older. Both Laila and Jamila were waiting to be in a position to allow them to finally reunite with their children. Moroccan women do not seem as prepared as their Filipino counterparts to endure long-term separation from their children, unless it is under exceptional circumstances. One such circumstance can be remarrying, in which case, as we have already noted, it can become difficult to bring children from a previous marriage into the new one. Salwa, who is a divorcee, decided to go to Barcelona with her son (who is now five) but she is aware that this will make it very difficult for her to marry again. Fhatiya left her child in Morocco and could marry again. However, it is now very difficult for her to bring her child into her new family. Below is how Salwa described her current situation:

> For the moment I can't marry because I have a son and I want somebody that is going to treat him well, because I already got married once, I have a child, what else do I need? I only need to work – but I would like to marry because I don't like the idea of ending up alone because when my son will grow up he'll get married, he'll not be on my side.
>
> But to find a man who will support you, who will be on your side and who will look after your child as if it was his own, it's difficult to find. If I have a husband with whom I'm in love but who shouts at my child, I wouldn't accept it, if he beats my child, I wouldn't accept it – and so a lot of problems will start for me: don't beat the child who's not your child, don't beat him! Don't shout at him! But can I tell him not to touch the child because he's not his son if I don't work and he is the one who works? When I'll ask him for money to buy something for the child he can reply, 'If I can't beat him, if I can't shout at him, I also can't buy him anything, he's not my son.'
>
> It's something that I have in my head that I can't get married if I'm not sure that the man I'm going to marry is not going to treat my child well. Since I'm here in Spain, if I work I don't need a husband [laughs], thus I only have to work, educate my child well, give him all he needs and that's all.

An issue that concerns all Moroccan mothers with children who are growing up in Catalonia is their education. Nadira feels that she has to transmit Moroccan culture and values to her five-year-old daughter. Every Saturday afternoon she takes her to Arabic classes. She is also teaching her the Koran and Muslim values. However Nadira finds it difficult to educate her daughter in such values, partly because Fatima is the only Muslim child in her school, and partly because she feels that such values are not appreciated and are actually looked down by Catalan society. Twice a week Nadira goes for coffee with the other mothers of children at her daughter's school. When they have these gatherings she feels that, in a way, they are chiding her and they recommend that she abandons her customs:

> The mothers tell me that I'm in a European country now and that I shouldn't do Ramadan. They also don't understand why my husband does it. They are not religious and they look at me as a bit odd. But I don't care, I prefer to carry on like this and to explain the Koran to my daughter.

When the children of Moroccan mothers grow older and become adolescent, many mothers start to worry about how they should deal with them now that they live in a society where the values that their children learn at school and with friends contrast with those which the mothers are accustomed to and would be the dominant ones if they still lived in Morocco. According to one of the teachers at Bayt Al Taqfa – an NGO which offers language courses to Arab women – an issue that her students were particularly keen to discuss was that of the parent–child relationship. What preoccupies several of the women I interviewed is the excessive liberty that in their view young people enjoy in Spain. Mbarka, who is recently married, hopes that she will have her children back in Morocco (after she has saved enough by working in Barcelona):

> To have children here means a lot of problems – here families give a lot of freedom to their children. Really a lot, we don't have the freedom to go out in the streets, to take drugs, to smoke, to have mini-skirts up to here, it's not like that.
>
> Here there are young girls of sixteen or eighteen who go and live with their boyfriends. We don't do this, we don't have these things. I don't like that. In Morocco if you have a boyfriend you can't go out with him and do what you like, you go to your house and he goes to his until the day of the marriage. Nothing more. Here it's not like that, here you can make love with him and do everything with him, that's not good.

As we can infer from the above extract, the problem of the education of children refers mainly to girls. Boys can enjoy much more freedom (as they do in Morocco); it is for girls that the difference between the way in which their mothers had been educated and the models that Spanish society offers are more divergent. Parents would like their daughters to be serious, respectful, conform to Muslim values and not flirt with boys until the time of a formal engagement that will lead to marriage. Most young Moroccan girls do respect the values and the teaching of their parents, are serious and studious, and wish to marry a Muslim partner. What they do not accept is the restriction of their freedom in comparison to their friends, the fact that they cannot go out like the others do, and also that they cannot be seen to be associating with boys by their families.

Some of these girls do well at school but often, once they finish the baccalaureate, prefer to leave their studies and work. In many cases this happens against the parents' will, who dream of having a child at university. Some of these Moroccan children see the sacrifices that their parents had to make for them and for their families, and now that they are older and have more tools (linguistic, educational, etc.) than their parents, they feel that they have to help them. Selma's son, whom she brought to Barcelona when he was sixteen and maintained for several years there, is now giving back his support to his mother. He now has a job as a waiter and together with his cousin (who has come to live with them) is now paying for the rent and some of the expenses of the flat where the three are living.

The two case-stories below exemplify some of the issues discussed above, in particular the changes and new challenges that migrant women have to face when forming a family and having children in the country of destination. Fhatiya remarried in Barcelona and had her second child there, whereas Batul remarried and divorced for the second time in Catalonia where she had her first and only daughter.

Fhatiya

As we have already seen, Fhatiya got married at eighteen, forced by her father:

> Our customs are different from here, you can't say to your father that you don't want to marry, if you say no they'll think that you have got somebody else, so I got married.

But Fhatiya could not cope with this marriage:

> You know when you get to your house – it's like if you eat a meal that you don't like, you make an effort to eat it, you can chew it, it goes down, you can do it, but then you throw it up. Out, I throw it out.

After eight years of marriage Fhatiya could not take it any longer and – unusual for a woman – asked for and obtained a divorce. From that union she had a son. After divorcing she went back with the child to her family of origin and subsequently decided to migrate to Spain, leaving him in the care of her parents. Once in Spain Fhatiya had no intention of marrying again but changed her mind and married a Moroccan man who had lived thirty years in Catalonia. When I asked her how this second marriage was turning out she replied: 'So-so' – but then added that it was better than the first one because she chose her own partner. But she now feels the isolation and the lack of family support in Catalonia:

> On the one hand Spain is good, on the other hand without family and without anybody – you are living like a foreigner and you don't have any family around you, it's not the same as if you were in your country with your family. I feel lonely.

Sometimes because of the loneliness she says that she thinks of going back to Morocco but then adds that she cannot do it, now that she has a daughter. Fhatiya did not want to talk much about her son in Morocco (he is now twelve) but admitted that it is hard to live apart from him. She keeps contact with him by phone and she visits him every one or two years. The boy apparently constantly asks Fhatiya why she is there and he is in Morocco and tells her that he wants to be with her. When I asked her what she replies to him she said:

Nothing. I always tell him that I cannot look after him here.

The economic reason is only part of the story since both Fhatiya and her husband have full-time jobs. Probably Fhatiya shares part of the doubts expressed by Salwa about bringing the child of a previous marriage to live with her new husband.

In the future Fhatiya hopes to be able to bring her son to Spain but she will do so 'when he's a bit older'. She hopes that both her children will study so that 'they'll turn out better than me and life will turn out better for them'. At present her life is quite hard, divided between her job and her domestic responsibilities. Although her husband provides for most of the expenses of the family, Fhatiya is the only one responsible for the domestic chores and the care of their child and she has to carry out these onerous duties on top of her daily nine hours of paid work. In order to be able to do it she is forced (like many Spanish women) to buy out at least two hours daily of her home-based tasks; and since that is seen as one of her responsibilities, she is the one who pays for the baby-sitter.

Batul

Three years ago Batul's second marriage ended and all of a sudden she found herself pregnant, without a husband, a job, and ill-prepared to deal with her new situation. As she herself explains:

He left me and – you know Moroccan men are not the same as Spanish men, they are hard. He wants that his woman doesn't work, that she doesn't go out in the streets a lot, you know? And the woman suffers, when her husband leaves her she' s like a child, she can't get out on her own – she's scared – she can't work, she can't speak very well, she can't – many problems. Now thank God I'm fine, not like before.

One day Batul discovered that he was seeing another woman; when she confronted him, he denied it and because Batul was persistent he gave her a slap:

One day he slapped me in the face because he didn't want to talk. 'I shut up? That can't be! You beating me, *cabron*!? That can't be. Take your things and get out of this house', I told him.

Batul sent him away and together with her cousin started to look for a cheaper flat in the village near Barcelona were she was living. The people of the village (Gavà) helped them a lot. When the baby was only two months old Batul started to work in a restaurant. In order to be able to do so she had to look for a baby-sitter. She coped like that for a year and then when she could not carry on any longer she decided to take Nadira – her daughter – to Morocco.

> I was working in the restaurant and earning 100,000 ptas and paying 50,000 ptas to this woman. Then I thought why do I have to suffer here, work really hard and then pay electricity, water, the baby-sitter and when it's the end of the month I don't have a penny!
>
> After a year I left this woman and called Morocco to say that my daughter now had all the papers and that I was going to leave her in Morocco for a while. My father and my family were all very happy! I left her in Morocco for three years. Now it's just two years that she's back here. I was calling her every day and crying. When I left her there I was really out of my mind! Then my family helped her, my brothers were very nice to her. She was loving my brothers and my father more than me, I swear it. Now when we go to Morocco she doesn't want to come back, she cries.

After some time spent in Gavà, Batul's cousin helped her to find a sizeable yet cheap flat in Barcelona. At that point she decided to bring Nadira back with her. Batul still did not have a regular job and was doing only sporadic hours of cleaning but she could cope with the help she was receiving from her family in Morocco and above all from her sister in France. At present Batul is doing a course of job training and because of that and because she has a child to bring up she is currently receiving a kind of unemployment benefit of 53,000 ptas per month. She hopes to be able to find a regular job soon.

Life for Batul in Barcelona has been hard at times but she has no intention of going back to Morocco, even though her family have asked her several times to do so.

> In my family they are all asking me why I don't go back to Morocco, but I don't want to go. You know what happens is that my daughter is from here, she has got a father who has Spanish nationality and she has Spanish papers. When my daughter grows older there will be a lot of problems, she would tell me that she doesn't like to work in Morocco, that she wants to work in Spain, a lot of problems. It's better for me to stay here, now I'm suffering but one day I'll be fine.

Living in Transnational Families: Constraints and Opportunities

In this section I have looked at the family as an important – although ambivalent – element that has to be taken into account when analysing female migration. It is ambivalent because it both constrains and enables immigrant women; that is to say the family is both the unit where some of the inequalities that force women to migrate are articulated, and the safe haven that provides support and protection at difficult times. Often these two elements coexist within the same family and become apparent at different moments of the women's migratory experience.

As for the two groups analysed, I uncovered changes in their familial arrangements that are the result both of the migratory experience itself and of the conditions in the receiving society. For Filipinas we can note changes in gender roles, with women acquiring more independence as a result of their jobs and control over the migratory networks, although often this independence is obtained at a high price and with extreme self-sacrifice. Women who migrated when single are marrying later than the average age in the Philippines and having fewer children. This is both a choice due to changed attitudes towards children and the desire to bring them up better, and a consequence of the difficulty of having children with little institutional support for full-time (and more) working mothers. Filipinas are at the centre of transnational families and networks: through their work they maintain family members in the Philippines and through their contacts and rights acquired in Spain (e.g., nationality) they can sponsor the migration of children and parents to Spain and beyond.

Migration is seen as an opportunity by Moroccan women of different types of civil status: for married women it is seen as enabling them to get away from the control of the extended family; for divorcees it is a possibility to start a new life by becoming economically independent; for single women it is an opportunity to earn more and achieve personal aspirations. My account has shown how the reality of life in Barcelona in part frustrates some of these aspirations. Like their Filipino counterparts, Moroccan women living in Barcelona tend to have few children (two on average), but in contrast to Filipinas they tend to keep them with them if at all possible. They leave their children in the care of their families of origin only for limited periods, unless the woman is a divorcee who has remarried. Moroccan mothers want to raise their children personally although their education (particularly of daughters) in the receiving society is an issue that worries many of them. An important change in family life brought about by migration is women's increased involvement in paid work, but without the corresponding involvement of Moroccan men in care and domestic work. Moreover these women have lost the help of the female kin they had in their country. The new burdens that these changes put on Moroccan women and their lack of satisfaction with the jobs they encounter in Barcelona results in the fact that some of them are now longing for the ideal of the full-time mother and wife.

Conclusions

The first section of this chapter introduced some of the women migrating to Barcelona and their reasons for doing so. Economic factors certainly play an important role in setting in motion these migration flows, but what seems to be more important for understanding female migration is the interplay between economic motives and other factors, such as women's roles and positions within families and kin groups. We saw how women of both national groups migrate in order to help various members of their families of origin; they move to save enough to create their own family; to reunite with their families (parents or husbands); they go abroad to get away from oppressive familial situations at home; they leave because their position (e.g., as single mothers or divorcees) is despised or simply because they want to remain single and avoid unwanted familial responsibilities in societies where this is not an accepted option. The chapter also explored how women have access to migration and exposed the arbitrariness of the categories illegal/legal in relation to the migratory experiences of the women at the centre of this study.

The second section discussed the settlement process of Filipino and Moroccan women in Barcelona, looking at the problems of housing and women's insertion in the local labour market. Both groups are highly involved in domestic work, providing important services for the city and playing a crucial supporting role for the maintenance of middle-class families. The section also revealed the different attitudes and perceptions towards paid work of the two groups. Domestic work is valued negatively by Moroccan women but not so by Filipinas, although there are changes underway, with Moroccan women beginning to look more favourably on domestic work (if done in the migration setting) and Filipinas getting fed up with their participation in this sector. The section also tried to document immigrant women's participation in other sectors (restaurants, shops, their own businesses, etc.) to provide a wider picture of their changing labour-market profile. The final part of the section identified some differences in the way women of the two groups manage and spend the money they earn, with Filipinas generally responsible for the family budget and Moroccan women considered as supplementary earners.

The final section addressed the issue of the family as an important – although ambivalent – element shaping female migration and settlement. In so doing I showed the inadequacies of the analysis that reduces Filipino women's migrant lives to their work functions and Moroccan women solely to their family role. Rather, both groups are involved in trying to combine and balance different roles and responsibilities, both productive and reproductive. Cultural norms influence the ways in which different women strike this balance but what my findings show is that conditions present in the immigration context (entry requirement, labour market opportunities, housing facilities, etc.) are also key in shaping the familial arrangements and choices of the women involved.

Notes

1. SURT (Associaciò de Dones per la Reinserciò Laboral) is an association of women funded through various sources (local authorities, government, EU) dedicated to the socioeconomic integration of women who belong to groups at risk of exclusion and social marginalisation (e.g., ex-convicts, immigrants).
2. 1 Euro equals L 2000 and 165 ptas (approximately). At the time of fieldwork one dollar was equivalent to 0.91 Euros.
3. Public housing is very limited in Barcelona and totally inadequate to meet demand. Besides, the Council does not consider housing as one of its priorities in its policies towards immigrants. In an analysis conducted by Zapata-Barrero (2002) on the planning documents published by the Council and on its specific actions in the field of immigration from 1984 to the present, it appears that no specific action has been planned or undertaken in the sphere of housing.

5
COMPARATIVE PERSPECTIVES ON FEMALE MIGRATION AND SETTLEMENT IN SOUTHERN EUROPE

This chapter summarises the results of the research and locates them in an explicitly comparative perspective both across locations and migrant groups so as to highlight the main similarities and differences among them. The first section addresses the reasons behind Moroccan and Filipino women's migration and the ways in which they accomplish their migratory projects. The second section deals with female immigrants' insertion in local labour markets. I consider both the characteristics and conditions of employment, and immigrant women's own valuation and perceptions of their jobs. The third section centres on immigrant families and women's roles in them, paying particular attention to changes brought about by migration. This section also describes different immigrant households and family forms emerging in Southern Europe, taking into account their transnational ramifications.

Why and How do Women Migrate?

Family Background and Origin of the Respondents

By summarising some information about the origin of my interviewees, this section explores whether it is possible to identify household characteristics at the point of migrant origin that make female migration more or less likely.

Filipinas

With regard to the geographical origin of Filipinos migrating to Italy and Spain, some of my key informants reported that they migrate from all regions of the Philippines. As far as my forty Filipino respondents were concerned, their origin was more variegated in the case of Bologna and more uniform in the case of Barcelona where they all came from Luzon island. A majority of respondents in both cities had a rural origin: 80 per cent of the women interviewed in Bologna and 50 per cent of those interviewed in Barcelona had a farmer father. However, the majority of respondents had already left the countryside: seventeen Filipinas in Bologna and eleven in Barcelona had undertaken rural–urban migration to study and/or work prior to international migration. Usually they went to live with relatives who were already residing in cities in the Philippines. A few lived at the work-place (factory and hospital workers, for instance). In some cases they had formed their own family with men whom they had met in the city.

The majority of Filipinas in Bologna and Barcelona came from large families with an average of more than six siblings. Another characteristic of these migrants is that they often come from female-headed households, created by the death or desertion of the father/husband. As regards their civil status upon international migration, fifteen women were single and five were married when they migrated to Bologna. Of the latter, three migrated together with their husbands and two went ahead alone. Of the migrants to Barcelona, twelve were single, six were married, one was a widow and one separated. Looking at the socioeconomic situation of the home-country families of these migrants, it seemed more variegated in the case of Bologna and generally lower for those going to Barcelona. However, in both case-studies the economic situation of the respondents and their families tended to be precarious and international migration was seen as a means of improving it.

Moroccans

The geographical origin of Moroccan women differs in the two cities. In Barcelona they tend to come mainly from the Rif, the northern part of Morocco, reflecting Spanish colonial influence on this region, although a number of Barcelona respondents came from Casablanca. The geographical origin of respondents in Bologna was more varied with a majority coming from Casablanca and a town called Khouribga (the latter probably as a result of chain migration). Contrary to their Filipino counterparts, Moroccan women had not been involved in rural–urban migration much although some experienced internal mobility, mainly as result of marriage.

Like the Filipinas, the Moroccan women tend to come from large families, especially those in Barcelona. In Bologna, some women came from smaller families; these were normally migrant families and female-headed families. In Barcelona, half of the sample were from female-headed households. As for the civil status of Moroccan women upon migration to Bologna, nine were single (five had a parent already living in Italy and migrated to reunite with them); five were married (four had married men who were already working in Italy) and four were divorcees. In Barcelona six were single, five were married (two left their husbands behind upon migration) and seven were divorcees. The socioeconomic background of the respondents seems more mixed in the case of Bologna, where I met both women from very deprived backgrounds and women from wealthy families; whereas in Barcelona they tended to come mainly from the urban working classes.

Comparison between the Groups

The main difference I identified between the two national groups of female migrants is the more homogeneous character of the Filipinas compared to the heterogeneity (in terms of class, education, origin, etc.) of the Moroccans. This enables me to generalise more easily about specific characteristics of Filipino migrants than about the Moroccan ones. For Filipinas such characteristics include: a rural origin, but urban residency prior to international migration; a poor background, but a family's aspiration for upward social mobility; a large number of siblings; and high educational qualifications (usually at university level). Such common traits are also found in analyses of Filipinas migrating to other parts of the globe such as Hong Kong, Singapore and Canada (see the studies respectively by Chang and McAllister Groves 2000; Yeoh and Huang 2000; Stasiulis and Bakan 1997). Another difference between the two groups relates to civil status, although this element has less importance than I had originally anticipated. Filipino migrants are commonly portrayed as single, surplus labour not involved in reproductive work and therefore better deployed elsewhere; and Moroccans as dependant wives becoming international migrants only as result of marriage. However, a considerable proportion of Filipinas I met were married, whereas the majority of Moroccan women I interviewed were either single or divorced. A characteristic shared by many migrants of both groups is that of being a female head of household or coming from a female-headed household, confirming what Moore (1988) and Chant and McIlwaine (1995) have noted for female rural–urban migration in the Third World.

Reasons for Leaving

Filipinas

Economic imperatives are almost always at the root of the migration of married women with children. The decision may be taken at the household level after appreciation of the fact that it is generally easier for women to find jobs in feminised sectors of the labour markets in the countries of Southern Europe (and elsewhere) where there are quotas for categories of immigrants such as domestic workers. Husbands may depart subsequently or they may remain in the Philippines and retain their job. In virtually all the interviews conducted in Bologna and Barcelona, the main reason articulated for married women's migration was the need to pay for their children's education. In synthesis, women give up their qualified jobs at home in order to undertake manual jobs in Europe for the well-being and futures of their children. Gender roles clearly play a part here since it is the mother who is the one who has to 'sacrifice' for the family; her job is invariably considered more disposable than that of her husband (even if she is a professional). But married women can also use their responsibilities towards the family to their own advantage, for example to get away from unhappy relationships without incurring the local social stigma that a separation would entail.

Single women too may migrate for economic necessity but in their case such need does not generally originate within the household. These women often migrate to support members of their extended family who do not necessarily live with them and who do not count on such support. Older siblings feel responsible for their parents (particularly if they in turn had earlier made sacrifices for supporting their child's studies) and younger siblings and may sacrifice their own interests to improve the family situation. In these cases migration is not a household's strategy but can be rather framed within wider kinship relations and obligations.

Once they have undertaken international migration, these women are often the ones putting pressure on other family members to become migrants too in order to share the burden of remittances. They do so playing on the same kinship duties that motivated their own move. What is interesting is that they almost invariably favour the migration of female members of the family before that of male members. Some respondents commented that their sisters would accept and adapt more easily to the kind of jobs that are available in Italy and Spain than their male kin. Such a pattern shows on the one hand how women can contribute to gender-selective processes of migration, and on the other hand it points to the control that women are exercising over current migration flows. The opportunities opened up by these 'early' female migrants and the consolidation of these channels of migration from the Philippines offer women escape routes in a variety of situations, something that we can also find in Moroccan female migration. The economic motor lies at the heart of Filipino migration but this interacts with a number of other reasons. Filipino women exercise their agency on the one hand by complying with their gender-ascribed roles of dutiful daughters and sisters, and on the other hand by using such roles as an 'excuse' to undertake international migration. Such migration may 'mask' more personal goals such as the desire to leave unsatisfactory living and working conditions, the desire to enjoy more freedom and independence, the desire to pursue personal objectives, the wish to remain single, and so on.

Moroccans

Moroccan married women tend to migrate to reunite with their husbands – the typical 'family reunion migration' described in the literature. However, what this literature does not explore is how this form of migration may mask more personal goals on the part of the woman. For instance, many – particularly the younger ones – see and live their migration as a hard-won achievement usually gained despite family (that of the husband) opposition and state regulations that make it almost impossible to meet increasingly stringent requirements for family reunification (Kofman 1999). Their reasons for migrating go beyond the mere desire to be with their husbands; they often want to earn a wage, see the 'West', and/or run away from their allotted place in the extended family and from restrictive social control. The known availability of 'female' jobs in Southern Europe is used by the most adventurous women to subvert gender roles and start migrating ahead of their husbands. This is, however, still far more the exception than the rule and women who have done it feel very proud of it (even if they have to bear increased tensions with their partners who do not seem very supportive of their choices).

For single Moroccan women, migration is often a family project since in many cases they move to reunite with the head of their family who initiated the migration (normally the father, but if parents were divorced the mother). If the woman does not belong to such a 'transnational family' the most important factor governing her likelihood to migrate is the socioeconomic position of her family of origin. We saw how women coming from wealthy and progressive families migrate to study or look for a job in order to better themselves, and generally they have few responsibilities other than for themselves. If they come from poor working-class families their migration actually resembles that of Filipinas in that they are migrating to take up low-skill feminised jobs in Southern Europe that allow them to support their families back home.   However, this class-based dichotomy appears somewhat too rigid in the case of Barcelona, because there I met women from working-class backgrounds who chose to migrate when single not to fulfil responsibilities towards their natal families but to secure an economic independence for themselves as an alternative both to marriage and to dependence on their natal family, a possibility rarely enjoyed by women in Morocco. As already pointed out, divorcees seem to be present in large numbers in the migration both to Bologna and to Barcelona, proving their vulnerable position (both in ideological and economic terms) within Morocco.

Comparison between the Groups

In this book I argue that structural *and* individual factors are at the root of women's migration in both groups. Such factors are linked to gendered roles and positions within households, families and kinship groups. But the ways in which Moroccan and Filipino women can and do articulate their agency differ. Contrary to common assumptions that portray them as passive victims, Moroccan women often see and undertake migration with a clear emancipatory goal. Their aims are studying, having an income, enjoying more freedom, eluding social control, starting a new life and so on. In order to render such goals socially acceptable, if they are married they frame them within a family project, and if they are single they justify their migration as a temporary measure to accumulate capital for things such as helping their family of origin or for their own dowry. Class and education are important factors shaping the likelihood and the form of their migration, and, to some extent, the jobs and activities pursued in the destination cities.

For Filipinas, migration tends to be more in line with their roles as dutiful daughters, sisters and mothers who have to 'sacrifice' for the family well-being by working abroad. Yet they too, even if more subtly, exercise their agency and try to fulfil personal objectives. They tend to opt for conflict-free ways of bettering their position within families and kinship groups; such strategies allow them both to maintain their role expectations and at the same time allow them to gain more control and independence over their lives.

Accessing the 'Fortress'

This section looks more closely at the interconnections between countries of origin and destination. It considers wider migratory networks both informal – constituted by family, kinship and friends – and formal – such as those involving agencies and the organisations that make up the 'migration industry' (Castles and Miller 1998; Kofman et al. 2000). Understanding the functioning of these mechanisms that provide information and facilitate individual movements acquires relevance in the context of the consolidation of a 'Fortress Europe' whereby stricter rules are passed in all of the member states to 'protect' them from what public opinion and policy makers perceive as waves of 'dangerous' Third World immigrants threatening the stability of a supposedly homogeneous

Europe. The consequences of such rules are clearly not a halting of immigration but the creation of an increasing number and variety of undocumented migrants. As Koser and Lutz (1998:13) have pointed out, 'Any effort to provide an overall view of the new migration must also take into account the numerous strategies adopted by people to overcome regulations, limitations and borders, and must fully appreciate the risks that are being taken to this end.'

In the previous two chapters I documented just this by addressing the following questions: how do Filipino and Moroccan women manage to arrive in Bologna and Barcelona? Which networks do these women have access to? What is their role in them? What are the similarities and differences that women from these two 'Third Word' countries encounter in accessing Southern Europe?

Filipinas

A great number of my Filipino interviewees in Bologna arrived illegally in spite of the existence of quotas for domestic workers: sixteen out of twenty respondents entered the country illegally. What is more, in at least two of the remaining cases there was some kind of circumvention of the rules, such as using 'contacts' in a selection centre or having an offer of domestic work from a cousin who was a naturalised Italian and who was not the real employer of the immigrant. The others paid agencies that organised their entire trip from the Philippines across several countries using various means of transport to access Italy.

Although both Italy and Spain are said to need foreign domestic workers, the presence of different regulatory systems impacts differently on the immigrants and this is reflected even in my small sample. The privileged entrance accorded to Filipinas in Spain due to colonial ties results in the fact that illegal migrants are fewer in my sample (ten out of twenty respondents). In this context, what is interesting about Filipino immigration to Southern Europe is that, whether the migration happens legally or illegally, networks play an important role. The networks are formal (such as agencies) when the migrant has few contacts in the country of destination. In this event she will go to an agency which will arrange the placement for her. If in that particular moment the country chosen has a recruitment policy, the migrant will be able to arrive legally; if not, additional money will have to be paid to arrange for an illegal entry. If the migrant already has a consolidated network in the country of destination she can bypass these agencies and organise the migration with the help of relatives and friends who will provide her with a job through the contacts of their employers, thereby giving her the possibility of entering as a legal domestic worker. The case of Victoria is illustrative in this respect: she was the first of her family to migrate and she had to borrow a substantial sum of money to pay an agency that arranged her illegal migration; her younger sister also came this way shortly afterwards. Then they both acquired more information and contacts in the city and were able to sponsor the migration (this time legal) of a third sister. As their network in Barcelona consolidated they were able to find contracts for their remaining sisters and brothers, sisters-in-law, cousins, even neighbours and friends, up to a total of eighty people. All except the first two arrived legally thanks to the contacts, information and 'skills' of Victoria and her sister.

Moroccans

The situation of legal versus illegal entry reverses with this group, with more Moroccan women having entered Spain illegally than Italy. Seven out of eighteen respondents in Bologna had been illegal; twelve out of eighteen in Barcelona. Their illegal status includes a number of situations ranging from entering on tourist visas and then overstaying (six cases in Italy and five in Spain), entering and eluding border checks by hiding in a car or getting on the ferry without a visa (three cases in Spain), getting 'false' job requests (one case in Spain), or paying agents for fake documents (one case in Italy and three in Spain). The last of these options is the last resort for the potential immigrant since it is the most expensive and also the one that involves the highest risks of jeopardising one's position if discovered or in the event of a regularisation – as we saw in the case of Jamila (Chapter 4).

Comparison between the Groups

A point that has emerged from the case studies is how the majority of my respondents of both groups moved from one migrant status to another with little control over their situation – which is strongly characterised by precariousness. For example, they went from tourist to illegal immigrant when their visa expired, from illegal to legal immigrant after an amnesty was granted, and from legal to illegal immigrant again when for instance the elderly person for whom the migrant was working died and the residency could not be renewed. Such switches occur not only because of changes in the circumstances of the individual migrant but also, as we have seen, because legislation can change abruptly, modifying the conditions by which one person can acquire residency or taking away rights that were previously enjoyed, as happened with the introduction of the restrictive Spanish immigration law 8/2000. As Staring (1998: 237) concludes, 'seen this way, undocumented migrants truly are products of restrictive migration policies'.

The main difference between the groups in relation to women's access to Southern Europe is the more organised and 'institutionalised' nature of Filipino migration in relation to the Moroccan one. In order to migrate 'successfully' (both legally and illegally), networks are vital and women of both groups rely heavily on them. But whereas the networks to which Moroccan women have access are mainly loose ones based on the information of friends, relatives or neighbours who have moved before, those used by Filipinas are true 'international organisations' that work for profit and can place Filipino workers in countries located in several continents in exchange for a fee. This means that, for Moroccan women, getting access to Southern Europe is more unpredictable (it depends on whom they know, if they have some contacts there, etc.), but is also a project which is cheaper to realise and which requires less prior planning. Geographical proximity (especially in the Spanish case) eases these less organised forms of Moroccan migration.

The New Breadwinners: Immigrant Women in the Southern European Labour Market

This part of my comparative analysis draws parallels between the ways in which Moroccan and Filipino women get inserted in the region, paying particular attention to their labour market incorporation. Drawing on the material presented in the two previous chapters, I address the following questions: how do different groups of foreign women get access to the Southern European labour market? What are different groups of women's positions and conditions of employment in the two cities studied? What are the causes of such differences? How do different groups of women experience and value the type of jobs that are currently available to them? In line with the model proposed in Chapter 2, this account is concerned not only with the structural conditions shaping contemporary female immigration to Southern Europe but also with the views and experiences of immigrant women of these processes, and their ways of making sense of, adapting to and acting on, the structural constraints that they find.

Supporting Southern European Families: Access, Position and Conditions of Work

Filipinas

Filipinas tend to arrive in Southern Europe already with a job contract fixed up, normally to work as domestics. Whether they obtained the contract through a consulate, a recruitment agency or relatives already residing abroad, Filipinas know what the job prospects in Southern Europe are and usually start working within the first week of their arrival. Filipinas' labour market participation in Southern Europe is remarkable for its intensity and their unemployment rate is extremely low.

The fact that care and domestic work represent the principal occupations of Filipinas both in Bologna and Barcelona confirms the similarities existing between these two Southern European urban labour markets. Alternative employment options open to Filipinas are few and are slow to develop, in spite of their high educational levels and quite long-established presence. There seems to be only two possible ways out of domestic work for Filipinas. The first one is represented by all those service activities catering specifically for other immigrants ranging from call centres and banking to cultural mediation in the sphere of public services. The other one is getting involved in so-called 'ethnic business', mainly in restaurants and shops. Another option for young Filipinos (both females and males), particularly in Barcelona, is the restaurant sector where increasing number of foreigners are finding employment especially in labour-intensive outlets with high turnover and long shifts that 'local' workers find unattractive. The mainstream labour market, however, is still closed to these foreign-born workers.

As documented in the two previous chapters, the way in which many Filipinas initially access Southern European labour markets is through live-in work. As Andall has shown (1998, 2000b), this is the most exploited and disadvantaged sector of domestic work and is therefore the one with the highest demand for foreign workers. Working hours are long and unpredictable, the contact with the employer is constant and the privacy of the worker is reduced. Filipinas use it as a way of learning the job and getting established locally, and as soon as they can they try to leave it for forms of live-out work. At the time of the interviews thirteen out of the fifteen Filipinas engaged in domestic work in Bologna and thirteen out of sixteen in Barcelona were live-out domestics, showing that Filipinas are quite successful in moving from live-in to the preferred live-out mode in both cities studied.

The high employment rate of Filipinas in both locations is a reflection of the ease with which they find jobs. As the two case studies show, and as other studies confirm, they are at the top of the foreign domestic worker hierarchy in Southern Europe (Chell 1997, 2000; Lazaridis 2000); they are rarely unemployed, they manage to secure legal and even indefinite contracts, they manage to move to live-out work, and since they are more in demand they normally command higher wages than other immigrant workers. The reasons for this consolidated position are complex: other studies have pointed out that Filipinas in Southern Europe are preferred by employers because they are seen as docile, hard-working and polite and because they are Catholic. These aspects emerged also from the cases studied by myself. However, the reasons for their 'superior' position in the domestic service sector are, I believe, more complex than this and are also related to the particular form that their migration to Southern Europe has taken. Their migration originated as contract work to fill specific positions in the live-in sector of domestic work. As Chell (2000) has noted, Filipinas are making a career out of domestic work and have become highly specialised in this sector. While it is certainly the case that employers are making racist assumptions about Filipinas, it is also true that Filipinas themselves are contributing towards the perpetuation of these stereotyped ideas about themselves, in a way because they see it in their own interest to do so. Many Filipino informants repeated to me the supposed qualities of Filipinas and explained that the possession of such qualities is a bonus in the increasingly competitive domestic sector. Filipinas are therefore playing on the racist assumptions prevalent in the host society to their own advantage, using them as a form of marketing strategy to sell their labour more expensively than other groups in the domestic service labour market. Filipinas in both Bologna and Barcelona seem to spend a great deal of energy in preserving the good reputation of the group, since such a positive image is seen as an asset for securing good working conditions and higher rates of pay.

The 'community' has an important role to play in this respect. Communal activities in both cities tend to pivot around the churches, both Catholic and Protestant. Through such activities church figures exert some degree of control over the behaviour of the members of their community and take seriously the task of 'rescuing' members who have left the 'good path'. In Bologna, Susan and her husband said they changed after the leader of a Protestant charismatic group took interest in them. She stopped playing cards and her husband stopped drinking and they are both now active members of the group. A local priest in Bologna reported the example of a Filipina who was found working in prostitution and who was first beaten up and then sent away from the city by other Filipinos. In Barcelona the Filipino priest publicly criticises men who abandon their families for other women, thereby contributing to the preservation of specific moral values within Filipino families and by extension within the community.[1] Another way utilised by Filipinas to maintain the good reputation of the group is through the use of Filipino mediators in the case of labour conflicts. The President of the Association of Filipino Workers in Barcelona acts in this way in conflicts that may arise between workers and employers, trying to impose conciliatory resolutions whenever possible. Open conflict is preferably avoided since it is believed to be detrimental not only for the individual worker but also for the 'community' more generally. The same pattern has been identified by Lazaridis (2000) in her work on Filipinas in Greece.

Moroccans

Moroccan women arrive in Italy and Spain for a variety of reasons and not necessarily with the prime goal of working. However, whatever their reasons for migrating to Southern Europe, the majority of them seek employment soon after their arrival in the same feminised sectors occupied by their Filipino counterparts. At the time of my fieldwork, eleven out of eighteen of Moroccan interviewees in Bologna and ten out of eighteen in Barcelona were in employment. Most of the others were actively looking for a job. The majority of those working were employed in the domestic sector. Few Moroccan women, like their Filipino counterparts, manage to escape the domestic and cleaning sector niche. For those who have completed their education in Italy and in Spain, there are some possibilities in low positions in the service sector (as shop assistants, cashiers, etc.) or in services targeting immigrants, where their bilingual skills are appreciated. For first-generation migrants the only alternative job in Bologna seemed to be the better-valued care worker position in nursing homes. As one of my informants explained to me, the work there is not any better than that of carer in a private household, but she valued having an agreed timetable, clear tasks, and good contractual arrangements, in particular in relation to sick leave and pension rights. In Barcelona, the main area of employment for Moroccan women outside domestic work is in the restaurant sector. However, in contrast to Filipinas who work as waitresses, Moroccans are employed mainly in the kitchens.

If outside the domestic sector the situation of both groups of immigrant workers seems to be similar, inside this racialised sector their position is different. Moroccan women find it more difficult to get a consolidated position in the domestic sector. They are heavily discriminated for their national origin and their Islamic religion when looking for a job. Employers hold a number of prejudices against them such as being lazy, stealing, being backward, being religious fanatics, etc. The discrimination against Moroccan women, although present in both cities, seemed more acute in Bologna than in Barcelona: in the former city few of my respondents succeeded in even entering the domestic sector, the majority of them being employed by cleaning companies. All this reflects on Moroccan women's position and conditions in the domestic work sector. First of all they find it more difficult than Filipinas to get employment. When they do manage to find a job, it is either for lower wages than other workers, or it is without a legal contract, or both. In Bologna undocumented Moroccan women are employed as live-in carers for elderly people for wages that are up to a third lower than average, and without any contract. In Spain stricter controls apparently make it more difficult, at least in Barcelona, for undocumented workers to find employment.

Moroccan women's position in the Southern European labour market is therefore strongly influenced by racism, although there are other elements that should be kept in mind. Differently from the Filipinas, some of them did not migrate to Southern Europe with the goal of engaging in domestic work. As with the Somalian women in Rome studied by Chell (2000), the involvement of many Moroccan women within the sector is often out of necessity and not out of choice. It is something that many women had not planned before migrating, but it is a job that they are forced to take up because of the inadequate earnings of their husbands or because they have lost the economic support of a male figure, for instance as a consequence of divorce or separation. Moreover, the involvement of Moroccan women with domestic service is more recent than that of Filipinas and they lack their organisation. Rather than cooperate for securing advantages as a group within a specific sector of the local labour market, the approach employed by Moroccan women is more individualistic. They are unconcerned of the reputation of Moroccans in general, although they often feel offended and negatively affected by stereotypes and assumptions about Moroccans circulating in both Italy and Spain. Particularly in Bologna, where the city is smaller and Moroccan families have been concentrated in degraded housing schemes, women tend to compete against each other. Contrary to Filipinas, who exchange information first of all with other Filipinas, Moroccans seem to hold the deepest distrust towards other Moroccan women and it is against them that they measure themselves and their families' achievements. This behaviour is clearer for married women; whereas women who are on their own and who are primary migrants exert forms of solidarity and cooperation.

My work shows that in order to understand the hierarchical pattering of the domestic work sector in Southern Europe it is therefore important to take into account not only the racist assumptions and stereotypes present in the receiving societies, but also the reasons for migrating and the evolution of the insertion of different groups in the sector. Linked to this is how different groups of women value the jobs they are doing and how they see their position in the labour market, elements of which in turn are influenced by the cultural values of the group. These are aspects that will be explored further in the next section.

Economic Agents or Servants of Globalisation? Immigrant Women's Perceptions of their Work

How do women belonging to different national groups evaluate their jobs and see their positions in the Southern European labour markets? Which aspects of their jobs do they value positively and which negatively? What are the consequences of their involvement in such labour markets on their lives? Answering these questions will help shed some light on the different patterns of labour market participation of the two groups of women studied. In line with the theories presented in Chapter 2, this section will analyse immigrant women's labour market participation taking into account important non-economic factors such as kinship relations and gender ideologies.

Filipinas

Literature on the gender division of labour in the Philippines points to a relative fluidity in the domestic allocation of productive and reproductive tasks. Contrary to what happens in Morocco, in Filipino society, particularly among lower-income groups, women engage in paid work and this involvement accords them approval and prestige by both their male and female peers. Men and women thus share the task of generating household income, and they also share some household chores. Another aspect characteristic of Filipino society is the strong role of women in managing the household budget (Chant and McIlwaine 1995).

This apparent gender egalitarianism is questionable (Chant and McIlwaine 1995) and my own fieldwork confirms the subordinate positions of Filipino women vis-à-vis Filipino men, but what remains valid is that Filipino women's economic function is recognised, valued and never ostracised. As my case-studies show, it is even encouraged, so much so that mothers and wives can leave their families in search of a job and stay absent from home for periods up to ten and even twenty years. Research conducted in the Philippines quoted by Chant and McIlwaine (1995: 23) shows that 'in the current period of economic restructuring for most poor Filipino families women's income-generating efforts are now crucial to household livelihood'.

Gender ideologies and visions of female work present in the society of origin clearly reflect on the attitudes of Filipino women immigrating into Southern Europe and their relationships to the local labour market. Filipino women arrive in Italy and Spain to fulfil their economic function for the well-being of their families. The resources that they remit to the family justify their absence from home and because of that they will be relieved of a number of reproductive tasks. The female emigrant remits the money necessary for the family's survival but the day-to-day activities of child-rearing are carried out by other female members of the family with the help of her husband. Even when she has her own family in the immigration setting, her work function is privileged over her reproductive function and even when pregnant or having small children she is not expected to reduce the number of hours worked or to quit her job. Her husband (if present) will share some domestic tasks as will other family members. If such help is not sufficient, she will resort to paying for baby-sitting, bringing the children to her work and, if all this does not prove feasible, she will take her children back to be raised in the Philippines. The work function will always be prioritised over the maternal one since it is believed that through the money earned a better future for her children and family can be achieved.

Filipinas interviewed in both Bologna and Barcelona do not hold negative views about domestic work, which they generally consider a dignified profession. They complain about specific jobs or instances but not about the profession as such, at least in its live-out form. Live-in work is seen somewhat more negatively, particularly for the minimal control that the worker has on the hours worked, but they all tend to consider the live-in arrangement as a necessary step in the domestic worker 'career'. Also some women, particularly those recently arrived in the two cities, see it as a safer and more protected form of employment.

What makes Filipinas of both Bologna and Barcelona talk positively about domestic work are factors such as the opportunity to learn new things, having the trust of their employers and above all being treated 'like one of the family'. In the opinion of one of my respondents, a caring relationship on the part of the employer can alleviate the hard work carried out in the house. Having a contract and a long-term working relationship are also considered important. But the aspect of their work that they appreciate the most is the wage they receive which, compared to Filipino standard, is high. Through domestic work Filipinas can achieve goals that are unthinkable for them in their country, even with professional salaries. As we have seen, such goals are normally family-oriented and involve the sending of substantial remittances. It is this capacity of sending money home and achieving specific objectives that makes domestic work a worthwhile occupation in the eyes of Filipinas. My interviewees do not feel themselves as victims of global economic forces, rather they see themselves as courageous workers who, by working as domestics abroad, can fulfil their own and their families' aspirations for upward social mobility.

But not all accept their destiny as domestic workers passively, especially those with fewer responsibilities. Although few succeed, many try to leave the domestic sector. Those who have managed to get other occupations, such as restaurant workers, value positively the possibility of leaving the boredom and isolation of the employer's house and the fact of having clearer and fewer tasks. Some highly qualified Filipinas have tried hard to find jobs matching at least partly their qualifications, but they have been confronted with what they perceive as clear 'racial discrimination'. This is why some of my informants undertook or are considering further migration in order to achieve better working conditions. Some women, who realised that changing their occupation will be unfeasible and who have achieved part of their economic goals, are now reducing the hours worked and engaging in voluntary and community activities. Women in both Bologna and Barcelona have become the pillars of very organised and internationally linked Filipino associations. These bodies cover cultural/recreational activities, campaigns for the protection of worker's rights, and are active participants and sustainers of various Church groups. All those women involved in such organisations talked about the personal fulfilment brought to them by these activities. Contrary to what happens for most other immigrant groups, for Filipinos the so-called 'community leaders' chosen as preferential interlocutors by the local institution are usually women. They are operating from groups and associations where their activities in favour of Filipino migrants have brought them popularity and respectability among their compatriots.

In contrast to what seems to be the norm in the Philippines (Chant and McIlwaine 1995), Filipinas employed in Southern Europe continue to support the family of origin even after marriage. Marital status did not seem to be the main factor determining the sending of remittances. The amount of money sent correlates directly with the situation of the family back home. Women with children – and if they never married these would be nieces and nephews – still at school or at university in the Philippines will send almost their entire salary. The amount decreases if the immigrant has created her own family in the country of immigration, but by no means does it stop. Married women will still send regular remittances to various members of their family of origin. As we have seen in Chapters 4 and 5, domestic workers' wages (apart from supporting children's education) will be spent for things such has helping relatives to start an economic activity in the country of origin or to subsidise their migration, both strategies aimed at enabling these persons' economic independence. Another frequent objective is that of buying land and above all building brick properties that will replace the bamboo bungalows where most of my informants lived prior to migration. Nineteen of the twenty Filipinas in both Bologna and Barcelona declared sending remittances. As documented by the literature on the Philippines, it is the woman who keeps the family earnings and this remains so when her family has joined her in the immigration context. It is she who has an important say on the family's spending and above all on the projects to which such resources are to be dedicated.

The main difference identified between management and spending patterns of Filipino women as between Bologna and Barcelona is that the latter group invests resources also in the immigration city and not only in the country of origin, which is the case for those in Bologna. The more established character of the Filipino community of Barcelona and the easier criteria of getting nationality (which in turn facilitates all bureaucratic transactions) are possible explanations for this difference.

Moroccans

As far as Morocco is concerned, Gregorio and Ramírez (2000) point out that women's role there is considered to be mainly that of homemakers, mothers and wives. Gender roles are clearly divided, with men having the responsibility of supporting the family economically and women of rearing children. Women's waged work – except in some instances of professional work – is not seen as desirable but rather is considered an obligation or a last resort that clearly marks the family's social class.

Many young women are entering the labour market in Italy and Spain and are valuing positively the possibility of earning a wage and acquiring a certain degree of economic independence. But whereas for Filipinas the norm (that is to say what is expected from them) is to work, for Moroccan women this is not the case. If they do not come from very deprived families, they have to justify their desire to work and convince their husbands of the benefits of such work. In an immigration context characterised by a very precarious labour market and where men often find themselves underemployed or having gaps in their employment (due to the temporality of some of the jobs done by them – such as agricultural or construction work), the usefulness of women's involvement in paid work is not difficult to be argued for. Added to this there are increasing housing and living costs making it impossible even for men in stable occupations, such as factory work, to be able to meet all the household's expenses. This is why the majority of Moroccan women in both Bologna and Barcelona are currently working or seeking employment.

However, since Moroccan women often have to fight within their household to get out and work, they tend to quit jobs that are unsatisfactory to them. If a job is too exploitative and too poorly paid they lose the incentive to fight for it and prefer to step back to a more traditional role where their husband has to support them while they take care of domestic duties, at least until they have found a more suitable occupation. Having said this, it is worth remembering that few women are in the privileged position of having a husband in employment who can fully support them. Those who are divorced, widows and those who have family members dependent on them cannot afford the luxury of being full-time housewives or of being too choosy with the types of employment they perform. These women's work function becomes as prevalent as it is for their Filipino counterparts, since like them they have no safety-nets which they can fall into.

Moroccan women I interviewed in Bologna and Barcelona valued positively the greater possibilities that exist in Southern Europe for them to work. Yet, on the whole, they dislike domestic work and are quite critical of it. Almost all of them complained bitterly about present and past jobs – on issues such as the relationship with their employers, the hard nature of the tasks given to them, the humiliation of having to do what they considered a dirty job. The cleaning part of the job is what they resented most and what they found most degrading. Several valued more positively jobs that involved looking after elderly people and above all children (see Hondagneu-Sotelo 2000). Another element which Moroccan women resent is their lack of rights and the precarious conditions of domestic workers. However, whereas Filipinas try to improve their contractual positions within the service, Moroccan women hope to leave it altogether and to find employment in better-protected sectors of the labour market, albeit with limited success. Although domestic work in emigration loses the negative connotations associated with it in Morocco, Moroccan women still tend to prefer other types of occupation although, as we have seen, the possibilities open to them both in Bologna and Barcelona are few. In Barcelona a preferred occupation is restaurant work. Contrary to Filipinas who are ambivalent about it, Moroccan women unequivocally prefer this to domestic work. Although they admit that it can be harder than working in a house, they see it as a less stigmatised profession and lacking the servile relationship present in domestic service.

In spite of a generally shared negative opinion about domestic work, Moroccan women who managed to have full-time live-out work and in some cases also live-in jobs with good contractual arrangements and good working conditions, showed higher levels of job satisfaction. They valued the role they had in their employer's home and the possibility of having a relatively good and secure wage. Yet those who had their own family in Bologna and Barcelona felt drained by the double shift that they had to do at work and at home. This is why those with a family and with non-satisfactory working conditions did not think twice about the possibility of quitting or refusing a job, even if the extra income was necessary for the family budget. For these women the maternal role is always the one to prioritise vis-à-vis an economic role that gives them few satisfactions. Rather than engaging in full-time jobs that put too many strains on them, they opt instead for occasional and hourly paid jobs that are more compatible with their domestic duties. By privileging their reproductive role these women are jeopardising further their position in the labour market since the part-time jobs that these women go on to accept are those with the lowest security, protection and working conditions, and moreover are extremely poorly paid.

Young Moroccan women and those who had access to better types of jobs have a different attitude towards the balance between productive and reproductive work. They are prepared to give more prominence to their labour function since the jobs they do and the wages they earn give them satisfaction and self-value. Generation has emerged as an important element for framing Moroccan women's attitudes to paid work (see Brah 1996 on Muslim Asian women in Britain). Women of the younger generations, including those arriving directly from Morocco for family reunification, give more importance to waged work and economic independence than older Moroccan women do. Often these women's retreat into more traditional gender roles is the result of their frustrated aspirations due to the conditions that they found in a racialised and ethnically differentiated labour market, rather than their uncritical adherence to specific cultural norms.

As for the issue of household budget management and remittances, Moroccan women's situation differs sharply from that of their Filipino counterparts. As said previously, the support of women is the responsibility of the father first and then of the husband upon marriage. Women therefore are generally not expected to send remittances back home unless it is for the keeping of children, or the situation of the family of origin is particularly vulnerable. It is not unusual for the women I met to receive economic support from family members resident both in Morocco and in other countries. This does not mean that Moroccan women do not send remittances home. Seven out of eighteen Moroccan women interviewed in Bologna declared that they were sending remittances, but none said that they did so regularly. In Barcelona four women declared sending regular remittances and another two send money occasionally. As Gregorio and Ramírez (2000) have noted, some Moroccan women buy their independence by sending money home. For married couples the household's budget should be constituted mainly by men's wages with women's salary viewed as an additional contribution to the breadwinner's income. The male wage is used to pay for the main expenses related to rent and bills whereas the woman's wage is normally used for 'additional' things for the house and children. The idea that motivates many young married women to work is that of contributing to realising the family's projects, the main one being that of buying or building properties in Morocco. However, many realise that living costs in the two cities are high, and therefore that their wages are not a mere 'help' but a fundamental part of the family's survival.

Comparison between the Groups

Filipino and Moroccan women are clearly positioned differently within the Southern European labour market. Filipinas have remarkably higher levels of labour market participation and job stability than Moroccans, who find it difficult to get stable jobs with good contractual arrangements. Their ways of accessing the labour market also differ: Filipinas have a clear strategy that involves passing various stages of a consolidated 'career' that goes from live-in to live-out work, whereas Moroccans find it hard to accept that all their aspirations are reduced to an under-valued domestic job. Such differences are partly linked to Filipino and Moroccan women's different relationships with paid work. Whereas the former were involved in it prior to migration, the latter still tend to consider it as a sign of poverty and something which sets them apart from the ideal of the housewife/mother kept by a breadwinning husband. Another important difference between the two groups is their different view of the acceptable balance between productive and reproductive work. Whereas Filipinas tend to privilege the former, Moroccans give more prominence to the latter.

In the light of all this, making generalisations on the impact of the jobs that immigrant women do in Southern Europe on their lives seems difficult. As Gregorio and Ramírez (2000) have noted, Moroccan female engagement in paid work in Southern Europe represents a change and a challenge to their traditional gender role, whereas for the Dominican women studied by them (but also for the Filipinas at the core of my study) it represents a continuity and a reinforcement of their role as those who have to provide and sacrifice for the family. As Chant and McIlwaine have highlighted, 'labour force participation is often a double-edged sword … with gains in one domain often contradicted, if not cancelled, in others' (1995: 302).

Immigrant Women in Transnational Families

Few studies have dealt with the changes to families brought about by migration. As Zlotnik (1995: 5) has noted, 'it is both ironic and very telling that, although women have traditionally been considered as "family migrants", that aspect of their migration experience had generally been disregarded'. Many questions relating to immigrant families thus remain unanswered. The following subsections address some of them including the following: how are immigrant families forming and evolving to adapt to the situations they find in Southern Europe? What are the different forms of immigrant families and households emerging there? Are there differences between Filipino and Moroccan women's arrangements? What are the effects of women's employment on their family life? What are the implications of the structural factors that condition female migration on the roles that migrant women play within their families? Is immigrant women's agency enhanced or constrained by their position in so-called transnational families?

Immigrant Families and Households

This section will map the different family forms of Filipino and Moroccan women in the two destination locations. We saw in an earlier section of this chapter that some women formed their families in the Philippines and in Morocco prior to migration but several arrived single in Southern Europe. Did these women marry? Whom did they or will they marry? Once new immigrant families are formed in the receiving context, what form do their household arrangements take?

Filipinas

One consequence of migration on Filipino family formation is that in some cases Filipinas are marrying out of their group and they do so both with Italian/Spanish nationals and also sometimes with other foreigners, including Muslims. The choice of their partners seems to be entirely their own since they either married in the immigration context – far away from family influence – or they married boyfriends they had met during the first leg of their migration from villages to large Filipino cities. Those who met their Filipino partners in the emigration context, and could afford the trip, went back to the Philippines to get married, taking advantage of one of their holidays and taking the opportunity to gather together family members scattered around the globe. Others, who had not yet saved enough money, celebrated the wedding in Bologna/Barcelona but generally had a second ceremony on their first trip back to the Philippines. Such a trip in some cases was possible only several years later than the 'first' wedding.

Among the single Filipinas I interviewed in Bologna, all but one were in a relationship and many hoped that such relationships (with Filipinos, Italians/Spanish and other immigrants) would lead to marriage. Some, however, were more uncertain on what to do since they knew that marriage would bring important changes to their lives. In Barcelona and in one case in Bologna some women chose to remain single, something that is apparently very rare in the Philippines.[2] Some did so as an extreme act of self-sacrifice to dedicate themselves totally to their family of origin. Others did so because, thanks to their newly acquired independence (both economic and social), they could become more choosy with their marriage partners or choose not to marry altogether.

Many women arrived in Southern Europe when their family had broken down as a consequence of separation or death of the partner. Among these women, some chose to form new families but the majority did not. Among married women only two of the total of my forty interviewees in the two locations were currently living away from their husbands – this demonstrates a tendency towards family reunion, at least among those couples who do not break up for good. As we saw in Chapter 4, the practice of men forming new families while their spouses are working abroad seems to be quite common and several unions ceased as result of these prolonged separations.

With regard to children, two women (one in Bologna and one in Barcelona) had them outside wedlock. Both women felt 'shame' for their situation and preferred to avoid the Filipino community. The number of children per woman was higher for those who formed their families in the Philippines and lower for those who formed them in Southern Europe, but this contrast could also be partially explained by age factors and the non-completion of the families of Filipinas who started them in Europe. Among the two locations it was higher for Filipinas of Barcelona. The majority of Filipinas tended to live separately from their children for a number of years but then to reunite with them when they had completed their education. At the time of interview the number of women who were separated from their children was relatively low, although the majority of them had had this experience in the past.

The Filipino family does not include only partners and children. If we include other kinship relations such as parents, siblings, aunts, uncles, cousins, sisters and brothers-in-law we are able to appreciate the 'true' international nature of the Filipino family. Filipino women – like most migrants – have family in at least two countries: that of origin and that of destination. But Filipino families normally span more than two countries. Within Filipino transnational families, husbands, wives and children move between the country of origin and those of destination at different times in the individual's life course and in the developmental stage of their household.

The arrangements and the distribution of family members between these dispersed 'residential nodes' (Bjéren 1997) vary, but the majority of interviewees stated that they were in regular contact with many of their family members. Examples of such transnational families linked to Bologna are the following. Melissa lives with her husband and brother-in-law in Bologna where also one of her cousins is; her mother, four brothers, one sister, various nephews and nieces as well as her aunts and uncles are in the Philippines; one of her brothers is in Japan and one of her sisters is in Canada; moreover she has a cousin in Northern Ireland and one in Australia. She says she is in regular contact with them all via email and telephone. Ester lives with her parents and two brothers in Bologna where also two of her aunts are; her youngest sister remained in the Philippines in the care of her grandmother and aunt together with her cousins; three of her aunts are respectively in Canada, the United States and Switzerland. Cristina lives with her husband, daughter and two sisters in Bologna; living permanently in the Philippines there is now only her grandmother who is looked after by a carer; her aunts and cousins are in the US, whereas her parents (who are former domestics) live between the Philippines, where they have now retired and Bologna, where they help out with the grandchildren.

As far as the Filipinas of Barcelona are concerned, Annaline is the one who has the most dispersed family, having several aunts and cousins in Barcelona, her parents and siblings in the Philippines and relatives in the US, Canada, UK, Italy and Germany; she is followed by Mirna who has her husband, a brother and a sister in Barcelona, her parents and other siblings in the Philippines, a sister in Hong Kong, two cousins in Italy (Milan), other cousins in Saudi Arabia and one uncle in South Africa; whilst Vivian has only her husband and daughter in Barcelona, her parents and six of her siblings are in the Philippines whereas one of her brothers is in Italy, four cousins are in Canada and two of her brothers-in-law are in the US.

There is no major difference in the distribution of family members of the Filipinas residing in Bologna and Barcelona (the majority of them having family resident in between three and five countries), apart from the fact that whereas in Italy some women had family in more than one Italian region, Filipino families in Spain tend to be a bit more concentrated within the country. What emerges clearly even from a relatively small sample like mine is the dispersed nature of the Filipino family. Family members migrate to different destinations according to opportunities to maximise the possibilities of success, and minimise the risks. The various groups do seem to keep in contact with one another and these networks may be used to frame further migrations or simply as safety-nets in times of difficulty. Margarita's brothers-in-law, for example, migrated to Saudi Arabia to support their children in school but when one of them found himself temporarily out of work, Margarita intervened and sent money to her nephew from Barcelona. Another example is that of Beatrice's brother, who migrated to Japan where he found a job in a factory but was unable to regularise his position. Not having any future as an illegal immigrant in Japan, he decided to use his sister's network and he was expected to arrive in Barcelona within months.

Filipino families are thus truly transnational, with members dispersed in several countries and aggregated in various 'residential nodes', one of which can be either in Italy or in Spain. Such residential nodes or households are not static but change periodically with the arrival of new family members or the departure of someone for a new location. Moreover, their composition often varies cyclically, even over the course of the week. While some members are stable occupants who sleep in the dwelling every night, others – who are live-in domestic workers – stay there only one or two nights per week. The living arrangements of my Filipino informants varied greatly, ranging from small households of only two occupants to much larger ones reaching ten occupants.

The receiving context clearly influences such arrangements. As we have seen, rents in Bologna are extremely high and in Barcelona they are increasing fast; therefore even if Filipinos earn good wages they can rarely afford a flat either on their own or with their nuclear family. Filipinos in Bologna and Barcelona share their flats with other families or groups of friends in order to be able to pay the rent. Sharing flats allows Filipinos to be able to cover all the living costs and therefore to be in the position to move from live-in to live-out domestic work. The long hours worked by most of my interviewees mean that they effectively spend very little time at home and therefore sharing their accommodation with many people becomes easier. These arrangements are the result of necessity and lack of alternatives but they are not really considered an ideal solution by the women I interviewed who, prior to migration, were in most cases living in nuclear households. Filipinas' living arrangements are not the result of 'cultural' preferences but rather of the consequence of the local housing market and the lack of policies in this field protecting vulnerable groups (Zontini 2001a).

Moroccans

As a consequence of migration some Moroccan women also marry out of their group but they do tend to marry within their religion. The only woman in my sample who married a Spaniard did so after he converted to Islam. On the choice of their partners, many women had arranged marriages but unlike some South Asians in Britain (e.g., Summerfield 1993) they tended to consider this practice oppressive. New 'imported spouses' often were 'chosen' by their future husbands but they had the final say on the marriage. Fatima, for instance, had received three propositions, all from emigrants (one living in Belgium, one in Germany and one in Italy). She eventually chose the man who worked in Italy because she felt he was the most suitable. The Belgian one was a non-practising Muslim 'with long hair who played in a rock and roll band' whereas the German suitor was a traditionalist Muslim. She opted for the one nearer to her personality and customs: 'a practising Muslim with open views'.

Regarding the marital status of Moroccan women, many of my interviewees were divorcees, particularly in Barcelona. Contrary to what happened for some Filipinas, separation was not the result of migration (except in one case) but the cause of it. Among the Moroccan sample there was one woman who chose to remain single. Having a full-time job and a rented flat, she felt free of not getting into an unwanted marriage. The same conclusion was reached by some of my divorced interviewees who refused marriage approaches and preferred not to form new families. When Moroccan families are separated due to migration, women are normally those left behind; but there are also some Moroccan women who are

211

becoming the initiators of migration, as their Filipino counterparts are, thanks to the growing presence of 'female' jobs in Italy and Spain. As for the number of children, Moroccan women tend to have fewer than their Filipino counterparts: rarely do they have more than two. They tend to live together with their children, although some do leave them for periods of varying length in the care of their families of origin.

The Moroccan women I interviewed in Bologna also belonged to transnational families. Three women in my sample had family only in Bologna and Morocco but the majority had family members in several countries, as the following examples testify. Nabila is the only one of her family living in Bologna, but she has two cousins in Treviso and one in Sicily; all her sisters and one of her brothers are in Morocco where there are also her aunts, uncles and cousins (her parents have died); one of her brothers lives in Tunisia and one in Belgium and she has uncles, aunts and cousins living in France. She sees her bothers and sisters every year or so when they all reunite during August at their family home in Morocco. Buchra lives in Bologna with her sister, and two of her brothers are also there; in Morocco she has her son cared for by her mother, and two of her siblings; in France she has some cousins. Fatima lives with her husband in Bologna; she has a divorced sister with a child in Genoa; her mother and four siblings are still in Morocco and one of her married brothers lives in Kuwait.

Seven of the Moroccan women interviewed in Barcelona had family only in Spain and Morocco, but the majority had family in at least three countries (normally Morocco, Spain and France) and in some cases in more. Nawal, for instance, lives alone in Barcelona but has a brother in Almeria; the rest of her family is still in Morocco with the exception of some cousins who are living in the UK and another cousin who is in France. Salwa is alone with her child in Barcelona but her former neighbours in Morocco are acting as her family in Spain, helping her to find work, accommodation and childcare; meanwhile her parents and sisters are in Morocco, one of her aunts is in France and she has an uncle in Germany. The main difference between Moroccan women living in the two locations is that Moroccan women in Bologna have family members more geographically dispersed within Italy than Moroccan women in Barcelona – an aspect identified also for Filipinas.

Moroccan women's household composition in Bologna and Barcelona is heterogeneous and changing, like that of their Filipino counterparts. Housing provisions are an obvious constraint. Women migrating on their own have few options: living with their employers, relying on charity structures or renting rooms in other people's homes. In Barcelona until recently a more accessible housing market meant that Moroccan women migrating alone had access to flats where they are now living either with their children or with friends in similar situations. Unlike the Filipinos, Moroccans are not generally inclined to share their flats with other families. What they do is to accept 'guests' who, although they may live with them for long periods, are not considered integral members of the household and are expected to leave once their situation in the migration context improves. Such hospitality had in some cases resulted in abuse, exposing the fact that Moroccan family networks do not always function harmoniously in transnational movement.

The fact that they are not willing to share with others means that Moroccan families that have managed to get access to a flat have to spend a large part of their income on accommodation. Housing has been a major problem for the Moroccan immigration to Bologna since its beginning whereas in Barcelona, thanks to the presence of working-class neighbourhoods with cheap flats, this problem was initially less evident. In Bologna where the problem was more acute, Moroccan women have acted directly to claim their and their children's right to housing by carrying out illegal occupations of empty public buildings. Such a strategy – centred on their gendered role as mothers and responsibility for their families – proved quite successful in the Bologna context, as in many other contexts world-wide (Afshar 1996). It is in fact largely thanks to these 'direct action' politics deployed by Moroccan women that the Bologna City Council was forced to address the issue of housing and eventually to open up the lists for council housing to foreign residents. The Council's responses to the housing needs of immigrant women are, however, still inadequate and directed only at solving emergency situations (Zontini 2001a, 2002).

Differences between the Groups

Filipinas are more inclined to international and inter-religious marriages than Moroccan women. The former are also freer to act over the choice of their spouse than the latter. However, young Moroccan women increasingly have a say on their future husband and can refuse a suitor whom they do not like. Both groups of women are under considerable social pressure to marry, but women of both groups are consciously postponing the event or refusing it altogether. A considerable number of women of both groups are divorcees but, whereas for Filipinas separation is often the result of migration, for Moroccans it is its cause.

Although slightly less geographically transnational than the typical Filipino family, the Moroccan migrant family is quite dispersed and the majority of my Moroccan respondents had family in three countries, normally Morocco, Italy/Spain and France. Both the Filipino and Moroccan family distribution reflects the geography of their group's migration. For Filipinos the countries of emigration are, in order of 'prestige', the US, Canada and Australia, followed by Southern European countries (mainly Italy, Spain and Greece) and to a lesser extent other European countries such as Germany, France, UK and Switzerland, then the Arab Gulf states and finally Hong Kong and Singapore. Moroccan migration is less 'global' and has mainly a European character. Countries that were destinations of the older wave of Moroccan labour migration are France,

Belgium and Holland, whereas new flows are directed primarily to Italy and Spain.

Although they have different preferences – e.g., Filipinas share flats with other families and Moroccans do not – both groups have to adapt their living arrangements to the housing conditions that they find in the receiving contexts. The scarcity of affordable places in both locations results in several adaptive strategies adopted by women in both groups, depending on their particular circumstances. Housing (or lack of it) emerged as an important structural variable that had the power to influence important family decisions and conditioned the lives of nearly all my informants. Both the Bologna and Barcelona city authorities provide insufficient support to vulnerable categories (especially immigrants) in this important sector. Both Moroccan and Filipino women have therefore to rely on their own initiatives. In this context the role of networks made up of family, co-nationals, former neighbours and new employers – although operating differently for the two groups – seems crucial in helping the settlement of these women. What also emerged from my analysis, however, is that such networks are not necessarily virtuous but they can also be exploitative and detrimental to its weaker members.

Changing Family Structures

Migration results in a number of important changes for family organisation. This section will summarise the main changes occurring to family structures, whereas the next one will deal with changes in roles and responsibilities between the genders and across the generations.

Filipinas

As far as the traditional Filipino family is concerned, we can define it as residentially nuclear but functionally extended. It is not rare for young married couples to live with one set of parents until the first child is born, and even afterwards they may live either in the same compound or close by (Chant and McIlwaine 1995: 15). Kinship ties are extremely important in Filipino society and distant relatives such as third cousins are often acknowledged; an average Filipino may regard up to 300 people as kin over a lifetime (Chant and McIlwaine 1995: 15). As far as the total fertility rate is concerned, in 1998 it was 3.7 children per woman, declining sharply from previous decades (it was 6.8 in 1965) (Philippines National Statistics Office 2000).

One obvious change for Filipino families and households occurring due to migration is the decline of the nuclear household. Only ten of the forty Filipinas I interviewed lived only with their spouse or their spouse and children. The local labour market and housing situation contribute to make this nuclear family structure not viable in the two cities. Added to this is the migrants' desire to save as much as possible in order to fulfil projects in the country of origin, which renders the nuclear household more expensive than other solutions and therefore economically non-viable. However, if the relevance of the nuclear family declines in emigration this is not the case for the kinship group, which maintains its centrality. In spite of the varied housing arrangements of my interviewees, the majority of households continue to be based on kinship relations. However, an important element of change is that of friendship-based households; these are uncommon in the Philippines but present in significant numbers both in Bologna and Barcelona.

Although the birth rate is decreasing in the Philippines, it seems to be lower among my interviewees in Southern Europe, particularly among those who formed their families after migration. As stated earlier, this is not necessarily a choice but is at times a forced decision influenced by the migrant's situation in the context of arrival (type of job, lack of housing, family responsibilities back home, etc.). It is also the case, of course, that migration, combined with delayed marriage and/or separation, reduces the chances of procreation leading to the birth of children.

Moroccans

'The traditional Muslim family model is of a patriarchal extended family consisting of a man, his sons and grandsons together with their wives and unmarried daughters, bound by legal, moral and religious parameters based on the Islamic family law, or *shari'ah*' (Husain and O'Brien 2000: 6). Marriage and children are very important for a Moroccan woman. The total fertility rate, however, is declining fast, due to urbanisation: in 2001 it was 3.3 children per woman (it was 7.0 in 1962) (Population Council 2001).

The patriarchal extended family model does not seem to reproduce itself in the context of migration; in both my samples I did not encounter any extended family of this type. The only three-generational family of my sample diverged sharply from what is supposedly the norm in Morocco since it included a married couple and the mother and brother of the wife rather than the parents and siblings of the husband, as it should be following patrilineal rules. The most widespread family form among my interviewees was the nuclear household (fourteen out of thirty-six cases), followed by a variety of combinations. Another element of change introduced in the immigration context is the emergence of households based on friendship rather than kinship (particularly in Barcelona). In these cases there may or may not be male members, but if they are present they are not the household head but rather 'guests'.

The fertility rate of Moroccan women residing in the two cities studied is quite low. A possible explanation for this could be that these women find it extremely difficult to bring up children due to a number of factors such as their new labour function, the changing structure of their households (with fewer female members at hand) and the lack of support and facilities in the context of arrival. Changing attitudes towards children among women of the younger generations should also not be disregarded, nor should the fact that some of my interviewees have come out of situations of divorce, separation and abuse which make them wary of starting new relationships and families.

Negotiating Roles and Responsibilities: Marriage, Children and Women-centred Households

Although some feminist literature has equated the family with the site of female oppression (Millet 1970; Mitchell 1971; Oakley 1972), in the migration context the family appears as an institution characterised by ambivalence, a site that it is at times beneficial and at other times detrimental to women – or both at the same time. This interpretation echoes to some extent that reached by other authors working on ethnic minorities and poor urban families who have noted how the family can carry out important functions such as that of mediator or barrier in racist and unsupportive environments (Andall 2000a; Brah 1996; Foner 1997; Standing 1991). My study shows that migration can weaken family relations as much as it can strengthen them, and can contribute to the fact that some families become more united in the face of what are perceived as difficult conditions. In a context such as Southern Europe where policies towards vulnerable categories are patchy and ineffective, the family represents an important cushion and a vital resource in a number of areas (e.g., for organising immigration itself, for accessing accommodation, for finding jobs, for providing childcare, etc.) (cf. Zontini 2001b). Here is how women I have studied negotiate their roles and responsibilities within such transnational families, taking in turn the realms of marriage, women-headed households and children.

Marriage: Filipinas

One obvious consequence of migration on couples is that it often involves them living apart. Such separation means that the 'traditional' marriage based on co-residency loses salience for many migrants and introduces new forms of conjugal union that bring with them new problems for the partners. For Filipinos, such separations are normally the result of women's departure to take up jobs abroad and are widely accepted within Filipino society since they are seen as carried out for the family's benefit. Such an arrangement may be beneficial to Filipino women, particularly for those who are tired of an unsatisfactory marriage and look for a legitimised way out of an oppressive situation (Moore 1988; Tacoli 1999). However, women and men's behaviour in these types of marriages is not expected to be the same. On the one hand men are 'excused' for being promiscuous in the absence of their wife, and many Filipinas live in fear that their husbands will form new families in their absence, as happened in many cases. On the other hand women are expected to be chaste and totally devoted to their distant partner and their family. Their respectability and moral virtues are controlled by the Filipino community in the destination and 'gossip' seemed a very important tool conditioning the life of my informants both in Bologna and in Barcelona. Chang and McAllister Groves (2000) report the same for Filipinas in Hong Kong.

After a period of separation, in many cases there is the process of reunion. This is an event that many of my interviewees have long wanted but which is not free of its own difficulties and strains. For instance, 'reunited' husbands may find it difficult to be economically dependent on their wives. Edna reported how this resulted in endless quarrels and disputes between her and her husband, who was becoming 'nervous' of staying at home all day with no job. Another issue is that men who had professional jobs in the Philippines find it more difficult than their wives to accept and engage in the types of jobs that Filipinos are offered in Italy and Spain. This is something that is anticipated by some of my interviewees who thus try to delay their husband's arrival and favour the migration of other family members instead whom they know will accept these kinds of jobs. When Filipino men are present they seem to work less than Filipino women, but this does not seem to bother their wives who take up the role of the main breadwinners. When that is the case Filipino men do seem to get more involved in domestic tasks, particularly in relation to childcare. Migration thus results on the one hand in a continuity for Filipinas with their role as those responsible for their families and on the other hand a shift towards becoming the main earners exempted from some domestic duties.

Another consequence of migration is that Filipinas are getting involved in mixed relationships, both with nationals of the country of immigration and with other foreigners. The Filipinas I surveyed seemed quite satisfied with their relationships with Italian, Spanish and Arab men. Their main problem in these types of relationships is that by having non-Filipino partners these women feel more sharply the decreased likelihood of an eventual return to the Philippines. Also some felt that the fact of having an Italian/Spanish partner was impeding their further migrations, condemning them to a life of domestic work. The most problematic relationships seemed to have emerged between Filipinas and sub-Saharan African men. One of my interviewees attributed the failure of her relationship to the 'cultural incompatibility' between her and her partner, particularly in relation to family formation. Filipinas wanted stable relationships leading to marriage, whereas their partners (who already had wives in their countries of origin) wanted more open relationships. However, I should stress that the small numbers in my sample who were involved in cross-national marriages implies caution in making generalisations about different types of problems of cross-cultural experience.

Marriage: Moroccans

The Moroccan family has often been looked at as the symbol of the problematic presence of Muslims in Europe, and women's supposed subordinate position within the family has been taken as an example of Muslim inferiority and backwardness in relation to more progressive and modern Western 'civilisation'. The Muslim family has been seen as static, resistant to change and inexorably linked to tradition. As some authors (Brah 1996; Husain and O'Brien 2000; Lacoste-Dujardin 2000) have pointed out, and as my own study confirms, that is not the case.

Quoting Husain and O'Brien (2000: 9), 'only a limited number of small-scale studies have been carried out to investigate the effects of migration, settlement, social exclusion and economic disadvantage on spousal relationships and gender dynamics within Muslim communities'. What my study found on this topic is first of all the importance of generation. I noted important differences between older women who grew up in the Moroccan countryside, young women from urban Morocco, and young women who had spent a considerable part of their life in the country of destination. Other important elements to bear in mind are class and education, since some women of higher socioeconomic status have fewer pressures to conform to what is supposedly the ideal model of the Moroccan family.

As with the Filipinas, migration results in many married couples having to live apart for a number of years. With Moroccans, it is normally women who are left behind while their husbands consolidate their position in the destination country. This constituted an extremely difficult period for the majority of my interviewees, because they were totally dependent on and controlled by their in-laws with whom they were living. Without the presence of husbands, they did not have anyone mediating between their wishes and the impositions of their mothers-in-law. Furthermore the absence of their husbands made them potentially 'loose' in the eyes of their families, and thus social control on them increased. Yet, as we have seen, some women may take advantage of their husband's absence to carry out activities that their husbands would not have approved of if present. Couples may live apart also as result of women's migration and this is another potentially difficult arrangement since Moroccan men do not see this inversion of roles positively. Mbarka commented how her fiancé did not talk to her for a year and almost cancelled the wedding when she decided to accept a job in Spain.

Reunion after a long separation is also a delicate phase. If those who are arriving are the wives, problems may arise because they have 'exaggerated' expectations of life in Southern Europe. Many find the housing arrangements that their husbands are able to provide unsatisfactory – either because the accommodation is too isolated (outside Bologna) or because of its poor quality (in Barcelona). They also expected their husbands to have better and less precarious jobs, and generally they hoped for a more comfortable life where they could improve their situation rather than being forced to take up jobs that in some cases are worse than the ones that they were doing in their country. If those arriving are the husbands, they may resent the freedom and independence of their wives and they may want to reinstate their male authority and control over family affairs. The process of migration may tend to weaken the power of the Moroccan husband as breadwinner. One consequence of this can be his clinging more to traditions where the male role is clearly defined rather than favouring the emancipation of the women in the family (Husain and O'Brien 2000; Lacoste-Dujardin 2000), but it can also lead to a new distribution of productive work between the spouses.

Families formed in the immigration context present fewer problems as partners seem to share a number values and expectations. Often, both partners accept the fact that women should work outside the home, and they agree on the primacy of the nuclear family and on the desire to control the interference of the kinship group. However, even in these families, 'the division of labour outside the family hardly affects the division of household tasks' (Pels 2000: 85), something that my interviewees (especially the youngest and most educated ones) felt as unjust.

Women-headed Households

Although not necessarily a consequence of migration, female mono-parental families are a reality of immigration for both Filipino and Moroccan women. Chant and McIlwaine (1995: 282) suggest that women-headed households can be advantageous structures, 'more likely to ensure that [women] will derive greater personal gains from their work, whether pragmatically or ideologically'. This is not so certain, judging from my two case studies. Such household structures do seem beneficial for some of my interviewees in the long run, but this seems to apply mainly to women who are without children or with grown-up children. For women living alone with young children in countries such as Italy and Spain with poorly developed welfare states, the benefits that they may derive from greater independence and control over their lives are to be seen against the hardship of daily lives characterised by extremely long work shifts both inside and outside the home. This is why for women in this situation married life is still seen as generally a preferable option.[3]

Children

For both Moroccan and Filipino women it has proved difficult to bring up children in the immigration context due to a number of interrelated factors. First of all female immigrants in Southern Europe are working much more than they would be in their countries of origin and their schedule leaves them little time for childcare. Second, they have very little help at hand. Filipinas, even though they live with a number of relatives, can hardly count on them since all the household's members work as much as they can in order to support family members elsewhere. Moroccan women too cannot benefit from the same kin support they would enjoy in Morocco since they now tend to live in nuclear households and their contact with relatives who live in the vicinity is often not that close.

Many Filipinas thus decide to have their children raised in the Philippines while they act as breadwinners abroad. Many of my Moroccan respondents also send their children to Morocco or left them there while they went to Italy and Spain. The difference lies in the fact that the period in which Moroccan women stay separated from their children is much shorter than the separation endured by Filipinas. Moroccan women tend to send their children away when they are very young, usually to cover the period prior to nursery school, and then generally take them back when they are one or two years old. Filipinas can stay away from them for periods of ten to fifteen or even twenty years, forcing them into new forms of distant parenthood. How to be a good distant parent is an issue that has started to be debated within the Filipino community since it is felt that it may bring new problems. Some have noted than giving children money instead of direct personal affection and parental guidance may result in the fact that these children get spoiled and do not take advantage of the possibilities that their parents are giving them through their work abroad, particularly opportunities in the field of education.

Undoubtedly the key issue that affected many of the mothers I interviewed is the relationship with their children. The majority of Filipino children have a great respect for their parents' choices and are grateful for all the efforts they make for the sake of the family. However, the connection to their parents has weakened as result of separation and their affection has often turned to other members of their families – such as grandmothers – with whom they have been more in contact. The lack of connection between parents and children has given rise to difficulties of reunion with teenage children in Southern Europe. Some of these youngsters have proved 'difficult', refusing the authority of their parents whom they consider almost strangers to them.

These kinds of problems do not seem to affect Moroccan women to the same extent since they tend to maintain a closer relationship with their children. 'Distant' relationships are also eased by the geographical proximity of Morocco to Southern Europe, which makes visits more possible and thus more frequent. The issue of education and that of parent–child relations does however concern

Moroccan and Filipino women equally. For Moroccan women their main concern is about the education of and relationship with their daughters (rather than sons who are supposedly able to look after themselves and are exposed to fewer risks). Many mothers expressed their fear about bringing up children in a society where, according to them, young people are 'too free' and therefore open to many dangers. Because of this, parents may resort to controlling their children (especially their daughters) more closely than they would have done in Morocco. Daughters – as we have seen especially in the chapter on Bologna – suffer from the restrictions that their parents impose on them and struggle to improve their position within the family. By and large these young women are not challenging their parents head on; generally they show understanding for the difficulties encountered by their parents. They tend to opt for a strategy of small steps that will lead them to more autonomy and independence. One of their tools is education and the other is work. Through school achievement and by working they are, on the one hand, pleasing their parents who feel that their own migration has had positive results for their children, and on the other hand they are getting access to spaces outside their parents' control where they can fulfil their aspirations and express themselves more individually.

Conclusions

This chapter has shown that, despite the differences between and across groups, women's reasons for migrating tend to be linked to their gendered roles and positions within families and kinship groups. Networks are crucial for reaching Southern Europe, legally as well as illegally. The difference between Filipino and Moroccan migration is the more instituionalised character of the former and the more spontaneous nature of the latter. The second section dealt with women's insertion in the local labour markets, highlighting how both groups are inserted by and large in the same sectors but with Filipinas enjoying, on average, better pay and working conditions. The ways in which the two groups perceive their work and the amount of time they dedicate to productive and reproductive work also differ. Filipinas tend to put the former before the latter whereas Moroccan women normally do the opposite. The last section analysed women's roles in immigrant families and the changes that migration has introduced in such families. Both groups live transnationally. Moroccan women however, try to reunite their nuclear family in Southern Europe whereas Filipinas often maintain their family scattered among various countries over long periods of time. Finally, it is important to notice new forms of parenthood and conjugal relationships as a result of this new form of migration.

Notes

1.   On the control of Filipino women exercised by community leaders and Church figures in Hong Kong see Chang and MacAllister Groves (2000).
2.   According to Chant and McIlwaine (1995:18), 'family continuity is important in Philippine society and high value is placed accordingly on both marriage and children. This is particularly the case for women, ... the possibility that a woman might voluntarily choose to perpetuate her single state rarely enters the Filipino mind'.
3.   On the difficulties of immigrant women-headed families in Italy see Andall (2000a).

6
CONCLUSIONS

The aim of this concluding chapter is to highlight the main findings of the book in relation to the questions posed in the Introduction and to the debates on gender and migration introduced in Chapter 2. This conclusions are organised thematically around the four aspects that were found to be crucial both from the literature review in Chapter 2 and from the empirical research presented in Chapters 3, 4 and 5. These aspects are: the structure vs. agency debate; the importance of a gender and family focus in migration studies; the effects of transnationalism on families; and the emergence of new forms of settlement.

The Interwoven Nature of Structure
and Agency in Shaping Migration

Applying the framework for studying female migration that I developed in Chapter 2, I have demonstrated during the course of my research that economic, cultural and personal factors all affect migration. Therefore, they must all be taken into account simultaneously when exploring the dynamics of migration. The macro-political dimension of migration is also undoubtedly important. As political economists remind us, migration has to be viewed within wider processes that are affecting contemporary societies. 'Migrant sending societies', such as Morocco and the Philippines, are enmeshed in these wider global transformations that affect their populations in a variety of ways. Both Moroccans and Filipinos are leaving countries that are struggling with economic restructuring, which suffer from high foreign debt, where there are enormous disparities between the rich and the poor and where unemployment and underemployment are endemic. To understand Moroccan and Filipino migration it is important to consider how processes of globalisation are impacting on the specific realities of migrants' home countries, although this is an aspect that this book did not set out to address.

I decided instead to pay more attention to the transformations affecting Southern European societies and to the impact that these transformations are having on immigration. Chapter 1 set the scene of the context of arrival, showing a number of structural elements that confer on Southern Europe its specificity as a region of immigration. It is clear that the rapid social and economic transformations undergone by Southern European societies in recent decades have been at the root of the arrival of foreign immigrant workers. The geographical position of Italy and Spain as first entry points into the European Union for migrants coming from the Southern and Eastern shores of the Mediterranean clearly makes them easy to reach and attractive destinations. It is also evident how immigration legislation (or the lack of it) has an impact on the type, nature and size of the immigration and how local conditions in the realms of labour market and reception policies shape immigrants' settlement.

Structural forces shaping migration have global, national and local dimensions. I was particularly interested in the local dimension since I wanted to provide a grounded account which took into consideration how specific cultural and political economic contexts shape the response to newcomers (cf., Cole 1997). This is why I compared the experiences of immigrant women in two cities. What has emerged from the comparison is that the similarities between Bologna and Barcelona as far as immigrant outcomes are concerned are remarkable. In both contexts the local labour markets absorb immigrant women in the same sector (domestic service) and with very similar conditions. Middle-class families in both cities rely heavily on the vulnerable legislative and economic position of these women in order to employ them for long hours and at lower salaries than native workers. Moreover, in both cities immigrant women are allowed very few job alternatives and are subjected to the same homogenising and inferiorising discourses depicting them as poor and resourceless. Finally, the role of local public authorities is also remarkably similar and is characterised by a general and vague rhetoric of inclusion of immigrants and practices of inertia if not exclusion. This confirms the sharp contrast between rhetoric and practice argued by Però in the case of Bologna (2001, 2007) and extends the validity of his point to the case of Barcelona (Però 2002b; Grassilli 2002). Housing, for instance, has emerged as an arena where immigrants are constantly discriminated against and encounter serious difficulties, yet public authorities are unwilling to commit themselves due to their fear of losing the support of the 'native' population.

My findings in relation to the local contexts of Barcelona and Bologna are broadly consistent with recent studies conducted in several Southern European locations also from a gendered perspective (see Anthias and Lazaridis 2000 and Ribas 2000). My work on Moroccan and Filipino women in Bologna and Barcelona confirms the presence of gendered, racialised and ethnically fragmented labour markets and the difficult conditions affecting immigrant women across Southern Europe.

Although crucial, structural factors (both at global and local levels) do not, however, seem wholly sufficient to account for the specificity of Southern European immigration. Economic imperatives are important to explain why women leave their countries in growing numbers and accept tough and low-paid jobs in Southern Europe. However, why some women migrate from a given country, and others do so to a lesser extent, is an aspect not accounted for in macro-economic analysis of migration. This research has shown how cultural and personal factors interact with economic ones in different ways in specific circumstances.

My empirical work demonstrates that only by combining all these elements can we achieve a fuller account of the specific immigration outcome that we are currently witnessing in Southern Europe, and elsewhere. In fact, in spite of the general characteristics of female immigration determined by the common structural conditions encountered in Southern Europe described above, some aspects seem to be group-specific. This points to the importance of cultural factors in understanding migration. My work shows that age and gender roles in source areas, expectation of 'proper' behaviour as well as kinship obligations (both are gendered), all shape the nature of a group's mobility and interact with individual and families' economic necessity. Other 'cultural' elements that might be determinant for setting migration in motion are those associated with the presence of human and social capital necessary for the circulation of information and resources that make migration possible.

The difference in normative roles and behaviours between groups and their effect on migration were clearly evident from my comparison of two groups of immigrant women. This shows the relevance of cross-group comparison and warns against a tendency to reach broad conclusions and make generalisations taking as a template the experiences of only a specific sector of the immigrant population. To give an example, whereas for Filipino women solo-migration may be in line with normative gender roles, for Moroccan women this form of migration directly challenges them.

What is worth stressing here, however, is that not all individuals respond to the same cultural and economic setting in the same way. My study has shown that there are important differences among women in broadly similar circumstances within each group, thus pointing to the importance also of individual and personal factors in shaping their migration. My approach confirms the strength of a research methodology that sees migrants as both subjects and actors and is attentive to their perspectives, strategies and points of view. One of the main contributions of this work has been to focus attention on the everyday experience of concrete individuals. Offering insights into the lives of often forgotten actors is not only important in itself but it allows us to enrich and at times modify existing theories on a number of aspects. By highlighting the personal biographies of a number of immigrant women I realised how they are far from passive and weak individuals tossed around by forces beyond their control (as implicit in much 'structuralist' literature); they are skilful and resourceful actors within transnational webs. My work thus offers valuable insights into the everyday lived experiences of 'globalisation'.

Few studies have applied structuration approaches – which stress the complementarity of human agency and social structures – to the study of migrants in Southern Europe. As discussed in Chapter 2, most research has hitherto focused on women's insertion in the labour market, thereby highlighting women's key economic role. Moving these analyses further, I have shown the relevance of both economic *and* non-economic factors influencing the migration of Moroccan and Filipino women. Paying attention to the interconnection of structural, cultural and personal elements in shaping migration, my research confirms the validity of structuration theories for the study of female migration to Southern Europe. I have shown how women are on the one hand forced to migrate by structural circumstances of poverty, underemployment and lack of alternatives, and on the other hand how they use the channels that globalisation offers them to escape patriarchal power and increase autonomy and control over their lives. Whether and to what extent they succeed in this is open for debate. Women, it seems, are simultaneously victims and main actors of globalisation.

The Gendered Nature of Migration: Family and Kinship Positions Shaping Women's Migration

This section deepens the analysis of 'non-economic' factors shaping migration and deals with the gendered dimension of migration decision making. As far as structuration theories are concerned, Chapter 2 pointed out how there seems to be disagreement among migration scholars as to which meso-level units – households, families, networks, etc. – should be considered for understanding migration decision making. This section goes back to this debate in the light of my empirical results.

My study reassesses certain accounts of the feminisation of migration which describe it as the result on the one hand of the demands of capital, and on the other of coercion on behalf of patriarchal household members (Castles and Miller 1998). In this interpretation, capitalism and patriarchy appear as allies, mutually reinforcing each other and leaving little space for autonomous action by the women concerned. My research points instead to a more complex relationship between capital forces and patriarchy in which some women may use opportunities offered by capitalism to escape patriarchal control over their lives. This is why many of my informants – both Moroccan and Filipino – often said they took their decision about migration against their father's will and implemented it thanks to the support of other women in their families. In yet other instances women may seek refuge from capitalist exploitation in patriarchal systems, notably in the Moroccan case.

My study has shown that migration decisions are rarely taken within the household and are more often than not negotiated outside it in wider family and kinship groups. Most of the Filipinas I interviewed had already left their household of origin either to form a new family or more commonly to work in the city. They did not have to ask the permission of anybody to migrate, rather they needed the economic support of family members to be able to meet the high migration costs. It is also interesting to note that many of my interviewees originated from female-headed households. Thus, my study shows the relevance of internalised behaviour – such as that of dutiful daughters/mothers dedicated to the social and economic well-being of their families – rather than externally imposed coercion.

In line with other studies (Hondagneu-Sotelo 1994; Tacoli 1999), my research confirms the importance of the family and kinship group over and above the household. It is in these units that normative age and gender roles are transmitted and played out, shaping the acceptability and likelihood of women's migration. In the Filipino case such roles are compatible with and actually favour the migration of women. Tacoli (1999) has stressed the importance of culturally specific ideological factors in determining who moves and who stays, and has called for further exploration of these issues in a comparative perspective. My comparison between Moroccan and Filipino women responds to this call and confirms the importance of culturally specific roles. However, my study has also shown that such roles do not remain intact but rather change and adapt to new circumstances such as those provoked by migration (see next section). And it also shows that normative gender roles can be effectively negotiated.

The malleability of such normative gender roles is evident in the Moroccan case. In Morocco, men are supposed to be income earners supporting their families and hence those undertaking international migration for work purposes. In my study men tended to have the control over the migration process although I witnessed important changes in this respect. Patriarchy dictates sequential migration whereby men migrate ahead of their wives and children, and in several cases men tried to delay the migration of their families. Women, however, bargain with their husbands and their families in order to be able to join them in Southern Europe, and in many cases they are successful. In other cases the decision to migrate is taken jointly by both partners even if the actual move may not be simultaneous. Following Hondagneu-Sotelo (1994) on Mexican migration, my study on Moroccan migration confirms that patriarchal authority is not fixed and can be successfully negotiated against.

Social networks – particularly female networks – seem to play an important role in Moroccan and Filipino female migration to Southern Europe. Several young women gathered information about potential destinations through the experiences of friends and relatives, who often then provided the capital necessary for migrating. The gendered nature of networks can be noted particularly in the Filipino context, where women have the control of such networks. It is they who have the contacts with employers in the destination country and who have the money to sponsor the emigration of other people. Often, they favour the migration of women over that of men. We are thus witnessing the emergence of a type of female chain migration, controlled mainly by women.

In the Moroccan case, networks are mainly male-dominated, although I have shown the partial development of female networks. Unattached women (single women, widows and divorcees) are migrating north in greater numbers, encouraged by tales of other women who have undertaken the same journey and by assurances of the availability of jobs. Although initially very different from Filipino migration, some Moroccan female migration ending up in the domestic sector is starting to assume similar characteristics to the Filipino one. In this particular sector of Moroccan migration, female networks seem to play a crucial role too.

My work has shown, especially in the Filipino context, how social networks interact with the 'institutionalised' ones that deploy labour abroad for profit. In the eyes of the women concerned there is no major difference between the two types of networks which, rather than opposed, seem to be located in a continuum. Once the decision about migration has been taken, the aspiring migrant will seek whatever means to accomplish her plan. She will use legal means if those are available and not too time-consuming, and illegal ones when she has no other option. Often the migrant is not even aware of the legality or illegality of the arrangements that will place her abroad. Her journey might be within the framework of international labour agreements or she may be smuggled into Southern Europe by experienced traffickers, depending on the agency she has approached or simply on the situation of the immigration legislation at the receiving end in that particular moment. Given the geographical proximity between Morocco and Southern Europe, the journey is much more straightforward for Moroccan women. Rarely do they have to rely on illegal networks to be smuggled into Southern Europe; their easier option is to overstay tourist visas.

It is clear that the reasons why women leave their countries of origin and become international migrants are heterogeneous, yet mostly gender-specific. Women move to fulfil prescribed gender roles, such as that of being responsible for the well-being of their family and children and that of being the accompanying wife, or they migrate precisely to escape their allotted place within their families and societies of origin. The latter is the case when women run away from unsatisfactory marriages, from the interference of the extended family or from the stigma of a socially devalued role such as that of divorcee, single mother or spinster. These motivations are not necessarily in opposition. This book has shown how women may use their prescribed role as a way to achieve other goals, such as diminishing patriarchal power over their life. This typically female 'resistance' strategy is used by both Filipino and Moroccan women in an attempt to gain further autonomy while protecting their social position at home, and in so doing maintaining their family's moral (and at times economic) support.

The Impact of Migration and Transnationalism
on Family Structures, Roles and Responsibilities

My study has shown how family roles and responsibilities shape the decision to move and are in turned shaped and partly changed as result of migration. The effects of migration and transnationalism on the family are little considered in current migration literature. This book contributes to this important yet neglected aspect of migration by providing empirically grounded theoretical observations on the changes that migration produces on the structure of the family, its functions and the roles of individual members within it.

The ethnographic chapters have shown how living in different and distant geographical locations leads to new ways of articulating family relationships, especially spousal and maternal ones. Productive and reproductive tasks may be conducted in different countries, with young adults working in Southern Europe and children and elderly relatives raised and cared for in the society of origin. Many migrant women working in Southern Europe are thus devolving some of their familial responsibilities to other family members. Generally such transfer of responsibilities does not happen across the gender divide since tasks tend to be allocated to other women, although this is not always the case, especially in the Filipino context. Due to migration, gender roles are slowly affected since women are becoming the main income generators of their families. This is not only the case for Filipinas but applies to some Moroccan women as well. What has to be highlighted, however, is that if women's roles are changing, men do not necessarily recognise/accept such changes and thereby take up new responsibilities. At times these changes may lead to spousal or parental conflicts, or simply to women silently taking up yet other burdens on top of their usual commitments.

Migration affects intra-familial relationships. The research presented here has documented the effects of both prolonged separations as well as reunions among partners and parents/children. Such circumstances have ambivalent consequences for women. On the one hand long-term separation from parents, husband and children causes considerable suffering to the women involved; on the other hand separation gives them increased freedom and control both over their time and their income. A similar ambivalence can be noted for the children of transnational migrants, who both benefit and suffer from the migration experience. They benefit from the increased economic possibilities acquired by their families through migration, but they also suffer from either prolonged separation from their parents when they are left behind or from the difficulties in adapting to a new and often hostile context when they get reunited with them in the immigration country.

Due to migration, families become more dispersed but not necessarily less united and less interconnected. Members are clustered in residential nodes located in different countries. The composition of these nodes varies not only periodically, as a result of the comings and goings of new immigrants or returnees, but also cyclically as result of the working and living arrangements of their members.

The way in which families can 'get together' in the immigration context is through 'family reunification', a migration form that, too, is still little-studied. My research contributes to this neglected topic in three ways. First of all, by documenting the experiences of Moroccan female family migrants. I have shown how they negotiate the ever-stricter conditions for family reunification and demonstrated that migration for family purposes is not in contradiction with other goals such as insertion in the local labour market. Second, I have shown how family formation is managed when the sponsor is female and the imported spouse is male (as is the case for Filipinos). I pointed out how, for women, it is more difficult to initiate procedures for family reunification; especially because, being in many cases live-in maids, they do not meet the requirements of having 'adequate housing'. Third, I have exposed the negotiated and contested nature of family reunification. In fact, I showed how the sponsors of family migrants may use their privileged position to their advantage.

Whatever the reluctance of some of the actors involved, new 'types' of families are emerging in Southern Europe. They are little studied and in the few existing studies they are described in a stereotyped fashion. The book shows that cultural norms about family relations are not transplanted intact from the societies of origin; rather, they are renegotiated and adapted to the new context. Such norms are at times resisted and openly challenged, whereas at other times they change slowly due to external influences. Economic, legal and demographic factors contribute to changes in family and kinship patterns.

Families seem to adapt quickly to new conditions and circumstances, and are crucial institutions for the success of the migration process, in spite of the problems previously mentioned. For women, families appeared in many cases as simultaneously constraining entities which are at the root of many of their current problems, but also as important safety-nets whose supportive role in difficult circumstances should not be neglected or undervalued. My study has shown the important role of the family in the settlement process, thus reassessing those accounts that depict immigrant families as intrinsically problematic (Favaro 1994; Tognetti Bordogna 1994). Such literature extends the characteristics of specific families to all immigrant families, which are thus seen as necessarily poor, lacking skills and resources, composed of many dependant members, inexorably at the margins of the societies where they are living and thus in need of 'integration' policies to help them to solve their many problems and to function in the receiving society (see especially the comprehensive critique of Santamaria 2002).

This book has tried to go beyond such stereotyped images of immigrant families. I have explored the characteristics of different types of new immigrant families ranging from mono-parental to extended ones. Some of these characteristics were found to be the result of cultural practices and specific traditions; others, however, were reflective of the requirements of the local job and housing markets which force women and men into new family arrangements and solutions. Other aspects, as I said before, are a direct result of transnational life itself. Ethnographic studies on immigrant families such as this one may serve to dispel the common pathologising descriptions of immigrant families mentioned above, and assert instead their resourcefulness and crucial role in the social life of immigrants.

Migrants and Settlers: The Participation of Immigrant Women in Transnational and Local Webs

My research has shown how migrant women are both migrants enmeshed in transnational webs and settlers who are involved in creating long-lasting links with the local contexts of reception. Their experiences not only seem to confirm Brah's (1996) point that transnational movement and the maintenance of strong ties with more than one society are not incompatible with settlement, but show that such transnationalism is the actual way that settlement takes place (see also Glick Schiller 2004; Levitt 2001). This type of settlement has implications for reception policies, which at present do not seem to recognise the possibility of multiple identities and different loyalties, nor recognise the primary role of women migrants in the settlement process. Both Filipinos and Moroccans live transnationally, maintaining close links with and participating in social and family life in at least two countries. This is not necessarily in conflict with their desire and efforts to establish themselves in Southern Europe. It may, however, be in tension with reception policies which tend to over-simplistically see migrants as inevitably 'excluded' and in need of being 'integrated' in the local society.

Women seem to have a crucial role in the maintenance of transnational links, as I have abundantly demonstrated. They are the ones who keep up the link with distant kin; manage family affairs from a distance; and, when situations so require, go back to their country of origin to help sick relatives or solve unexpected events. They are also reliable senders of vital remittances which support relatives scattered over a number of countries. Despite physical distance, they do seem to keep up contacts and relationships with home communities more successfully than men do. This crucial role is not always recognised and, while some women derive satisfaction and increased self-esteem from it, others feel that migration results in additional tasks and responsibilities stretching them beyond acceptable limits.

The recent rich international literature on Filipinas describes them as transnational migrants condemned to a situation of 'partial citizenship' (Parreñas 2001b) and 'provisional diaspora' (Barber 2000). Such concepts refer to Filipinas' supposed 'liminal' position both in the countries of destination as well as in that

231

of origin. Filipino migrants' constant talk (and yet postponement) of return, their spending of savings on the purchase of properties in the Philippines, their prolonged feeling of obligation towards kin left behind, and their constant sending of remittances which do not seem to decrease over the years, can all be seen as evidence of such a position of liminality in host societies.

Filipinas' strong ties and commitments towards their country of origin and their ambiguous position towards return certainly emerged from my own research. However, my work also shows that Filipinas, rather than being 'liminal', are in some respects quite rooted in their immigration contexts, especially in Barcelona. Their involvement in their societies of origin and their centrality in transnational links does not imply their passivity or their lack of interest in and concern with their situation in the receiving context. On the contrary: they buy properties there, they develop links with the local civil society, they assert their political and citizenship rights, and they reunite with family members. In this sense Southern Europe differs from other Asian contexts where family formation is strictly forbidden and where the Filipino community is composed almost exclusively by women (see Chang and McAllister Groves 2000; Constable 1997, 1999; Parreñas 2001a; Yeoh and Huang 2000).

Moroccan women, too, are far from passive victims. They lack the organisational capacity of Filipinas, but they are no less effective, especially when they use their maternal function as a political strategy to negotiate with local authorities. Their campaigns for access to housing have been quite successful in Bologna. As I pointed out in Chapter 3, Moroccan married women carried out occupations of empty public buildings to claim their children's rights to housing, forcing the Council to open new Centres of First Shelter for families and to open the lists for social housing to foreign residents. As documented by Hondagneu-Sotelo (1994) for Mexicans in the US, for Moroccans also it is the women who deal with the public services in order to obtain resources from them. This is one way in which women reinforce their position within the family and consolidate the process of settlement.

Helma Lutz (1997) has called for contextualised analyses of the situation of immigrant women which avoid focusing exclusively on the cultural resources of the immigrant but take into account the possibilities that the receiving society offers them. My study on Moroccan immigrant women shows how traditional gender roles may become politicised to obtain resources from local public institutions and also how patriarchy may become a refuge from a marginalised role in the economic system. Many Moroccan women find themselves faced by the choice between a low-paid, hard and (for them) degrading job, and a full-time position as wives and mothers in a patriarchal household. Many have chosen the latter option after disappointing experiences in the local labour markets. Few Filipinas have this choice. They are the economic pillars of their extended families, they have often incurred high debts in order to make migration possible, and their husbands are normally in low-paid jobs in the Philippines. My research

232

has demonstrated the importance of looking at the specific experiences of immigrant women, showing how women negotiate their limited possibilities and how they try to resist and change their roles in both the work and the family spheres.

The research has also shown how the role and position of women in their families affect their migration possibilities as well as their settlement. Hondagneu-Sotelo (1994) has demonstrated how women try to consolidate settlement since the immigration context reduces the patriarchal power of their husbands and increases women's autonomy. This analysis applies to Moroccan women who unequivocally work towards consolidating settlement, whereas Filipinas' position is more ambiguous. For Filipinas, having a paid job is not the new experience that it is for some Moroccan women since they generally had better jobs in the Philippines and their status changed from that of well-educated students and professionals to that of domestic workers. Their social position within the society they live in decreases with migration. What is new for these women is their increased earning power, which is what gives them self-esteem and increases their influence and prestige within the society of origin. Such earning power is significant, however, only in a Filipino context where their wages as domestics abroad exceed those of local professionals. In the immigration context they are low-paid workers. As Barber (2000) has pointed out, their migrant lives have meaning only when both the country of origin and of immigration are taken into account. Since the autonomy and prestige of Filipinas increase with migration thanks to the wages they earn abroad, it may be in their interest to perpetuate a transnational arrangement rather than get resigned to a lifetime as lower-class Southern European citizens.

These examples show that a transnational focus is necessary in order to interpret the experiences of immigrant women. An exclusive focus on the context of arrival may lead us to depict immigrant women as an oppressed group marginalised for reasons of class, gender and race. These women are indeed oppressed; however, such a focus obscures the agency and the personal story behind each of these women. By focusing exclusively on their oppression we do not explain why they accept these situations and often act in ways that from the point of view of the receiving society may seem irrational. Considering the commitments linking immigrant women to other members of their scattered families and their simultaneous involvement in different societies gives us clues to interpret and perhaps better comprehend some of their decisions and their migration experience in a broader sense.

This does not mean that the immigration context is not important. My work has shown that the possibility of enjoying full citizenship rights in the immigration country does not lose importance in the age of transnationalism: quite the opposite. The enjoyment of social and political rights has a direct impact on an immigrant's position in the receiving society. Their often insecure legal status has direct consequences for their position in the labour market and in relation to their family commitments and possibilities of conducting a transnational life. The lack of basic rights directly reduces the space of women's agency and conspires to render them the weak and powerless subjects some literature portrays and employers possibly desire them to be. The exclusion of resident workers from a number of rights shows the irresponsibility of some Western states in apparently endorsing the power of capital to engage in the super-exploitation of immigrant workers.

My research indicates that some transnational moves and arrangements are directly geared towards the attempt of negotiating and improving citizenship rights. A lot of effort was dedicated by my interviewees towards achieving some of their entitlements, such as nationality (for Filipinas in Spain), family reunion for all those who were potentially entitled, legal work contracts, and so on. Both Moroccan and Filipino women in Italy and Spain are actively involved in negotiating citizenship, in ways described by Stasiulis and Bakan (1997) in relation to immigrant women in Canada.

In a context of limited institutional support, immigrants have to rely on their own resources. Their social and personal networks are crucial. However they seem much more developed in the Filipino than in the Moroccan case. The latter tend to rely almost exclusively on the resources available either in their nuclear family or through charity structures. They tend to be in competition with other co-nationals rather than cooperating with them. Some Moroccan stories show that networks are not only virtuous but can exploit their weaker members.

My research has evidenced the different positions of the two groups of women in local labour markets. In both Italy and Spain Filipinas are at the top of the hierarchy of preferred domestic workers, whilst Moroccan women rank somewhere near the bottom. This has important consequences reflecting directly on the labour-market possibilities of the two groups and on their actual position. What I want to stress here, however, is the relativism of such preferences, which reveal more about the receiving societies than about the groups themselves. It is interesting in this respect to contrast the good 'reputation' of Filipinas in Southern Europe with the bad one that they have in other regions of the world such as Hong Kong, where many of the negative attributes that in Southern Europe are attached to Moroccan women are applied to Filipinas. They are in fact labelled as 'lazy, demanding, lacking commitment to their work, or "only in for the money"' (Constable 1997: 544). Other authors assert that in Hong Kong Filipinas are equated with prostitutes (Chang and McAllister Groves 2000). This is quite a difference from the reputation that the same workers have in Southern Europe, where in popular parlance the word 'Filipina' is synonymous with a supportive and sought-after domestic worker.

The analysis of the experiences of Filipino and Moroccan migrant women shows that there are different strategies deployed in the migration and settlement processes leading to different possible outcomes. My work has documented the lived experiences of 'globalisation', showing how concrete cases often defy grand generalisations. In spite of all their differences, the stories I have collected have important similarities and common threads. They all develop and get articulated in more than one context; they unfold in relation to people and realities beyond those of the place where they are residing. Nation-states exert their power over these women by controlling their moves, attaching degrading labels to them, denying them rights and facilitating their economic exploitation. Yet these women develop skills and build connections that allow them to bypass nation-states.

This study has dealt with the causes and consequences of migration and transnationalism for the small and often invisible – but extremely important – actors of globalisation who are the Filipino and Moroccan protagonists of this book. In the current European climate where migrants are so often talked about – in political and media discourses – but tend to be reduced to criminals, culturally incompatible 'others' and unwanted guests, I believe that is important to excavate below the surface of such images and provide alternative and 'deeper' accounts. It is also important to go beyond conventional stereotypes about specific groups of migrant women and take into account difference, diversity and commonality within and between groups. By so doing, we will uncover the skilfulness and resourcefulness of these actors who, in spite of all the obstacles, abuses and restrictions they encounter, manage to conduct their lives beyond national borders and become active members of more than one society, as well as showing different ways of conducting transnational lives.

BIBLIOGRAPHY

❦

Abdulrahim, D. (1993). 'Defining Gender in a Second Exile: Palestinian Women in West Berlin', in G. Buijs (ed.), *Migrant Women: Crossing Boundaries and Changing Identities.* Oxford: Berg, pp. 55–82.

Abella, M. (1993). 'Labor Mobility, Trade and Structural Change: The Philippine Experience', *Asian and Pacific Migration Journal* 2(2): 249–68.

Ackers, L. (1998). *Shifting Spaces: Women, Citizenship and Migration within the European Union.* Bristol: The Policy Press.

Ackers, H.L. and H.E. Stalford (2004). *A Community for Children? Children, Citizenship and Internal Migration in the EU.* Aldershot: Ashgate.

Afshar, H. (1996). *Women and Politics in the Third World.* London: Routledge.

Ajuntament de Barcelona (2001). *La Població Estrangera de Barcelona. Gener 2001.* Barcelona.

——— (2006). *La Població Estrangera de Barcelona. Gener 2006.* Barcelona.

Alicea, M. (1997). '"A chambered Nautilus": the contradictory nature of Puerto Rican women's role in the social construction of a transnational community', *Gender and Society,* 11(5): 597–626.

Andall, J. (1998). 'Catholic and State Constructions of Domestic Workers: The Case of Cape Verdean Women in Rome in the 1970s', in K. Koser and H. Lutz (eds), *The New Migration in Europe: Social Constructions and Social Realities.* London: Macmillan, pp. 124–42.

——— (1999). 'Cape Verdean Women on the Move: "Immigration Shopping" in Italy and Europe', *Modern Italy* 4(2): 241–58.

——— (2000a). *Gender, Migration and Domestic Service: The Politics of Black Women in Italy.* Aldershot: Ashgate.

——— (2000b). 'Organizing Domestic Wokers in Italy: The Challenges of Gender, Class and Ethnicity', in F. Anthias and G. Lazaridis (eds), *Gender and Migration in Southern Europe.* Oxford: Berg, pp. 124–41.

Anderson, B. (2000). *Doing the Dirty Work.* London: Zed Press.

——— (2001). *Reproductive Labour and Migration.* Transnational Communities Programme, University of Oxford, Working Paper No 02.

Anthias, F. (2000). 'Metaphors of Home: Gendering New Migrations to Southern Europe', in F. Anthias and G. Lazaridis (eds), *Gender and Migration in Southern Europe*. Oxford: Berg, pp. 15–48.

Anthias, F. and G. Lazaridis (eds) (2000). *Gender and Migration in Southern Europe*. Oxford: Berg.

Anthias, F. and N. Yuval Davis (1992). *Racialized Boundaries: Race, Nation, Gender, Colour, and Class in the Anti-Racist Struggle*. London: Routledge.

Aramburu, M. and M. Zegrí (1994). 'Un Programa en Favor de la Convivencia Intercultural en *Ciutat Vella* de Barcelona', *Extranjeros en El Paraíso*. Barcelona: Virus, pp.163–68.

Baganha, M. (1998). 'Immigrant Involvement in the Informal Economy: The Portugal Case', *Journal of Ethnic and Migration Studies* 24(2): 367–85.

Bailey, A. and P. Boyle (2004). 'Untying and Retying Family Migration in the New Europe', *Journal of Ethnic and Migration Studies* 30(2): 229–41.

Baldassar, L. (2001). *Visits Home: Migration Experiences Between Italy and Australia*. Melbourne: Melbourne University Press.

Baldassar, L. and C. Baldock (2000). 'Linking Migration and Family Studies: Transnational Migrants and the Care of Ageing Parents', in B. Agozino (ed.), *Theoretical and Methodological issues in Migration Research: Interdisciplinary and International Perspectives*. Aldershot: Ashgate, pp. 61– 89.

Barbagli, M. and C. Saraceno (eds) (1997). *Lo Stato delle Famiglie in Italia*. Bologna: Il Mulino.

Barber, G.P. (2000). 'Agency in Philippine Women's Labour Migration and Provisional Diaspora', *Women's Studies International Forum* 23(4): 399–411.

Basch, L., N. Glick Schiller and C. Blanc Szanton (1994). *Nations Unbound: Transnational Projects, Postcolonial Predicaments and Deterritorialized Nation-States*. Utrecht: Gordon and Breach.

Beckett, C. and M. Macey (2001). 'Race, Gender and Sexuality: The Oppression of Multiculturalism' *Women's Studies International Forum* 24(3/4): 309–19.

Beishon, S., T. Modood and S. Virdee (1998). *Ethnic Minority Families*. London: Policy Studies Institute.

Bergalli, V. (2001). 'La Reacción de la Sociedad Receptora a Nivel Local. Una Aproximación al Caso de "Ciutat Vella" de Barcelona', in C. Solé (ed.), *El Impacto de las Inmigraciones en la Economía y en la Sociedad Receptora*. Barcelona: Anthropos, pp. 213–45.

Bernardes, J. (1997). *Family Studies: An Introduction*. London: Routledge.

Bernardotti, A. and G. Mottura (2000). *Il Gioco delle Tre Case. Immigrazione e Politiche Abitative a Bologna dal 1990 al 1999*. Turin: L'Harmattan Italia.

Bjéren, G. (1997). 'Gender and Reproduction', in T. Hammar, G. Brochmann, K. Tamas and T. Faist (eds), *International Migration, Immobility and Development: Multidisciplinary Perspectives*. Oxford: Berg, pp. 219–46.

Böcker, A. (1995). 'Migration networks: Turkish migration to Western Europe', in R. van der Erf and L. Heering (eds). *Causes of International Migration*. Proceedings of a Workshop. Luxemburg, 14–16 December 1994, compiled by the Netherlands Interdisciplinary Demographic Institute (NIDI) on behalf of the European Commission.

Boyd, M. (1989). 'Family and Personal Networks in International Migration: Recent

Developments and New Agendas', *International Migration Review* 23(3): 638–69.

Brah, A. (1996). *Cartographies of Diaspora*. London: Routledge.

Brettell, C. (2000). 'Theorising Migration in Anthropology: The Social Construction of Networks, Identities, Communities and Globalscapes', in C. Brettell and J. Hollifield (eds), *Migration Theory: Talking Across Disciplines*. London: Routledge, pp. 97–135.

Bryceson, D. and U. Vourela (eds) (2002). *The Transnational Family: New European Frontiers and Global Networks*. Oxford: Berg.

Brooksbank Jones, A. (1997). *Women in Contemporary Spain*. Manchester: Manchester University Press.

Brusco, S. (1982). 'The Emilian Model: Productive Decentralisation and Social Integration', *Cambridge Journal of Economics* 6(2): 167–84.

Buijs, G. (ed.) (1993). *Migrant Women: Crossing Boundaries and Changing Identities*. Oxford: Berg.

Burholt, V. (2004). 'Transnationalism, Economic Transfers and Families' Ties: Intercontinental Contacts of Older Gujuratis, Punjabis and Sylhetis in Birmingham with Families Abroad', *Ethnic and Racial Studies* 27(5): 800–29.

Busato, B. (2001). 'Donne Maghrebine nel Veneto: Percorsi Lavorativi e Culturali', *Studi Emigrazione* 38(143): 539–63.

Campani, G. (2000). 'Immigrant Women in Southern Europe: Gender, Social Exclusion and Prostitution in Italy', in R. King, G. Lazaridis and C. Tsardanidis (eds), *Eldorado or Fortress? Migration in Southern Europe*. London: Macmillan, pp. 145–69.

Caritas di Roma (1994). *Immigrazione Dossier Statistico '94*. Rome: Anterem.

———— (1996). *Immigrazione Dossier Statistico '96*. Rome: Anterem.

———— (1998). *Immigrazione Dossier Statistico '98*. Rome: Anterem.

———— (1999). *Immigrazione Dossier Statistico '99*. Rome: Anterem.

———— (2001). *Immigrazione Dossier Statistico 2001*. Rome: Anterem.

Carmona, S. (2000). 'Inmigracion y Prostitucion: el Caso del Raval (Barcelona)', *Papers* 60: 343–54.

Carter, D.M. (1997). *States of Grace. Senegalese in Italy and the New European Immigration*. Minneapolis: University of Minnesota Press.

Castles, S. (1993). 'Migrations and Minorities in Europe. Perspectives for the 1990s: Eleven Hypotheses', in J. Wrench and J. Solomos (eds), *Racism and Migration in Western Europe*. Oxford: Berg, pp. 17–34.

———— (2000). 'Migration as a Factor in Social Transformation in East Asia', paper presented at the Conference on Migration and Development, Princeton University, May 2000, http://cdm.princeton.edu/workingpapers.htm. Accessed 15 March 2001.

Castles, S. and M.J. Miller (1998). *The Age of Migration*. London: Macmillan.

Catarino, C. and L. Oso (2000). 'La Inmigración Femenina en Madrid y Lisboa: Hacia una Etnización del Servicio Doméstico y de las Empresas de Limpieza', *Papers* 60: 183–207.

Chang, K. and J. McAllister Groves (2000). 'Neither "Saints" nor "Prostitutes": Sexual Discourse in the Filipina Domestic Worker Community in Hong Kong', *Women's Studies International Forum* 231: 73–87.

Chant, S. (ed.) (1992). *Gender and Migration in Developing Countries*. London: Belhaven.

Chant, S. and C. McIlwaine (1995). *Women of a Lesser Cost: Female Labour, Foreign Exchange and Philippine Development*. London: Pluto Press.

Chant, S. and S. Radcliffe (1992). 'Introduction: Migration: The Importance of Gender', in S. Chant (ed.), *Gender and Migration in Developing Countries*. London: Belhaven, pp.1–39.

Chell, V. (1997). 'Gender-selective Migration: Somalian and Filipina Women in Rome', in R. King and R. Black (eds), *Southern Europe and the New Immigrations*. Brighton: Sussex Academic Press, pp. 75–92.

———— (2000). 'Female Migrants in Italy: Coping in a Country of New Migration', in F. Anthias and G. Lazaridis (eds), *Gender and Migration in Southern Europe: Women on the Move*. Oxford: Berg, pp.103–23.

Clement, G. (1996). *Care, Autonomy and Justice: Feminism and the Ethic of Care*. Colorado: Westview Press.

Cole, J. (1997). *The New Racism in Europe: A Sicilian Ethnography*. Cambridge: Cambridge University Press.

Colombo, A. and G. Sciortino (2004). *Gli Immigrati in Italia*. Bologna: il Mulino.

Comune di Bologna (2000). Popolazione Residente Straniera per Cittadinanza, Sesso ed Età al 31 dicembre 2000, www.comune.bologna.it/iperbole/piancont/annuario/annuar2000. Accessed 15 March 2001.

Constable, N. (1997). 'Sexuality and Discipline Among Filipina Domestic Workers in Hong Kong', *American Ethnologist* 24(3): 539–58.

———— (1999). 'At Home But Not At Home: Filipina Narratives of Ambivalent Returns', *Cultural Anthropology*, 14(2): 203–28.

Dal Lago, A. (1994). 'La Nuova Immigrazione a Milano: Il Caso Marocco', in G. Barile (ed.), *Tra Le Due Rive. La Nuova Immigrazione a Milano*. Milan: IRER, Franco Angeli, pp.133–239.

De Bernard, M., L. Di Pietrogiacomo and L. Michelini (1995). *Migrazioni Femminili, Famiglia e Reti Sociali tra il Marocco e l'Italia*. Turin: L'Harmattan Italia.

De Filippo, E. (1994). 'Le Lavoratrici "Giorno e Notte"', in G. Vicarelli (ed.), *Le Mani Invisibili. La Vita e il Lavoro Delle Donne Immigrate*. Roma: Ediesse, pp. 65–72.

De Filippo, E. and E. Pugliese (2000). 'Le Donne nell'Immigrazione in Campania', *Papers* 60: 55–66.

Decimo, F. (1996). 'Reti di Solidarietà e Strategie Economiche di Donne Somale Immigrate a Napoli', *Studi Emigrazione* 33(123): 473–95.

———— (2001). 'Trapiantare il Focolare Domestico. Unità Familiare e Questione Abitativa tra Immigrati Marocchini a Bologna', in A. Bernardotti (ed.), *Con la Valigia Accanto al Letto. Immigrati e Casa a Bologna*. Milano: Franco Angeli, pp. 109–32.

Di Leonardo, M. (1984). *The Varieties of Ethnic Experience. Kinship, Class, and Gender among California Italian-Americans*, Ithaca and London: Cornell University Press.

Di Leonardo, M. (1992). 'The female world of cards and holidays: women, families and the work of kinship', in Thorne, B. with Yalom, M. (eds) *Rethinking the Family: Some Feminist Questions*, Boston: Northern University Press.

Domingo, A. and I. Brancòs (2000). 'Población Femenina de Nacionalidad Extranjera en la Provincia de Barcelona, 1996', *Papers* 60: 305–26.

Ehrenreich, B. and A. Hochschild (2003). 'Introduction', in B. Ehrenreich and A. Hochschild (eds), *Global Woman: Nannies, Maids and Sex Workers in the New*

Economy. London: Granta Books, pp. 1–13.

Erel, U. (2002). 'Reconceptualizing Motherhood: Experiences of Migrant Women From Turkey Living in Germany', in D. Bryceson and U. Vuorela (eds), *The Transnational Family: New European Frontiers and Global Networks.* Oxford: Berg, 127–46.

Escrivà, A. (1997). 'Control, Composition and Character of New Migration to South-West Europe: The Case of Peruvian Women in Barcelona', *New Community* 231: 43–57.

——————(1999). *Mujeres peruanas del servicio doméstico en Barcelona: trayectorias sociolaborales,* PhD dissertation, Barcelona: Universitat Autònoma de Barcelona.

—————— (2000a). 'The Position and Status of Migrant Women in Spain', in F. Anthias and G. Lazaridis (eds), *Gender and Migration in Southern Europe. Women on the Move.* Oxford: Berg, pp. 199–225.

—————— (2000b). 'Empleadas De Por Vida? Peruanas en el Servicio Domestico de Barcelona', *Papers* 60: 327–42.

Facchini, C. (1997). 'Gli Anziani e le Solidarietà tra Generazioni', in M. Barbagli and C. Saraceno (eds), *Lo Stato delle Famiglie in Italia.* Bologna: Il Mulino, pp. 281–89.

Faist, T. (1997). 'The Crucial Meso-Level', in T. Hammar, G. Brochmann, K. Tamas and T. Faist (eds), *International Migration, Immobility and Development: Multidisciplinary Perspectives.* Oxford: Berg, pp. 187–218.

Favaro, G. and M. Bordogna (1992). *Donne Dal Mondo. Strategie Migratorie al Femminile.* Milan: Guerini.

Faist, T. (2000). 'Transationalization in International Migration: Implications for the Study of Citizenship and Culture', *Ethnic and Racial Studies,* 23(2): 189–222.

Favaro, G. (1994). 'Avere Un Figlio Altrove', in G. Vicarelli (ed.), *Le Mani Invisibili. La Vita e il Lavoro delle Donne Immigrate.* Roma: Ediesse, pp. 141–53.

Finch, J. (1989). *Family Obligation and Social Change.* Cambridge: Polity Press.

Fisher, B. and J. Tronto (1990). 'Towards a Feminist Theory of Caring', in E.K. Abel and M.K. Nelson (eds), *Circles of Care: Work and Identity in Women's Lives.* New York: New York University Press.

Foner, N. (1997). 'The Immigrant Family: Cultural Legacies and Cultural Changes', *International Migration Review* 31(4): 960–74.

Freedman, J. and C. Tarr (2000). 'Introduction', in J. Freedman and C. Tarr (eds), *Women, Immigration and Identities in France.* Oxford: Berg, pp. 1–12.

Gabaccia, D. (ed.) (1992). *Seeking Common Ground: Multidisciplinary Studies of Immigrant Women in the United States.* Westport, CT: Praeger Publishers.

Gambaurd, M. (2000). *The Kitchen Spoon's Handle: Trasnationalism and Sri Lanka's Migrant Housemaids.* Itacha: Cornell University Press.

Ganguly-Scrase, R. and R. Julian (1998). 'Minority Women and the Experiences of Migration', *Women's Studies International Forum* 21(6): 633–48.

García-Ramón, M. and J. Monk (eds) (1996). *Women of the European Union: The Politics of Work and Daily Life.* London: Routledge.

García-Ramón, M. and J. Cruz (1996). 'Regional Welfare Policies and Women's Agricultural Labour in Southern Spain', in M. García-Ramon and J. Monk (eds.), *Women of the European Union: The Politics of Work and Daily Life.* London: Routledge, pp. 247–62.

Generalitat de Catalunya (2001). *Pla Interdepartamental d'Immigració 2001–2004.* Barcelona.

Giannini, M. (1994). 'Donne del Sud', in G. Vicarelli (ed.), *Le Mani Invisibili. La Vita e il Lavoro delle Donne Immigrate*. Roma: Ediesse, pp. 73–84.

Giddens, A. (1984). *The Constitution of Society*. Cambridge: Polity Press.

Gillies, V. (2003). *Family and Intimate Relationships: A Review of the Sociological Research*, Families & Social Capital ESRC Research Group Working Paper, No. 2. London: South Bank University.

Ginsborg, P. (1990). *A History of Contemporary Italy: Society and Politics 1943–1988*. London: Penguin.

Glenn, E.N. (1994). 'Social Constructions of Mothering: A Thematic Overview', in E.N. Glenn, G. Chang and L.R. Forcey (eds.), *Mothering: Ideology, Experience and Agency*. London: Routledge, pp. 1–29.

Glick Schiller, N. (2004). 'Transnationality', in D. Nugent and J. Vincent (eds.), *A Companion to the Anthropology of Politics*. Oxford: Blackwell Publishing, pp. 448–67.

Glick Schiller, N., Bash, L., Szanton-Blanc, C. (1992). *Towards a Transnational Perspective on Migration*. New York: New York Academy of Sciences.

Goddard, V. (1996). *Gender, Family and Work in Naples*. Oxford: Berg.

Goodhart, D. (2004). 'The Discomfort of Strangers', *Prospect*, February 2004.

Goulbourne, H. (2002). *Caribbean Transnational Experience*. London: Pluto Press.

Goulbourne, H. and M. Chamberlain (eds) (2001). *Caribbean Families in the Transatlantic World*. Basingstoke: Macmillan.

Grassilli, M. (2001). 'Festes, Ferias and Hip-Hop: Images of Multiculturalism in Barcelona', in R. King (ed.), *The Mediterranean Passage: Migration and New Cultural Encounters in Southern Europe*. Liverpool: Liverpool University Press, pp. 66–94.

——— (2002). *Representation of Diversity and Cultural Participation: Performances of Multiculturalism in Bologna and Barcelona*. DPhil thesis, University of Sussex.

Gregorio, C. (1996). *Sistemas de genero y migracion internacional: la emigracion dominicana a la Comunidad de Madrid*. PhD thesis, University of Madrid.

——— (1998). *Migración Femenina. Su Impacto En Las Relaciones de Género*, Narcea.

Gregorio, C. and A. Ramìrez (2000). 'En Espana Es Diferente? Mujeres Inmigrantes Dominicanas y Marroquies', *Papers* 60: 257–73.

Griffiths, M. (1995). *Feminism and the Self: The Web of Identity*. London, Routledge.

Grillo, R. (2002). 'Immigration and the Politics of Recognizing Difference in Italy', in R. Grillo and J. Pratt (eds), *The Politics of Recognising Difference. Multiculturalism Italian Style*. Aldershot: Ashgate, pp. 1–39.

Grillo, R. and J. Pratt (2002). 'Preface', in R. Grillo and J. Pratt (eds), *The Politics of Recognising Difference. Multiculturalism Italian Style*. Aldershot: Ashgate, pp. xii–xxi.

Hammar, T., G. Brochmann, K. Tamas and T. Faist (eds) (1997). *International Migration, Immobility and Development: Multidisciplinary Perspectives*. Oxford: Berg.

Hannerz, U. (2003). 'Several Sites in One: On Multisited Fieldwork', in T. Hylland Eriksen (ed.), *Globalisation*. London: Pluto Press, pp. 18–38.

Hartman, T. (2008) 'States, markets, and other unexceptional communities: informal Romanian labour in a Spanish agricultural zone', *Journal of the Royal Anthropological Institute* 14(3): 496–514

Hellermann, C. (2006).'Migrating Alone: Tackling Social Capital? Women from Eastern Europe in Portugal, *Ethnic and Racial Studies* 29(6): 1135–52.

Hellman, J.A. (1997). 'Immigrant "Space" in Italy: When an Emigrant Sending becomes an Immigrant Receiving Society', *Modern Italy* 1(3): 34–51.

Herranz, Y. (1996). *Formas de Incorporacion Laboral de la Inmigracion Latinoamericana en Madrid: Importancia del Contexto de Recepcion.* PhD thesis, University of Madrid.

——— (1998). 'La inmigración Latinoamericana en distinto contextos de recepción', *Migraciones*, 3: 31–51.

Hochschild, A.R. (2000). 'Global Care Chains and Emotional Surplus Value', in W. Hutton and A. Giddens (eds), *On the Edge: Living with Global Capitalism.* London: Jonathan Cape, pp. 130–46.

——— (2003). 'Love and Gold' in B. Ehrenreich and A. Hochschild (eds), *Global Woman: Nannies, Maids and Sex Workers in the New Economy.* London: Granta Books, pp. 1–13.

Hondagneu-Sotelo, P. (1994). *Gendered Transitions: Mexican Experiences of Immigration.* Berkeley: University of California Press.

——— (2000). 'Disturbing Jobs, Disturbing Gender: Latina Immigrant Domestic Workers and Articulations of Femininities', paper presented at the Conference on *Migration and Development,* University of Princeton, May 2000, http://cdm.princeton.edu/workingpapers.htm

Hondagneu-Sotelo, P. and Avila, E. (1997). '"I'm here, but I'm there". The meanings of Latina transnational motherhood', *Gender and Society, 11*(5): 548–71.

Husain, F. and M. O'Brien (2000). 'Muslim communities in Europe: Reconstruction and Ttransformation' *Current Sociology* 48(4) 1–14.

Indra, D. (1999). *Engendering Forced Migration. Theory and Practice.* Oxford: Berghahn.

INE (2006). www.ine.es

——— (2002). www.ine.es

Iosifides, T. and R. King (1996). 'Recent Immigration to Southern Europe: The Socio-Economic and Labour Market Contexts', *Journal of Area Studies* 9: 70–94.

Istat (2002). http://demo.istat.it

——— (2006). http://demo.istat.it

Jaggi, M., R. Muller and S. Schmid (1977). *Red Bologna.* London: Writers and Readers.

Jaquemet, M. (1999). 'From the Atlas to the Alps: Chronicle of a Moroccan Migration', in J. Holston (ed.), *Cities and Citizenship.* Durham and London: Duke University Press, pp. 242–54.

Juliano, D. (1998). *Las Que Saben. Subculturas de Mujeres.* Madrid: Horas y horas

Juliano, D. (2000). 'Mujeres Estructuralmente Viajeras: Estereotipos y Estrategias', *Papers* 60: 381–389.

Kertzer, D. (1980). *Comrades and Christians. Religion and Political Struggle in Communist Italy.* London and New York: Cambridge University Press.

King, R. (1987). *Italy.* London: Harper and Row.

King, R. (ed.) (1993). *The New Geography of European Migrations,* London: Belhaven Press.

King, R. (ed.) (2001). *The Mediterranean Passage: Migration and New Cultural Encounters in Southern Europe.* Liverpool: Liverpool University Press.

King, R. and J. Andall (1999). 'The Geography and Economic Sociology of Recent Immigration to Italy', *Modern Italy* 4(2): 135–58.

King, R. and R. Black (eds) (1997). *Southern Europe and the New Immigrations.* Brighton: Sussex Academic Press.

King, R. and E. Zontini (2000). 'The Role of Gender in the South European Immigration Model', *Papers* 60: 35–52.

Kofman, E. (1999). 'Female Birds of Passage a Decade Later: Gender and Immigration in the European Union', *International Migration Review* 33(2): 269–99.

——— (2000). 'Beyond a Reductionist Analysis of Female Migrants in Global European Cities. The Unskilled, Deskilled, and Professional', in M.H. Marchand. and A.S. Runyan (eds), *Gender and Global Restructuring: Sightings, Sites and Resistances*. London: Routledge, pp. 129–39.

——— (2004). 'Family-Related Migration: a Critical Review of European Studies', *Journal of Ethnic and Migration Studies* 30(2): 243–62.

Kofman, E., A. Phizacklea, P. Raghuram and R. Sales (2000). *Gender and International Migration in Europe. Employment, Welfare and Politics*. London: Routledge.

Koser, K. and H. Lutz (eds.) (1998). *The New Migration in Europe: Social Constructions and Social Realities*. London: Macmillan.

Lacoste-Dujardin, C. (2000). 'Maghrebi Families in France', in J. Freedman and C. Tarr (eds), *Women, Immigration and Identities in France*. Oxford: Berg, pp. 57–68.

LARG (2005). *Transnational, Multi-Local Motherhood: Experiences of Separation and Reunification among Latin American Families in Canada*, http://www.yorku.ca/cohesion/LARG/html/largindex2.htm

Lazaridis, G. (2000). 'Filipino and Albanian Women Migrant Workers in Greece: Multiple Layers of Oppression', in F. Anthias and G. Lazaridis (eds), *Gender and Migration in Southern Europe*. Oxford: Berg, pp. 49–79.

Levitt, P. (2001). *The Transnational Villagers*. Berkeley: University of California Press.

Levitt, P. and Waters, M. (eds.) (2002). *The Changing Face of Home. The Transnational Lives of the Second Generation*. New York: Russell Sage Foundation.

Lim, L.L. (1993). 'Effects of Women's Position on their Migration', in N. Federici, K. Mason Oppenheim and S. Sogner (eds), *Women's Position and Demographic Change*. Oxford: Oxford University Press, pp. 225–42.

Lim, L.L. and N. Oishi (1996). 'International Labour Migration of Asian Women: Distinctive Characteristics and Policy Concerns', *Asian and Pacific Migration Journal*, 51: 85–116.

Lister, R. (1997). 'Citizenship: Towards a Feminist Synthesis', *Feminist Review* 57: 28–48.

Loizos, P. (2000). 'Are Refugees Social Capitalists?' in S. Baron, J. Field, and T. Schuller (eds), *Social Capital: Critical Perspectives*, Oxford: Oxford University Press.

Lutz, H. (1991). *Migrant Women of "Islamic Background": Images and Self-Images*, Occasional Paper No. 11, Middle Eastern Research Associates.

——— (1997). 'The Limits of European-ness: Immigrant Women in Fortress Europe', *Feminist Review* 57: 93–111.

——— (2002). 'At Your Service Madam! The Globalization of Domestic Service', *Feminist Review* 70(1): 89–104.

Lutz, H., A. Phoenix and N. Yuval Davis (1995). *Crossfires. Nationalism, Racism and Gender in Europe*. London: Pluto Press.

Mackenzie, C. and N. Stoljar (eds). (2000). *Relational Autonomy: Feminist Perspectives on Autonomy, Agency and the Social Self*. New York: Oxford University Press.

Maffioli, D. (1994). 'Il Matrimonio e la Nascita dei Figli', in G. Vicarelli (ed.), *Le Mani Invisibili. La Vita e il Lavoro delle Donne Immigrate*. Roma: Ediesse, pp. 110–27.

Magli, I. (1999). 'L' Invasione dei Musulmani in Italia', *Resto del Carlino*, 18 August 1999.

Maher, V. (1984). 'Work, Consumption and Authority Within the Household: a Moroccan Case', in K. Young, C. Wolkowitz and R. McCullagh (eds), *Of Marriage and the Market: Women's Subordination Internationally and its Lessons.* London: Routledge, pp. 117–35.

Maher, V. (1996). 'Immigration and Social Identities', in D. Forgacs and R. Lumely (eds), *Italian Cultural Studies. An Introduction.* Oxford: Oxford University Press, pp. 160–77.

——— (2002). 'Place, Gender, Power in Transnational Sikh Marriages', *Global Networks* 2(3): 233–48.

Mand, K. (2006). *South Asian Families and Social Capital: Rituals of Care and Provision,* Families & Social Capital ESRC Research Group Working Paper No. 18.

Marcus, G. (1995). 'Ethnography In/of the World System: the Emergence of Multi-sited Ethnography', *Annual Review of Anthropology* 24: 95–117.

Marqués, M., R. Santos and F. Araújo (2000). 'Ariadne's Thread. Capeverdean Women in Transnational Webs', paper presented at the Conference on Migration and Development, University of Princeton, May 2000 http://cdm.princeton.edu/workingpapers.htm. Accessed 22 June 2001.

Mason, J. (2004). 'Managing Kinship Over Long Distances: The Significance of the "Visit"', *Social Policy and Society* 3(4): 421–29.

Millett, K. (1970). *Sexual Politics.* New York: Doubleday.

Mingione, E. (1995). 'Labour Market Segmentation and Informal Work in Southern Europe', *European Urban and Regional Studies* 2(2): 121–43.

Mitchell, J. (1971). *Women's Estate.* Harmondsworth: Penguin.

Modood, T. (1997). 'Introduction: The Politics of Multiculturalism in the New Europe', in T. Modood and P. Werbner (eds), *The Politics of Multiculturalism in the New Europe: Racism, Identity and Community.* London: Zed Books, pp. 1–26.

Moore, H. (1988). *Feminism and Anthropology.* Cambridge: Polity Press.

Morgan, D. (1996). *Family Connections: An Introduction to Family Studies.* Cambridge: Polity Press.

Morokvasic, M. (1983). 'Women in Migration: Beyond the Reductionist Outlook', in A. Phizacklea (ed.), *One Way Ticket: Migration and Female Labour.* London: Routledge and Kegan Paul, pp. 13–31.

——— (1984). 'Birds of Passage are Also Women', *International Migration Review* 18(4): 886–907.

——— (1991). 'Fortress Europe and Migrant Women', *Feminist Review* 39: 69–84.

——— (1993). 'In and Out of the Labour Market', *New Community* 19(3): 459–83.

Oakley, A. (1972). *Sex, Gender and Society.* London: Temple Smith Gower.

Observatori Permanent de la Immigració (1998). *La Immigració Estrangera a Barcelona. 1994–1997.* Barcelona: CIDOB edicions.

——— (1999). *Dades del Punt Informatiu del SAIER V.* Barcelona: Ajuntament de Barcelona.

Orsini Jones, M. and F. Gattullo (2000). 'Migrant Women in Italy: National Trends and Local Perspectives', in F. Anthias and G. Lazaridis (eds), *Gender and Migration in Southern Europe.* Oxford: Berg, pp.125–44.

Osservatorio Comunale delle Immigrazioni (1998). *I Residenti Stranieri Nella Città di Bologna. Analisi Dei Dati dell'Anagrafe al 31 Dicembre 1997,* http://www.2.comune.bologna.it/bologna/immigra. Accessed 7 March 2001.

Palomba, R. (1997). 'I Tempi in Famiglia', in M. Barbagli and C. Saraceno (eds), *Lo Stato Delle Famiglie in Italia*. Bologna: Il Mulino, pp. 163–72.

Parella, S. (2000). 'El Trasvase de Desigualdades de Clase y Etnia entre Mujeres: Los Servicios de Proximidad', *Papers* 60: 275–89.

Parlament de Catalunya (2001). *Document de la Comissio d'Estudi sobre la Política d'Immigració a Catalunya*. Barcelona: Publicacions del Parlament de Catalunya.

Parreñas, R.S. (2001a). *Servants of Globalization. Women, Migration, and Domestic Work*. Stanford University Press.

——— (2001b). 'Transgressing the Nation-State: the Partial Citizenship and "Imagined (Global) Community" of Migrant Filipina Domestic Workers', *Signs* 26(4): 1129–54.

——— (2005). *Children of Global Migration: Transnational Families and Gendered Woes*. Stanford: Stanford University Press.

Pascual de Sans, A., J. Cardelús and M. Solana Solana (2000). 'Recent Immigration to Catalonia: Economic Character and Responses', in R. King, G. Lazaridis and C. Tsardanidis (eds), *Eldorado or Fortress? Migration in Southern Europe*. London: Macmillan, pp. 104–24.

Pels, T. (2000). 'Muslim Families from Morocco in the Netherlands: Gender Dynamics and Father's Roles in a Context of Change', *Current Sociology* 48(4): 75–94.

Però, D. (1997). 'Immigrants and Politics in Left-Wing Bologna: Results from Participatory Action Research', in R. King and R. Black (eds), *Southern Europe and the New Immigrations*. Brighton: Sussex Academic Press, pp.158–81.

——— (1999). 'Next to the Dog Pound: Institutional Discourses and Practices about Rom Refugees in Left-Wing Bologna', *Modern Italy* 4(2): 207–24.

——— (2001). 'Inclusionary Rhetoric/exclusionary Practice: An Ethnographic Critique of the Italian Left in the Context of Migration', in R. King (ed.), *The Mediterranean Passage: Migration and New Cultural Encounters in Southern Europe*. Liverpool: Liverpool University Press, pp. 162–85.

——— (2002a). 'The Left and the Political Participation of Immigrants in Italy: The Case of the *Forum* of Bologna', in R. Grillo and J. Pratt (eds), *The Politics of Recognising Difference: Multiculturalism Italian Style*. Aldershot: Ashgate, pp. 95–114.

——— (2002b). 'Anthropological Perspectives on Governance in Multi-ethnic Contexts: The Case of Barcelona', paper presented at 4th Conference of European Urban and Regional Studies (EURS), Barcelona, 4–7 July 2002.

——— (2005). 'Inclusion Without Recognition: The Socialist Left and Immigrants in 1970s Italy', *Focaal* 45: 112–28.

——— (2007). *Inclusionary Rethoric/ Exclusionary Practices: Left-wing Politics and Migrants in Italy*. Oxford: Berghahn Books.

Pessar, P. and S. Mahler (2001). *Gender and Transnational Migration*, Transnational Communities Programme, University of Oxford, Working Paper No 20.

Philippines National Statistics Office, http://www.census.gov.ph/index.html. Accessed date Month Year.

Phillips, M. (2006). *Londonistan: How Britain is Creating a Terror State Within*. London: Gibson Square.

Phizacklea, A. (1998). 'Migration and Globalization: A Feminist Perspective', in K. Koser and H. Lutz (eds), *The New Migration in Europe: Social Constructions and*

Social Realities. London: Macmillan, pp. 21–38.

——— (ed.) (1983). *One Way Ticket: Migration and Female Labour.* London: Routledge and Kegan Paul.

Population Council (2001). News Release, http://www.popcoucil.org. Accessed 28 January 2002.

Portes, A., L. Guranizo and P. Landolt (1999). 'The Study of Transnationalism: Pitfalls and Promise of an Emergent Research Field', *Ethnic and Racial Studies* 22(2): 217–37.

Pratt, J. (2002). 'Italy: Political Unity and Cultural Diversity', in R. Grillo and J. Pratt (eds), *The Politics of Recognising Difference: Multiculturalism Italian Style.* Aldershot: Ashgate, pp. 26–39.

Pribilsky, J. (2004). '"Aprendemos a Convivir": Conjugal Relations, Co-parenting, and Family Life among Ecuadorian Transnational Migrants in New York City and the Ecuadorian Andes', *Global Networks* 4(3): 313–34.

Proyecto Xenofilia (1996). *Diagnóstico Sobre las Condiciones de Alojamiento de la Población Inmigrante Extracomunitaria en el Districto de Ciutat Vella de Barcelona.* Barcelona: Mimeo.

Pugliese, E. (1993). 'Restructuring of the Labour Market and the Role of Third World Migrations in Europe, *Society and Space* 11(4): 513–22.

Ram, K. (1998). 'Introduction: Migratory Women, Travelling Feminisms', *Women's Studies International Forum* 21(6): 571–79.

Ramírez, A. (1997). *Migraciones, Genero e Islam: Mujeres Marroquíes en Espana.* PhD thesis, Autonomous University of Madrid.

——— (1998). 'Relacionarse en Madrid: Mujeres, Hombres y Asociacionismo Marroquí', *Ofrim/Suplementos*: 103–24.

Reher, D.S. (1998). 'Family Ties in Western Europe: Persistent Contrasts', *Population and Development Review* 24(2): 203–34.

Reyneri, E. (1998). 'The Role of the Underground Economy in Irregular Migration to Italy: Cause or Effect?', *Journal of Ethnic and Migration Studies* 24(2): 313–31.

Reynolds, T. (2004), *Families, Social Capital and Caribbean Young People's Diasporic Identities*, Families & Social Capital ESRC Research Group, Working Paper Series, No. 11. London: South Bank University.

——— (2005). *Caribbean Mothers: Identity and Experience in the UK.* London: Tufnell Press.

——— (2006). Caribbean families, Social Capital and Young People's Diasporic Identities, *Ethnic and Racial Studies* 29(6): 1087–1103.

Reynolds, T. and E. Zontini (2006). *A Comparative Study of Care and Provision across Caribbean and Italian Transnational Families*, Families & Social Capital ESRC Research Group, Working Paper Series, No. 16. London: South Bank University.

Ribas, N. (1996). *La Heterogeneidad de la Integración Social: una Aplicación a la Inmigración Extracomunitaria (Filipinina, Gambiana y Marroquí) en Cataluña (1985–1996).* PhD thesis, Autonomous University of Barcelona.

——— (1999). *Las Presencias de la Inmigración Femenina. Un Recorrido por Filipinas, Gambia y Marruecos en Cataluña.* Barcelona: Icaria.

——— (2000a). 'Female Birds of Passage: Leaving and Settling in Spain', in F. Anthias and G. Lazaridis (eds), *Gender and Migration in Southern Europe.* Oxford: Berg, pp.173–98.

———— (ed.) (2000b). *Inmigración Femenina en el Sur de Europa*, Special Number of *Papers*, 60.

Riccio, B. (2001). 'From "Ethnic Group" to "Transnational Community"? Senegalese Migrants' Ambivalent Experiences and Multiple Trajectories', *Journal of Ethnic and Migration Studies*, 27: 583–99.

Root, B.D. and G.F. De Jong (1991). 'Family Migration in a Developing Country', *Population Studies* 45(2): 221–33.

Sabaté-Martínez, A. (1996). 'Women's Integration into the Labour Market and Rural Industrialisation in Spain: Gender Relations and the Global Economy', in M. García-Ramon and J. Monk (eds), *Women of the European Union: The Politics of Work and Daily Life*. London: Routledge, pp. 263–81.

Salih, R. (2001). 'Moroccan Migrant Women: Trasnationalism, Nation-states and Gender', *Journal of Ethnic and Migration Studies* 27(4): 655–71.

———— (2003). *Gender in Transnationalism: Home, Longing and Belonging Among Moroccan Migrant Women*. London: Routledge.

Santamaría, E. (2002). *La Incógnita del Extraño. Una Approcimación a la Significación Sociológica de la 'Inmigración no Comunitaria'*. Barcelona: Anthropos.

Saraceno, C. (1997). 'Le Politiche per Le Familgie', in M. Barbagli and C. Saraceno (eds), *Lo Stato delle Famiglie in Italia*. Bologna: Il Mulino, pp. 301–10.

Sartori, G. (2000). *Pluralismo, Multiculturalismo e Estranei. Saggio sulla società multietnica*. Milan: Rizzoli.

Schmidt di Friedberg, O. and C. Saint-Blancat (1998). 'L'Immigration au féminin: les Femmes Marocaines en Italie Du Nord. Une Recherche en Vénétie', *Studi Emigrazione* 35(131): 483–97.

Schuster, L. (2005). 'The Continuing Mobility of Migrants in Italy: Shifting between Places and Statuses', *Journal of Ethnic and Migration Studies* 31(4): 757–74.

Serrano Martínez, J.M. and R. King (1994). *Urban Systems and Regional Organisation in Spain*, University of Sussex Research Papers in Geography, No. 12. Lewes: University of Sussex.

Sevenhuijsen, S. (2000) 'Caring in the Third Way: The Reflection Between Obligation, Responsibility and Care in the Third Way Discourse', *Critical Social Policy* 20(1): 5–37.

Smart, C. and B. Shipman (2004). 'Visions in Monochrome: Families, Marriage and the Individualization Thesis', *British Journal of Sociology* 55(4): 491–509.

Smith, M.P. and L.E. Guarnizo (eds) (1998). *Transnationalism from Below*. London: Transaction Publishers.

Solé, C. (ed.) (2001*). El impacto de la Inmigración en la Economía y en la Sociedad Receptora*. Barcelona: Anthropos.

Sorensen, N. (2005). 'Trasnational Family Life Across the Atlantic: The Experience of Colombian and Dominican Migrants in Europe', paper presented at the International Conference on Migration and Domestic Work in a Global Perspective, Wassenar, the Netherlands, 26–29 May 2005.

Standing, H. (1991). *Dependence and Autonomy: Women's Employment and the Family in Calcutta*. London: Routledge.

Staring, R. (1998). '"Scenes from a Fake Marriage": Notes on the Flip-side of Embeddedness', in K. Koser and H. Lutz (eds), *The New Migration in Europe: Social Constructions and Social Realities*. London: Macmillan Press, pp. 224–41.

Stasiulis, D. and A. Bakan (1997). 'Negotiating Citizenship: The Case of Foreign

Domestic Workers in Canada', *Feminist Review* 57: 112–39.

Stolke, V. (1995). 'Talking Culture: New Boundaries, New Rethorics of Exclusion in Europe', *Current Anthropology*, 16(11): 1–23.

Suárez-Orozco, C. and M. Suarez-Orozco (2001). *Children of Immigration*. Boston: Harvard University Press.

Summerfield, H. (1993). 'Patterns of Adaptation: Somali and Bangladeshi Women in Britain', in G. Bujis (ed.), *Migrant Women: Crossing Boundaries and Changing Identities*. Oxford: Berg, pp. 83–98.

Tacoli, C. (1999). 'International Migration and the Restructuring of Gender Asymmetries: Continuity and Change among Filipino Labor Migrants in Rome', *International Migration Review* 33(3): 658–82.

Thorne, B. with M. Yalom (eds) (1992). *Rethinking the Family: Some Feminist Questions*. Boston: Northern University Press.

Tognetti Bordogna, M. (1994). 'La Famiglia Che Cambia', in G. Vicarelli (ed.), *Le Mani Iinvisibili. La Vita e il Lavoro delle Donne Immigrate*. Roma: Ediesse, pp. 128–40.

Trifiletti, R. (1997). 'La Famiglia e il Lavoro delle Donne', in M. Barbagli and C. Saraceno (eds), *Lo Stato delle Famiglie in Italia*. Bologna: Il Mulino, pp. 163–72.

—— (1998). 'Restructuring Social Care in Italy', in J. Lewis (eds), *Gender, Social Care and Welfare State Restructuring in Europe*. Aldershot: Ashgate, pp. 175–206.

Vaiou, D. (1996). 'Women's Work and Everyday Life in Southern Europe in the Context of European Integration', in M. García-Ramon and J. Monk (eds), *Women of the European Union: The Politics of Work and Daily Life*. London: Routledge, pp. 61–73.

Vertovec, S. (1999). 'Conceiving and Researching Transnationalism', *Ethnic and Racial Studies* 22(2): 447–62.

—— (2006). *The Emergence of Superdiversity in Britain*, Centre on Migration, Policy and Society, Working paper No. 25. Oxford: University of Oxford.

Vicarelli, G. (ed.) (1994). *Le Mani Invisibili. La Vita e il Lavoro delle Donne Immigrate*. Roma: Ediesse.

Vinay, P. (1996). 'From Informal Flexibility to the New Organisation of Time', in M. García-Ramon and J. Monk (eds), *Women of the European Union: The Politics of Work and Daily Life*. London: Routledge, pp. 202–16.

Wichterich, C. (2000). *The Globalized Woman: Reports from a Future of Inequality*. London: Zed Books.

Wilding, R. (2006). '"Virtual" Intimacies? Families Communicating Across Transnational Contexts', *Global Networks* 6(2): 125–42.

Wimmer, A. and N. Glick Schiller (2002). 'Methodological Nationalism and Beyond: Nation-state Building, Migration and the Social Sciences, *Global Networks* 2(4): 301–34.

Wright, C. (1995). 'Gender Awareness in Migration Theory: Synthesizing Actor and Structure in Southern Africa', *Development and Change* 26(4): 771–91.

Yanagisako, S. (1979). 'Family and Household: The Analysis of Domestic Groups', *Annual Review of Anthropology* 8: 161–205.

Yeoh, B. and S. Huang (2000). '"Home" and "Away": Foreign Domestic Workers and Negotiations of Diasporic Identity in Singapore', *Women's Studies International Forum* 23(4): 413–29.

Young, I.M. (1990). *Justice and the Politics of Difference*. Princeton: Princeton University Press.

Yuval Davis, N. (1991). 'The Citizenship Debate: Women, Ethnic Processes and the State', *Feminist Review* 39: 58–68.

———— (1997). 'Women, Citizenship and Difference', *Feminist Review* 57: 4–27.

Yuval Davis, N. and P. Werbner (eds) (1999). *Women, Citizenship and Difference*. London: Zed Books.

Zapata-Barrero, R. (2002). *L'Hora dels Immigrants. Esferes de Justícia i Polítiques d'Acomodació*. Barcelona: Proa.

Zinn, D. (2001). *La Raccomandazione. Clientelismo Vecchio e Nuovo*. Rome: Donzelli Editore.

Zlotnik, H. (1995). 'Migration and the Family: The Female Perspective', *Asian and Pacific Migration Journal* 4(2–3): 253–71.

Zontini, E. (2001a). 'Immigrazione al Femminile e Domanda Abitativa. Donne Filippine nella Città di Bologna', in A. Bernardotti (ed.), *Con la Valigia Accanto al Letto. Immigrati e Casa a Bologna*. Milano: Franco Angeli, pp. 133–54.

———— (2001b). 'Family Formation in Gendered Migrations in Southern Europe: Moroccan and Filipino Women in Bologna', in R. King (ed.), *The Mediterranean Passage: Migration and New Cultural Encounters in Southern Europe*. Liverpool: Liverpool University Press, pp. 231–57.

———— (2002). 'Female Domestic Labour Migrants and Local Policies in Bologna: The Story of a Filipino Woman', in R. Grillo and J. Pratt (eds), *The Politics of Recognising Difference: Multiculturalism Italian Style*. Aldershot: Ashgate, pp. 159–76.

———— (2004a). *Italian Families and Social Capital: Rituals and the Provision of Care in British-Italian Transnational Families,* Families & Social Capital ESRC Research Group Working Paper, No. 6. London: South Bank University.

———— (2004b) 'Immigrant Women in Barcelona: Coping with the Consequences of Transnational Lives', *Journal of Ethnic and Migration Studies* 30(6): 1113–44.

———— (2006). 'Italian Families and Social Capital: Care Provision in a Transnational World', *Community, Work and Family* 9(3): 325–45.

INDEX